Climbing Life's Mountains

Overcoming Challenges of Biracial Birth, Adoption, Gender Identity, and Depression

Jala A. McKenzie-Burns

New Friends Publishing, LLC

Climbing Life's Mountains

Overcoming Challenges of Biracial Birth,
Adoption, Gender Identity, and Depression

ISBN-13: 978-0-9856813-3-3

Cover design by
Anne Cote

Published by
New Friends Publishing, LLC
Lake Havasu City, AZ
www.newfriendspublishing.com

Printing history
First edition published in August, 2012

Dedication

In the beginning God created the Heavens and the earth. Before going any further I must give honor and glory to God. Without him my story would not be possible. When I say my story, I mean more than just the writing of my book. I am a firm believer that God preordained my life. Many years prior to my life He knew exactly how it would shape out. God knew the many struggles that I would encounter before I was even born. Without him none of this would be possible. He is the guide to all guides and has allowed me the opportunity to help others. Therefore I thank God for the continual blessing of my book *Climbing Life's Mountains.*

Special Thanks

There are many people that I want to thank. So in my efforts to reach everyone I proudly say thank you all. Everyone is special to me and has played an important role in my life. Without those people in my life and without God I would not have a story. I encourage each of you to share my vision to "Do something for somebody every day. Go scatter a blessing along life's way."

In keeping my remarks brief I must recognize a few people. Derrick, thank you for being my mentor and supporting me through my life. I love you more than anyone could imagine. Gina, many thanks for your nurturing spirit. You are wonderful. Patricia and Karen, you ladies are wonderful and a true blessing to have in my life. I'm glad that I met you and that we now share each other's story. Both my adopted and biological families have been instrumental in shaping me into the person that I am today. During my lonely days, without my immediate family, I created a family that includes Blythe, Jamie, Ericka, Yaria, Sam, Nadine, Valerie, Ashley and so forth. You all are wonderful. If I named everyone I would end up writing for days.

President Carter, you are a very strong person and I thank you for your mentorship in terms of fighting for employee rights. You were very instrumental in getting me involved in labor politics. Mary Clark you helped raise me as a young adult and taught me how to stand up for what is right. A.F.S.C.M.E. was very important in allowing me to learn how to protect my rights and the rights of others. Felicia thanks for your assistance and leading me to the Pride Committee. Mr. Lawrence A. Roehrig, you were wonderful when I met you back in 1990 and 22 years later I still hold you in high regards. I also thank Council 25 President Albert Garrett.

Tori, your photography is outstanding. Amanda, thank you for your help with my pictures as well. The Picture People are blessed to have you both as vital employees for their organization. Effie your artistry for Mac is outstanding. Lee, you always do a wonderful job with my nails and I appreciate you and the nail salon.

The Donaldsons, my God Family, I love and treasure you. You are very important people in my life. All my cousins and everyone else in my family I truly appreciate your support and I ask that we continue to press forward to help other people. Maya and Jamil, you make your Aunt Jala proud of you because you both are amazing. My Eastern Michigan University family, you have taught me many lessons within the classroom and in life. Verizon Wireless, many thanks for being an important part of my life and allowing me the opportunity to have a career with you. Kimball Sargent and the Diverse Solutions have been instrumental in my journey through transition and I will forever appreciate you. Many thanks to my transgender friends Sila, Rachel, and Cindy for sharing their experiences of transition so that both non-transgender people and transgender people could fully understand the issues that we go through. I know that I missed many people and I apologize.

I would fall far short of the mark if I did not make a special remark about Denise and Ace. When people suffer from depression they do not recognize the pain they cause others. It takes a special person to deal with the agony that others may have caused while suffering through the illness. My depression and my gender transition were difficult for Denise and Ace to experience. Ace, my son, you are a special person and as I watch you grow, I grow also. I am very proud of you and advise you to stay focused and to continue to move forward. Denise you, my friend, are a wonderful person and I thank you for being there.

A special thanks to my editor Cody Pace. Mr. Layne Walker and New Friends Publishing, I am forever indebted to you. Thanks for teaching and working with me on this publication. Bill Greenleaf, I truly appreciate your guidance towards my work.

May God add a blessing to the reading of *Climbing Life's Mountains.*

In Memory of Howard L. Burns, Willa Martha Burns, Aunt Mae, Uncle John, Aunt Agnes, Uncle Bubba, Aunt Mildred, Aunt Net, Kimberly Donaldson and my other relatives that are deceased. I also want to remember my Verizon customer and good friend Freda Springs who recently transitioned. I will forever love you.

Table of Contents

SECTION 3

SECTION 4

SECTION 5

Preface

Although this book is considered an autobiography, its purpose is to encourage people to overcome obstacles in life. My purpose is not to bore you with the specific details of my life but to encourage you to overcome obstacles such as racism, gender, adoption and depression. All of these touch our society in various ways. Before I begin, let me first recognize and give honor to God; give thanks to my brother and mentor Derrick R. Burns; and express my thanks and remember my parents Howard L. Burns and Willa Martha Burns. My father was very supportive of me throughout my life and we developed a very close relationship. My one regret is that I never told him about my gender issues. I did disclose that a psychological exam deemed that I had a lot of feminine traits. We didn't go any further into the conversation due to me being so close to him and not knowing what to expect if I informed him of my gender. Now I believe that he would have been okay with me regardless. My brother supported and continues to show his unconditional love for me. My mother was a different story. We struggled in our relationship even prior to me disclosing my internal gender conflict to her. My mother played a disappearing act during my wedding; she had other engagements during my college graduation; and once I disclosed to her that I was transgender she kicked me out of her life. But still, my mother influenced me to stand up for my beliefs and to become politically active within the community. Her inheritance for me included building a solid foundation in Christianity and education.

November 11, 1965 was a very special day because God graced us with a very special gift, Dave Edward Morris was born. Now there are two versions of this gift. The beginning of each version is consistent, which is that I was left at the hospital after my biological mother, Carla Morris, gave birth to me. She and my biological father were both institutionalized. Carla was clinically depressed and it was common in that day to treat depression by placing individuals in an institution. My biological father was institutionalized due to his illness of alcoholism. Non-identifying information from my research shows that my biological father was a well dressed African-American. My biological mother was Caucasian. She was described as having a very low IQ and being childlike and immature. This background information is vital information that leads to both versions on how and why I was put up for adoption.

After doing extensive research, including contacting The Children's Aid Society (Detroit, Michigan) in July 2003, I was reunited with my biological mother and sister. I must also add that my sister, Patricia, did a lot of work locating me. I nicknamed Patricia "Glue" for her hard work of trying to bring our family back together. There were a total of six siblings and four of us are back together. I was the oldest and was the only black child. After speaking with my biological family, I was advised that I was conceived while my mother was institutionalized. She stated that "while out on furlough" she delivered me at Detroit's Children's Hospital. After giving birth she escaped and left me at the hospital. She told me that her reason for leaving me was because she didn't think it was fair to me to keep me on the run while she was hiding and not planning on returning to the institution. Therefore this was version number one.

Version number two goes as follows. Throughout my childhood my adopted mother Willa Martha Burns would tell me that I was given up because of racial reasons. After speaking with Patricia she also said that she thinks that I may have been given up because of racial reasons. She did say that she wasn't 100% certain but she thought that racial circumstances were the cause of my being placed up for adoption. I was told that my maternal grandparents may have pressured my mother to put me up for adoption. This second version stands to reason, especially in the 1960's. At this time I was taboo, being a biracial child.

My life story is told in this book in my effort to show that we are capable of overcoming obstacles. In my opinion God has placed each of us here on earth with a purpose. It is up to us to determine that purpose. My mother once told me that my life will be a testimony for someone in the future. I now present my story in my effort to help others make it through their trials.

I present a "Bringing It All Together" chapter in each section of the book to further illustrate my understanding of the experiences that I travelled. It is not my intent to be condescending to my readers; but my goal was to further highlight my lessons learned and to share them with my readers. Please enjoy.

In an effort to protect the identity of some individuals, I have used some fictional names. The following autobiography is 100 % accurate in terms of everything that I remember (or at least as close to account as I can remember). Please enjoy and remember that this book serves to help others overcome similar challenges in their lives.

Jala A. McKenzie-Burns

Tribute to My Favorite Poet Langston Hughes

During my high school days I became endeared to African-American literature and fell in love with Langston Hughes' poetry. I lay awake during the night many times and I think whether it's about my profession, about life in general, or about helping others and after reading Mr. Hughes' poetry I envisioned him as a warm hearted person whom also loved helping people. While writing my book I awoke from a deep sleep and decided to add a tribute to my all-time favorite poet, Langston Hughes.

Although I enjoy all of his poems I think of several that I became endeared to. As I wrote my book I thought about several of his poems and saw a fit for certain aspects of my life. The poems by Hughes affected my life in a positive manner. My favorite poem is "Me and the Mule." After reading the poem I soon learned to recite it for it touched my inner feelings about me being an African-American. As you will soon find out I have the utmost respect for people that fought for civil rights. This poem was very fitting as for what I was taught at an early age "I'm black and I'm proud."

As a labor leader that fought for the rights of employees I soon could appreciate Mr. Hughes' poem "My People." The poem reflects on the beauty of "My People." Well as a union leader I felt that the A.F.S.C.M.E Local 1583 members were "My People." Color, nor greed, nor gender would matter because everyone I represented was "My People." I would often proudly relate to our members in this fashion.

Fitting my experiences with my 10 years of depression (and some of my family would say longer) I find the poem "Still Here" as one that matches my outcome. August 6, 2002 was the lowest day of my life. For the first time I was admitted to the University of North Carolina Hospital due to being suicidal. For many years and for several reasons I found myself in a deep depression. People hurt for many reasons and use many things to attempt to cope with their pain. Once they have exhausted all of their coping mechanisms and the pain is still there they often become suicidal. My friend, I found out that was true of me. No matter how many pills I swallowed; no matter how I wanted to jump off the mezzanine level of my doctor's office; although I stopped eating for a week even though I was diabetic; no matter what my doctor's observations were I am "Still Here." God moves me as he sees fit. Today I give honor to Him.

The poem "Troubled Woman" reminds me of my emotions as I decided whether to continue to fight my gender issues or decided to live as who I truly am. As I lay in the hospital bed during those sixteen days in August 2002, I gave thought to what my doctors had told me. They advised me that I had a choice. I could either accept who I was or continue life being miserable. My decision cost me my marriage but it added a sense of happiness to my quality of life. The same pain that this woman felt in the poem was similar to the pain I felt wanting to be Jala. As Mr. Hughes stated in his poem, "...like a wind-blown autumn flower that never lifts it head again..." I was like that flower in that I would not question the decision of who I am because I could no longer live with the pain of my inner conflict referencing my gender. I am no longer a "Troubled Woman" for now I am a happy woman.

Langston's poem "Garden" fits my siblings. My biological mother gave birth to six children, all of which are different. I was the only biracial child. My adopted brother, Derrick, was also given up due to racial reasons. This was a major issue during the sixties. Each one of my siblings represented a different blade of grass in the garden. As I reflect, I truly appreciate that we all are different. We all are God's "Distorted Tulips" that fit in the "Garden."

Finally, the poem "Midnight Raffle" represents a total picture of my life. I live by faith, "For the things that are unseen..." and therefore we live life as a "Raffle." Sometimes our paths do not turn out exactly as we had hoped. For example, my labor experiences directed my thought process towards my wanting to become an U.S. senator. I went in a different direction and still continue to help people just as I would have if I would have reached that goal. During our "Raffle" called life we go through ups and downs and we lose out on certain things but we can turn these losses into gains.

My favorite poems by Langston Hughes are:

"Me and the Mule"
"My People"
"Still Here"
"Troubled Woman"
"Garden"
"Midnight Raffle"
"The Negro Speaks of Rivers"

I invite you to enjoy the reading of my book. I ask for you to use my life to help you overcome your obstacles and pains in life. Use the information to help you climb mountains and reach your mission in life. I ask God to bless you as you read the following materials.

Racism: A Biracial Product

The Civil Rights Movement was something near and dear to me. African-Americans have worked hard and have come a long way in society. Let's stop and think for a moment: Where would we be if not for our predecessors who fought for our equality? Hopefully I am wrong, but I don't think that the younger generation (those born in the mid 1970's and later) truly appreciates the gains that African-Americans have made. Sometimes things like drinking from the same water fountain as our white friends could be taken for granted. When we ride the city bus and we want to sit in the front of the bus, do we actually think of the great Rosa Parks? African-Americans had to protest and fight for the right to be educated, the right to vote, the right to be politically active, and for overall equality. As being a biracial product I am very concerned with my role in society. In the pages that follow I will discuss the accomplishments, experiences, and opinions of an African-American female. (Yes, this is who I am and I will discuss that in depth as this book unfolds.)

SECTION 1

EDUCATION

Willa Martha
Burns
Educator

Aunt Agnes Baily
Educator

Virginia Donaldson
A educator in the
Detroit School
System

The Value of Education

An important right that we as African-American people have earned is education. As a graduate of Eastern Michigan University I studied several African-American classes which range from African-American Literature to South African Effects on America. On April 26, 1997, I earned a bachelor's degree in history and political science. This is a major accomplishment because many of our African-American predecessors fought for the right of education. Dating back to slavery, black people have been beaten, killed and arrested for the right to learn how to read and write. In earning my degree I wrote several papers on Dr. Martin Luther King, Jr. and the Civil Rights Movement. Among all of my essays and research papers that I wrote, two papers are treasured the most, and now to think both papers were written in my historical research class (a graduate level class). The first "Derrick R. Burns –The Most Influential Person in My Life" was about the influence my brother, Derrick, had on my life. Derrick (also adopted – different biological parents) graduated from Princeton University with honors (1986). Derrick earned his degree in Computer Science and Electrical Engineering. Through Derrick's mentorship I am proud to say that my last 18 classes resulted in 15 "A's," 2 "A-'s," and a "B." My second most recognized paper, "The Philosophical Difference between Dr. Martin Luther King, Jr., Malcolm X, The Black Panthers, and The Student Non-Violent Coordinating Committee," described the ideas that each had in helping African-Americans progress in society. After my professor graded this term paper he told me that I was indeed ready for graduate school. At this point I hope everyone can see that I value a solid education.

Other examples of successful people when it came to education include my relatives, in particular my adopted mother, Willa Burns; Aunt Mae; Aunt Agnes; and my godmother, Virginia Donaldson. Now in order to truly understand and value these accomplishments we must understand that these four women were born in the early 1900s. My mother was born in 1923. My hope is that after reading this information the younger audience will take heed and believe that obstacles can be overcome.

My mother and her sisters had a huge impact in education; as well as my mother's longest standing friend, Virginia Donaldson. At the time that these four young ladies were growing up it was unheard of a "nigga earning an education." Negros, especially women, performed domestic work for "white people." My mother and her sisters lost their mother at an early age. My Aunt Mae was left with the responsibility, as a surrogate mother, of raising my mother and their sister. From what I see Aunt Mae did an excellent job; both sisters became school teachers. As a young child my mother would tell Derrick and me how Aunt Mae wanted her to get an education to avoid having to "scrub white folks' floors" and "raise white folks' babies." Both my mother and their sister earned their bachelor's degree and master's degree in education. My Aunt Mae taught Bible School in both her church and at McDowell Elementary School (she taught during the After School Program). Virginia Donaldson, recently shared stories of her friendship with my mother during their early years of teaching. They both taught at Mt. Moriah, in Climax, Georgia. Mrs. Donaldson, like my mother, retired from the Detroit Public Schools system. Aunt Agnes was a very successful school teacher in Chicago and she was very talented when it came to working with children. I often appreciated the support that she gave me. Again, this is a testament of the obstacles and achievements that African-American Women in my family had with education. In my humble opinion, African-Americans of this age who became educators could be compared to today's CEOs.

Now through my education and my family's education we have become successful members of society. I can hear my audience now. "Wait just because people have book smarts that doesn't mean that they have common sense." While this is certainly true, if a person applies both book smarts and common sense then the person should become a powerful individual whatever their mission. For example, I have a degree in history and political science, but I am a highly successful sales person.

My Early Education

My memory in terms of the early stages of my education takes me back to my experience in foster care. After being given up for adoption I remember going through several foster homes. I am a firm believer that a child's education begins at home prior to pre-school. Although it is not clear to my teachings prior to pre-school I do clearly remember that while growing up in the Burns' household, I was often reminded that I was a "Special Needs" child. I remember going through various experiences with different families. For example, I clearly remember being beaten by a foster mother with a brush while I was standing on a stairwell. I also remember, as a small child, holding salt and pepper shakers over the stove and turning the stove on and catching them on fire; and I remember the spanking that resulted. One memory was the fighting that occurred between my last foster parents. I remember knives being thrown through the sliding kitchen door that was made of a paper like material. I also remember my foster father getting drunk on a daily basis after his work was completed at "the factory." He would often pass out and a friend of his would have to make sure that a cab brought him home from the bar. Whenever he was partying, his friends would give me 25 cents to dance like Michael Jackson. One memory that stayed with me all my life was when my foster father, foster mother and I stood in a circle. He took a gun and put it in the middle of the circle and told me to shoot whomever I wanted. This memory is clear and vivid. It is as clear as day. We were standing in the corner of the living room near the black and white console television. Another formative lesson that stayed with me is that he always told me that since I acted like a girl and was always crying that he would put a barrette in my hair, put a diaper and a dress on me and make me sit on the porch. He would also call me a sissy because I would play with my female cousins and their dolls. Today, I am a transgender female (I will discuss that later). All of these memories and many more added to my early education and my formation.

My foster mother also taught me quality things of which most stayed with me. She would often sit with me on the floor and make paper-hats. This was both fun and entertaining. I never was good with my hands but I would always try. We would often make firemen hats. She also would teach me at a young age how to do chores. I remember standing on a stool and trying to wash dishes. My foster mother used to like to bake and I would always position myself in the kitchen while she made her Pineapple Upside Down Cake. These early lessons were truly a mixed bag. While I learned to enjoy cooking and baking, I am not very good at cleaning house. I did however learn how to stand up for what I believed was right.

Still prior to me starting kindergarten, I remember being taught about the Civil Rights Movement. I remember watching several marches and speeches led by Dr. Martin Luther King, Jr. These marches included the "March on Washington." I remember listening to the "I Have a Dream" speech on the radio. My foster parents would watch the evening news every night, while I sat on the floor playing and doing other activities. There were two events that I remember that shaped history; both events occurred in 1968. I remember watching the news when Dr. King was assassinated. I remember the hurt that many people felt at that time. A more pleasant memory was sitting on my foster father's knee watching the Detroit Tigers win the World Series. I remember when the batter on the other team popped the ball up and the Detroit Tigers' catcher caught the foul ball. To this day I still love baseball.

Therefore, I point out that children begin their education prior to attending school. Their behaviors and attitudes are formed at a very early age. A lot of these behaviors that I learned were things that I carried with me throughout life. Some are good and some are not so good.

While in kindergarten, I remember fighting because other kids called me "white boy." I have always considered myself as a Black American. I remember several things which occurred during my kindergarten school year and I also remember the teacher told my foster mom that if I didn't learn how to stay within the lines while coloring that I would not pass on to first grade. I remember participating in a Christmas program. The students would stand on a platform and sing Christmas songs for the audience. My most feared memory, which is still a phobia, was during a "Show and Tell." This adult visitor brought a snake to the classroom. I remember the yellow and black snake being wrapped around this Caucasian man's neck. I remember screaming and crying and being frantic. To this day I am terrified to even watch a snake on television. I actually remember getting in trouble in my high school biology class because while watching a movie on reptiles, I turned my desk around while other students watched a section of the film which pertained to snakes.

In 1971, at the age of five, I began my transition to the Burns' household. I remember hiding under the bed and in the closet on several occasions whenever Anne Taylor, the lady from the Children's Aid Society, would come and take me for visits. Ms. Taylor was a Caucasian lady in her early to mid-twenties. She was very nice but I was scared because I had gone from foster home to foster home and didn't want to leave my last foster home. However, during a visit to the Burns' household, I was in the basement playing on Derrick's toy piano and Mr. Burns was very kind and gentle towards me. He was truly an amazing man who made me, this little scared child, feel his love that he had. I grew so comfortable with him and the Burns' family that I did not return to the foster home. Mr. Burns asked if I wanted to stay at their house or return to foster care. My reply was to stay with them. My adoption was finalized on March 24, 1972.

While this transition took place I was in Ms. Parkers' first grade class at Atkinson Elementary School. My memory serves me that I often got picked on because I was "a little white boy." Other kids made fun of me saying things like "I saw you on television where they were trying to give you away and no one wanted you." I was often told that I was retarded. I remember a classmate told me that I could be his friend but I was either white or I was a girl. Internally I thought well I'm a girl but at that time I was afraid to say anything. My grades were pretty good; however my mouth seemed to be a problem. As one progress report stated "Dave talks too much." Well the gift that God gave me was a mouth and I was to use it to talk. I needed to learn how to control my mouth. To no one's surprise, to this day, I am still working on controlling my mouth.

Throughout elementary school my pattern of getting good scholastic and attendance awards continued, however I could not master the art of citizenship. I remember my second grade teacher would sit me in the corner of her classroom with a petition around me so I would be by myself and would leave other students alone. She would also make me sit under her desk so I would not bother other students. She told me since I acted like a baby and couldn't behave she would sit me next to her. I often had to hold her hand when the class would line up to walk down the hallway to the restroom. Although my behavior was a problem, my grades were decent. I remember when my teacher told the class that I was going to be a math teacher in the future. As my behavior improved she assigned me task of erasing and washing the chalkboard. I became what was known as a "future teacher."

Activities crucial to my elementary education included fashion shows, Christmas programs, and other performances. Back in the day, every morning began with the teachers and students standing up and repeating the Pledge of Allegiance. The teachers focused on teaching us about "Black Power" and would also tell us to proudly say "I am somebody special." Our second grade class actually had an "African-American Fashion Show." I proudly strutted myself across the auditorium stage wearing my African-American attire. I remember being one of the three kings during a Christmas program. As my elementary education progressed I participated in many school programs. My highlight was my fifth grade graduation. I was in a school program about the Declaration of Independence. My role was to be the best little Benjamin Franklin that one could be. I was so proud I thought that I was even better than the real Benjamin Franklin. Not only did I sign the Declaration of Independence, I also played the drums.

My musical talents were something else. It all started because my big brother, Derrick, was a decent clarinet player. I said that I wanted to be like Derrick, but I wanted to be better. Well during my fourth grade year our homeroom teacher asked the students for their interest in playing musical instruments. I said that I was interested and went down to meet the music teacher. Well, I was so proud I volunteered to be the first student to try and learn to play the trumpet. There was one major problem: I lacked a very special talent called rhythm. The music teacher, although he tried to keep me encouraged, urged me to learn to try to play the drums. He stated that while learning how to play the drums I could learn how to get rhythm. This was hilarious. I remember my father was very talented with musical instruments. The family would really appreciate listening to him play the piano. He also helped Derrick become a better clarinet player. Guess what? Derrick had rhythm. My father cut strips from a bicycle inner tube and nailed it to a piece of wood in an attempt to make an instrument so that I could practice playing the drums. I also took music lessons at McKenzie Music School and I remember playing the part of the Little Drummer Boy at Vernon Chapel Church. My rhythm was still off but I was impressed with myself.

Two other major contributing factors during my elementary education helped shape me into the person I am today. I was blessed to be adopted by a family deeply rooted in Christianity. The second factor was the attempt to implement busing during my elementary school days.

Although I had attended Sunday school and church with my last foster mother, I was too young to understand what was really going on. However, as I became a member of the Burns' family I truly began to understand what church was about. We attended Metropolitan Baptist Church in Detroit, Michigan. My parents were both very active in the church. My father was a Trustee and was very good with numbers and money. My mother was very active in Sunday school and was the Director of the Primary Church. My parents kept Derrick and me very active in the church. The funny thing is that I once was the groom in a Tom Thumb Wedding. When the preacher asked the bride if she took me to be her husband she wouldn't answer and finally I answered for her. I said "she does." The same behavior that I displayed in elementary school was consistent in Primary Church (whenever my mother wasn't the Primary Church teacher for that Sunday). Many spankings awaited me when I got home.

While in Primary Church I learned a song, which I have adopted throughout my life and strongly feel the true meaning of this song is my niche in life. The song "Do Something for Somebody Everyday" is special to me. A verse of the song is as follows, "Do something for somebody every day. Go scatter a blessing along life's way. Do something for somebody every day. Be watchful and pray. Do something for somebody every day." This is a lesson which I live by. I can't emphasize the importance of carrying out its message in my walk of life. My sister-in-law (whom I refer to as my sister due to the closeness that I feel to her), Gina Gregory-Burns often tells me "Jala, you have a heart as big as Texas." I have always wanted to help others. As a matter of fact, my mother passed on December 19, 2010 and in order to get me thru my grief my manager at Verizon Wireless delivered to me a very strong message. She said, "Jala, I know that this is hard for you; but I want you to get on the sales floor and do what you do best… I want you to focus on helping others. This will help you meet your sales and help you with grieving your mother's passing." As I mentioned, God has rewarded me with being one of our district's top sales representatives because my focus was to earn the trust of my customers by helping them. I either help them save money; help them learn to use the highest level of technology; or just help them by being the warm, compassionate sales lady that they need. I firmly believe that if "everyone does something for somebody every day" this world would be a better place. Now I also say make sure that you can do for yourself as well. Again this piece of education is as valuable (if not more valuable) than anything that a textbook could teach.

The attempt to bus students from Atkinson Elementary to Wilkerson Elementary School took place when I was in the third grade. Racial tensions grew between the black and white students. The black students often told me to take my "white self over across the city to the white school where I belonged." I was also accused of throwing a brick through a school bus window. Many of the students at Atkinson could not understand "why the white kids coming to our school." A lot of the students did not want to have to change schools and go to Wilkerson. My memory does not serve me on how that issue was actually settled. I do remember that some students had to switch schools. There was a lot of tension and fights between the black and white kids. Me, being biracial, got caught in the cross fire. Many of the kids, both black and white, didn't like me and I often got in a lot of fights.

Speaking of fights, my brother would often have to walk away from fights. As he got older he figured out that his mouth got him in trouble too. Well, Derrick was one of those gifted and hardworking students. Due to Derrick's academic achievements he was double promoted during his elementary education. Throughout Derrick's school years it was not uncommon for him to receive straight "A's" on his academic reports. There were many students that grew jealous of Derrick due to his success. However, Derrick admitted later on in life, that his problem was that he was a "smart ass" to many of his peers. This caused many issues for him and many students wanted to beat him up. Kids also wanted to beat Derrick up because of his skin complexion. Derrick was also called "white boy" and "honky." While Derrick followed my parent's advice and found a way to walk away from fights I didn't learn that craft. I seemed always to either come home with a black eye or bruises on my face. Two brothers actually jumped me one day and threw me into a tree trunk. It's a funny thing, and it always seemed strange, but I would often become friends with most of the children that I had fought in the past. The biggest fight that I ever had was with a boy named John Strong. He and Stanley Joyner kept calling me "honky" and other derogatory names. Stanley was too big for me to fight so I decided to fight John. I called him "Bald-head." Well as soon as I got the insult out of my mouth I felt a punch in my chest. I went wild and swung and punched John in the eye. I thought my troubles were over. Well, I was wrong. The whole school was after me. Stanley was very popular and it appeared that he and the entire school were saying, "Let's kick that white boy's ass." I must have punched John Strong really well because one Sunday afternoon John and his family showed up at my parents' house. His parents told mine that I punched him in the eye and he had just had eye surgery. My mother was extremely upset with me and told me that I was in trouble and that our family might get sued. Nothing further resulted. John and I became friends before the end of the school year.

The informal training that Derrick and I received was very valuable. As I mentioned earlier our mother was a school teacher. She taught Special Education at McDowell Elementary School. So in my opinion we felt the brunt of her career. For example, my mother would always have us do homework during the summertime. I detested this because in my opinion I had worked hard enough during the school year and I couldn't understand why I was doing school work when other kids were outside playing and enjoying themselves. Derrick and I were a lot different. He would enjoy reading books and doing writing exercises. I, on the other hand, would rush through assignments; whether they were math problems, writing exercises, or reading. I can hear it now. My mother would say, "Dave put that stupid ball down and read a book." My response was, "Uh I don't want to read." She would make me sit there until I successfully completed the work which she assigned me. That meant sometimes doing the work three or four times. Derrick would do his work correctly the first time and then proceed to an activity which he enjoyed.

Most of the time, Derrick would enjoy watching television. People have called the television the "idiot box." Well Derrick is not an idiot and he enjoyed watching boring things like "Star Trek" or the "Planet of the Apes." I hated those shows. I felt that he always controlled the TV but when I complained my mother would tell me to stop whining or to stop squealing. She couldn't stand my squealing voice. I would go downstairs and play with my stuffed animals or toy soldiers while Derrick would watch TV. Derrick also did other things that he thought were interesting; I thought that they were boring. He would collect stamps, comic books, and coins. He also had a microscope. I'd rather play with other things.

It was nothing for our father to load our car up at 4 a.m. and drive us on summer vacations. He would take us to places like Orlando, Florida; Denver, Colorado; or Omaha, Nebraska. While riding in the car we would play family games. For instance, he or our mother would ask us to name state capitols. We would also play the sign game. Whenever we saw a mile marker we had to say the next number in that sequence. We also played board games. I thought that Derrick was an outstanding chess player. He actually won a few tournaments during the Parks and Recreation Youth Programs. If you think about it chess is a thinking game, which means you have to use logic. I wasn't that good. Even though I would rather stay back at the hotel and swim, my parents would take us to Cape Kennedy or The Omaha Boys Home. I thought that these things were boring; little did I know that they were actually educational.

I remember lying in bed during Christmas break worrying about how my report card would turn out. I would be scared that my marks in citizenship would be bad and that I would get in trouble once my parents read the report. I worried about a lot of things throughout life (I will explain later in our book.) I do, however, remember my father always saying, "Dave you worry too much…

you worry about things after you have done something that you shouldn't have done." Derrick often told me the same thing later in life.

In 1976, I graduated from the fifth grade and began to feel old. Wow, little ole me was feeling old. My elementary education had a huge impact on my future. Patterns are formed at an early age and they followed me throughout life. My education at Atkinson Elementary School had served its purpose.

My Middle School Years
Shirley Temple Had Arrived

After fifth grade, I headed to Law Middle School where my pattern of fights and struggles continued. My sixth grade class was called Section 65. Our class always had fights with other sections in order to prove that "we were the baddest of the sections." We would always fight either Section 63 or Section 64. This continued in the seventh and eighth grades as well. Wow so let's get this right. Instead of concentrating on a valuable education we focused on fighting. We would meet in the restrooms in between classes and fight. We also had many food fights in the lunch room. I clearly remember sitting on the right side of the lunch room and as I looked up a chocolate milk carton was flying in my direction. My "bad ass" tried to catch the milk carton because I was going to throw it back. Wrong answer. What was I thinking? After catching the chocolate milk carton the proof was on my white shirt and I had chocolate milk dripping from my head. The school counselor ordered me to his office immediately. Let me tell you, once I got home I was greeted with the belt that my mother had in her hand.

There was this huge white boy, named Buff, who started off as my friend. My big mouth ruined that friendship. One day while we were sitting in science class he was sitting across the table from me and I looked up and he was digging in his nose. He proceeded to eat the booger. I yelled out "yuk...that's nasty." I said my friends don't dig in their nose and eat boogers. If I knew what was in store for me I would have kept my mouth shut. He commenced to kicking my butt and I cried afterwards.

I also could not control my mouth when it came to Reggie. During the summertime this boy had an unfortunate accident occur. He was shot in the eye with a BB gun and had lost his eye. When I saw him I called myself being funny and opened my trap and called him "Glass Eye Reggie." Again, I got beat up. I was in a lot of other fights throughout my middle school years.

Not only did I often get beat up by the boys, I also got beat up by the girls. One incident happened while riding the school bus from Law Middle School to our drop off point at Atkinson Elementary School. Although I was in the sixth grade and was new to Law Middle School I still did not know how to control my mouth. I got in a dispute with a girl that was in the eighth grade. She knew my brother, Derrick, because they had previously been in the same class. The girl knew that I was Derrick's little brother. She asked me if I was a "little white bitch like my brother." I responded to her with something like "Fuck you, you big foot bitch." She got up from her seat on the bus and walked across the aisle and slapped my face bright red. Everyone laughed. I cried and my friend, whom I later called my cousin, told me to stop crying and not to worry about it because the girl was an eighth grader and I was only in the sixth grade. Needless to say I didn't mess with her anymore.

So the sixth grade was kind of tough for me. There was this huge girl that was trying to prove to everyone that she was tough and that I was a little sissy. She started calling me Shirley Temple and started saying other rude things to me. One day she said that Shirley Temple needs to go to the restroom with the other girls. Everyone laughed at me and I felt belittled. My classmates called me Shirley Temple because I had curly hair. One day while trying to walk from one class to another she walked into me and pushed me. I pushed her back and before I knew it she had slammed me on my back in front of a lot of students. I was looking at the ceiling while lying on my back on the floor. From that point forward I got harassed through the rest of middle school. During one art class I was sitting across the table from another girl, named Sandra, and she actually called me Debbie. She said that I cry like a girl. It got so bad that two other girls, Donna and Shavonne, became my friends and protected me from both the boys and girls.

Now, I know exactly what you are thinking. If I spent all my time fighting when did I have time to learn anything. Well, I do have a lot of memories learning a lot of cool things. I remember being appointed the chief editor in our sixth grade journalism class. This was super exciting and I learned how to produce a quality newspaper. I also have fond memories of our Shop teacher, Mr. Jon Jackson. Although I was not good with my hands I appreciated Mr. Jackson's encouragement. He would urge his students to do their best. I actually remember the quote that Mr. Jackson wrote in my eighth grade memory book. He stated, "No matter what always focus on the finish line; for it is forever moving forward." My interpretation was to keep moving forward and never stop trying to become the best at whatever I do. Another fond memory was in Mrs. Lewiston's language arts class. Our assignment was to write a book and my book, "Space Odyssey 2001" was featured in the Detroit Newspaper. It was about a man playing golf in outer space. Mrs. Lewiston was also in charge of the Drama Club. Although I participated in a lot of drama productions my favorite was Arsenic and Old Lace. My rhythm didn't get any better but I continued to take drum lessons throughout middle school. At this point I had grown accustomed to being the Little Drummer Boy. This was routine every Christmas. Another fun activity took place in our math class. Mrs. West was in charge of the Equation Club. This club took part in a city wide competition where the various middle and junior high schools competed. This was a game where the students would create different mathematical equations by playing with dice. Our team was so good that we were invited to the State Tournament at Eastern Michigan University (I had no clue that I would end up earning my college degree from Eastern Michigan). Another memory that wasn't as fun took place in Mr. Jones' social studies class. Mr. Jones told the class to stop talking; but guess what? My big mouth got me in trouble. I kept talking and no sooner than I knew Mr. Jones was standing behind my chair shaking it abruptly. His words were "You are not to disrespect me and when I say stop talking I mean exactly what I say." Overall, I thought that Mr. Jones was pretty cool because a few years prior he had taken my brother and some of his classmates to London, England to perform a Shakespearean play "Coriolanus."

Although classroom learning is very important I also enjoyed extracurricular activities. Thanks to my father, both my brother and I were very active in the Junior Achievement program. The purpose of this activity was to help the youth learn business concepts. Our Junior Achievement organization met in Hamtramck, Michigan. My brother and I were in two different groups. The groups were set up as businesses. Derrick was the president of his organization and I was elected vice president of my organization. Derrick and I interviewed at the Hamtramck Chamber of Commerce for the Youth Business Leader of the Year. Derrick was very organized and won the achievement. I was sort of jealous but thought that if I didn't win that I was glad that he won. Derrick was a student at U of D High School and I was in the eighth grade at Law Middle School. My group project was to design a project that involved different color sand and vases. The officers of our organization had to give weekly reports. Once our project was done we would sell the vases and give the money to the Junior Achievement Directors in order to fund the program. This was a very exciting activity. Even more exciting was that every Monday after the Junior Achievement meetings our father would take us to Pizza Hut.

Furthermore, our parents continued to keep Derrick and I involved in church activities. Derrick is two years older than I am and I always wanted to follow in his footsteps. He was chairman or president of several groups in the church. We both served on the Junior Usher Board, Altar Boys, and several other groups. We both were active members of Metropolitan Baptist Church.

Overall, I learned many different things during my middle school years at Law Middle School. I learned that mathematics was a strong subject for me, but I was reading on a level two grades below my class level. Reading has always been a challenge for me; however I also learned how to overcome that obstacle. I graduated from the eighth grade in 1979 and was the co-chairperson of the Middle School Graduation Program. Our graduating colors were lavender and grey. I had a lot to do with getting my classmates to agree on lavender. I knew that it was a pretty color and was happy that my classmates went along with it. Mrs. Lewiston retired in 1979 so the event was very special to us all. I received many awards at the graduation. I remember receiving awards for scholastic achievement, attendance, the drama club, the equations team, and even citizenship. I received other awards as well. The students signed each other's memory books as an attempt to remember one another. One comment I received was "Congratulations to the Yellow Banana." I was called that due to my skin tone. At least people were no longer calling me "whitey" or "honky." I felt prepared to go forward to high school.

High School Times During the '80s

Well my high school years started out with a lot of fun. I was a student at Osborn High School in Detroit. During my first days of high school I decided to try out for football. What me? Football? Wow, this was funny. During these years I was searching for an identity and felt that I wanted to live my life as a girl. I knew that society wouldn't accept me so I needed to find activities to fight this conflict. If anything, I felt that if guys knew that boys were gay or transgender then the other boys would beat them up. In case you aren't aware there is a difference between being gay and being transgender. Well after a few days of practicing football, I quit. I think that the guys that I was practicing against were too big and too strong so I couldn't hang. During the homecoming week, I was elected Freshman Homecoming King (Mr. Freshman). I distinctly remember being at the homecoming dance and thinking that the Freshman Homecoming Queen had a pretty dress and I wish that I was wearing that dress. It was a long frilly mauve color dress. During the fall semester, I became a member of the Spirit Club and I proudly wore my red color Osborn Knight Spirit Club shirt. My nickname was Dr. Burns. Friends called me this because my best friend at the time, whom I called my cousin, was a great football and basketball player. Also I did like basketball and my favorite basketball player was Dr. J. As you can tell I was and still am a sports fan. Later that fall semester I tried out for the freshman basketball team. I wasn't that good and got cut from the team. I also tried out for the baseball team in the early spring. Guess what? I also got cut from the baseball team. I made the track team and ran long distance. My events were the one mile and two mile runs. My father showed up to my first track meet at Pershing High School. I was super excited and wanted to show him that I was good. I started out so fast that everybody was saying, "Wow Dr. Burns is going to set a record." Guess what? As I finished the first turn, I ran out of gas. Before the race was complete I had been lapped. Oh well, I tried. I always think back and ask myself why I tried out for the male sports teams. My answer to myself was that I was trying to fight against my wishes to be a girl.

My first tragic event occurred during my freshman year of high school. My Aunt Mae died. When I say tragic; I mean that I was devastated. Ever since I became a member of the Burns' family I was attached to Aunt Mae. She was a devout Christian. She was a member of the choir and very active in Sunday school. I believe that she was the director of the Sunday school at First Corinthian Church in Hamtramck, Michigan. Aunt Mae would often take

Derrick and me to her church's roller skating parties. She also would take us to her Summer Vacation Bible School. I also remember going with her to a Christian Convention to hear Billy Graham at the Pontiac Silver Dome. Aunt Mae gave Derrick the nickname of "Shug." Derrick and I would go over Aunt Mae and Uncle John's house (her husband) during the weekends and play a game called Pokeno. She would also make the best peach ice cream. One day Aunt Mae was braiding her hair and I said that I wanted to braid my hair too. She said that girls braid their hair and if I was a sissy then I could have my hair braided. I'm thinking that I should have had her braid my hair. I also remember when my brother was dating this girl during his high school years. Aunt Mae stated that Derrick should be careful dating white girls because anything could happen to him. I remember the Sunday in 1980 when Aunt Mae passed. The U. S. hockey team had just won the Gold Medal in the Olympics. It was about 4 pm.

In terms of academics I was performing at a decent rate. My grades were basically "A's," "B's," and "C's" during my freshman year. Since my reading level was a couple grades lower than my actual grade level I was required to take a reading comprehension class. During my first year I was required to take physical education. My favorite part was the swimming portion of the class. Coach Thompson, the football coach, challenged me and told me that if I dog paddle for the entire swim hour he would give me an "A" on my report card. He didn't think I could do it but because my mouth was so big and I kept bragging about how I could tread water he challenged me. I earned that "A." I remember that Coach Edwards, the Junior Varsity Football and Basketball Coach, told me during my first semester that I talked too much. Unlike Coach Thompson, I think that Coach Edwards liked me as a person. My feelings were mutual; I looked at Coach Edwards as a big brother. He would always stay on me about my grades and my behavior. Another fond memory is Mr. Ford's world history class. Due to my mouth, me talking too much, and my behavior he would call me a "character." I would really misbehave in his class but I had fun. He would always threaten to put me out of his class but instead would often tell me that I would like that. Mr. Ford would make me write "I will not talk in Mr. Ford's class" a whole lot of times (I think at least 500 times). He also made me write an essay on "Why I will not talk in Mr. Ford's class." My favorite part of his world history class came on Mondays when we had to present current events. He would always pick on me and tell the class since "David wants to talk so much I will let him start us off with his current-event report." I normally got "A's" on my report.

My sophomore year started off during the summer when I was attempting to make the Junior Varsity Football Team. Coach Edwards would often laugh with me, saying, "What is Doctor Burns going to do today to make us laugh?" I would often try to hit the blocking sled and I would hit it too high and the springs from the sled would knock me down on the ground. One time one of the football players, I think his name was Reggie Boyd, hit me so hard that my helmet turned sideways and I was looking out of the ear hole. I ended up making the Junior Varsity Football Team as the last player on the roster. Coach Edwards would call me "Dr. Fuck Up." Overall, he was really cool though. One special memory that I have is when our team messed up and Coach Edwards made us do push-ups. He stated something like, "Ladies you are going to learn to listen and do what your coaches tell you. Isn't that right ladies?" I was the only one that said yes sir. I really wanted to be a female. (I actually snuck and dressed up at home when my parents weren't home. I will elaborate on that later in the book.) I think that he allowed me to make the team so that I would gain more confidence. As I think about it I only played in one game and that was when the game was way out of hand. By the way, I would always tell my family that I was great and make it seem like I was better than I actually was. In fact, my father showed up to one of our games and of course I didn't play. Somehow my father made it inside of the building and saw the final cut list that was posted on the locker room door. My father told me that I was the last one that made the team.

As my sophomore year continued I stayed involved in extracurricular activities. I continued to be a member of the "Spirit Club." I again won the homecoming pageant contest. I was "Mr. Sophomore" and wished that I was "Miss Sophomore." I was also in the Drama Club and I continued to enjoy being in school plays. I actually tried out for "The Wiz" but because I refused to sing I did not get the part of the Lion. I also remember going through the hallways with my Spanish class singing Christmas Songs in Spanish. That was fun. However, after my first semester in the 10th grade, my grades brought a halt to my extracurricular activities. I had a 3-dimensional report card. Actually it was the first time that I ever had a "D" on my report card. That wasn't good enough. So I had to set a record. I actually got 3 "D's."

Well Big Bad Dr. Burns, (well actually I was the smallest person on the football team) thought that I was all that because I was on the football team. I was so out of control that my behavior hit rock bottom. There was a television show in the 1970s called "Welcome Back Kotter" which featured a group of students known as the "Sweat Hogs." Well there were several members of the J.V. football team who thought they were members of the "Sweat Hogs." Tommy and Donald were the leaders and so was Dr. Burns. I actually thought that I was the character "Arnold Horshack." Some of our other friends formed a group called the Holiday Players and they included me in that group. The Holiday Players would go to parties and dance. No matter what, the dances would seem to end up with the Holiday Players fighting other groups like the Davidsons. My parents were strict so they didn't let me hang out a lot. If I did hang out it was usually when Derrick was hanging out. For some reason Derrick was allowed to hang out more than I was.

No matter if I was in Mrs. Green's class or Mr. Abraham's class or anyone else's class I was the class clown. One day in my biology class, I asked if I could go to the restroom. The teacher told me that I couldn't so I got loud with him and said that my father told me that I could go to the bathroom anytime I needed to. Well one day I was bragging about the incident on the telephone and my mother was eavesdropping on my conversation. She rudely interrupted the phone conversation and told me to get off the phone and come see her immediately. She scolded me and put me on punishment for my behavior. I behaved poorly during my sophomore year. For example, I actually got kicked out of our Spanish class for calling my teacher a "bitch." My Spanish teacher stated on the first day of class that she didn't know how to curse (in Spanish). One day a few of my friends were in the back of the class talking. I turned around and joined them and started to laugh. The Spanish teacher called me out in front of the class. She told me to stop talking or she would have to move my desk. Since she said that she didn't know how to curse, I called her a "bitch." I thought that I said it under my breath; really I did. She heard me and told me that I "would not be able to digest those words." Well not only did she say that, she kicked me out of her class and I was sent to the principal's office. Mr. Evans was probably the coolest principle ever. Well, he told me that the Spanish teacher stated that she did not want me back in the class unless one of my parents met with her. Well, when my mother came to Spanish class the teacher and my mother hit it off perfect. My mother would have had to be a teacher so no matter what I did I was wrong. You can only imagine how this went. My teacher had beautiful flowers in the windows and she offered my mother some flowers. Then my mother said hello to Glen, whom she knew, and then she and the teacher spoke about how well behaved he was. Well long story short, I was put on punishment for the rest of the semester. My mother stuck to the punishment. It seemed like I was in my room for about three months. All I could do was go to school, go to church, eat my meals, and clean the house. Other than that I was not allowed out of my room and at that time we were not allowed to have televisions nor phones in our bedroom. Needless to say I got good grades the rest of the school year.

Although my issues dealing with race and adoption had quieted down, there were still times when I got teased about my skin color. For example, a boy from our neighborhood who had previously picked on Derrick was in my biology class and he kept calling me a "peckerwood." In return I called him a "hood rat." At this point I thought he was cool because another friend of mine and I would purchase marijuana from him. Other students would pick on me by calling me a white boy. But the racial issues that I faced in elementary and middle school had calmed down.

Speaking of drugs and alcohol, I began experimenting with them when I was in the tenth grade. A neighborhood friend and I used to get high while listening to music or watching television. "On Television" was our first experience of cable television. My friend and I would gather our money and go purchase weed and 40 ounce beers and Champale. After drinking and smoking I would make sure that I used his toothpaste and cologne so I would cover the smell. I would be careful to sneak in the house and head straight downstairs so that my parents would not know what I'd been doing.

As mentioned before, my first semester grades were my worse ever (3 D's). I got D's in my great expectations class (reading –yuk), personal health and hygiene, and geometry. Although I was strong in math, I didn't do well in geometry because I was busy being the class clown. Well, if I had not clowned in geometry and paid more attention I would have become a great student in mathematics like my second grade teacher Mrs. Bridgette had predicted. Since I didn't pay attention and learn my geometry in high school I struggled in my first calculus class at Eastern Michigan. I could be making a whole lot more money than I'm currently making if I had a degree in mathematics.

During the summer of my junior year my mother agreed to let me play football again. I guess she felt that I learned my lesson and that my grades in the second half of my tenth grade year had improved. It was typical that we held our summer practices inside in the gym. Well I wasn't very good so Coach Thompson directed me to hold a blocking dummy so the offensive team could run their plays. One of the players had warned me that I would get hurt unless I held the blocking dummy lower. I thought that I was holding it lower but apparently I wasn't holding it low enough. Crack…boom…awe… shit. I got hurt. As I lay on the floor in the gym, with my leg locked and while I was rocking back and forth on my back, the football coach said let's move our practice down some so the "Crip" would be out of the way. I thought that this was a messed up thing to say. Once he found out that my injury was serious he apologized. The injury that I received was a torn Anterior Cruciate Ligament.

Although I was injured my extracurricular activities continued. The football coach asked me to be the team equipment manager. I accepted, but I didn't know that the equivalent of this job was actually being the water boy. I refused to carry water out to the team because I was too cool and the coaching staff often got on my case because of that. One of my friends, whom I called "Daddy," was a great football player and I also thought that he was cute. I never told him for fear of losing our friendship. He would often tease me and tell me that I acted like a girl. We became really good friends and I ended up going to Eastern Michigan University because he had transferred from Alabama State University to E.M.U. I was voted "Mr. Junior" Homecoming King for my eleventh grade year. My mother began to let me hang out a little bit more and I was allowed to go to some parties. One time The Holiday Players were hanging out at a party and got into a fight. My cousin, who stood 6 feet 3 inches tall and was about 250 pounds, told me to get in the car and not to get out because a fight was taking place. When I heard that I thought that I was being treated like a little girl. Anyway I did as I was told.

My behavior improved during my junior year. I guess I learned my lesson during the previous year. As my behavior improved so did my grades. I was actually earning "A's" and "B's" and occasionally, I would receive a "C." My classes included Chemistry, Trigonometry, English, and Typing. During this time I fell in love with poetry written by Langston Hughes. "Me and the Mule" became my favorite poem because as I read the poem I reflected on my pride of being an African-American. My counselor, Mrs. Edith Dean, would tell me that she was very proud of me for finally getting my act together. She said that she had confidence in me and knew that I was pretty smart. She also stated that if I didn't clown in class and if I paid more attention and applied myself that I could become very successful. Two friends, Damon and Charlie, were good athletes and good influences for me. Damon was on the basketball team. Charlie played both football and baseball.

One matter that I need to discuss is how God blessed me and kept me out of trouble. During my junior year a few of my friends wanted me to hang out with them. We were going to ride around in their father's van and get high. For some reason I didn't go (I can't remember if my mother told me that I couldn't go out or if there was another reason that I didn't go.) Well anyway, I didn't go and it was a true blessing that I didn't hang out with them this time. According to the newspaper they got high while joyriding and became hungry. They robbed a country style store, where the store was on the bottom and an apartment or living quarters was on the second level above the store. Well the police were called and the boys were spotted on a scaffold. According to reports one of the boys had a gun and got scared. As he lifted his hands the gun went off and he killed a police officer. I was devastated when I got the news about this. He was quoted in the Detroit Newspaper saying that he was not a murderer. The boy was an excellent student at a local community college. I think the report said that he was a straight-A student. Again, God was watching over me because I could have gotten caught up in this matter.

As I was transitioning to my senior year I had heard that a lot of students were not graduating from school on time because they failed Government and Economics. Therefore, during the summer of my senior year I decided to take both Government and Economics. I took both of these classes very serious and the results showed. I received an "A" in both classes. Therefore I was off to a great start for my senior year. My extracurricular activities included me being in the Drama Club and Spirit Club. Since I had previously worked for the Athletic Director, Mr. Rutherford, I was allowed to be the Public Address Announcer during the basketball games. I earned class credit for working for the athletic department. The Athletic Director's office was right across the hall from the dance classroom and I would often look at the students that were in dance class and wonder how I might feel if I were in the class and if I could be the girl that I wanted to be. I really fantasized about wearing tights and being in the dance class. Due to society's norms and the fact that I would probably get beat up if I made my desires known I kept quiet. I decided not to try out for the cheer team nor enroll in dance class due to my lack of rhythm. During my senior year I was invited, by our Senior Coordinator, to the Detroit Economic Conference. Mr. Rutherford also invited me to a conference and parade for high school students that were interested in becoming sports announcers. No one showed up for the Sports Announcer Conference and the weather was very cold during the parade. Mr. Rutherford told me to toughen up and quit complaining about being cold. I had also participated in the Senior Basketball Game; we lost to the teachers by at least 20 points. I was the so called "Player-Coach." I started off coaching and when I got ready to go into the game the crowd started giving me a hard time by "booing" me. They were actually teasing me. So I further amused the crowd. As I ran down the court for the first time, I slipped and fell flat on my face. Everyone started laughing and finally the crowd started chanting "Sit down Dr. Burns." Finally I took heed and took myself out of the game. I received the loudest cheer as the crowd showed their appreciation that I finally sat down.

I decided to join the United States Marine Corps during the winter semester and was to report to boot camp in July. My mother was not pleased that I had wanted to join the Marine Corps and since I hadn't turned eighteen years of age I needed my parent's signature. At first my mother refused to sign the papers. I kept pestering her and telling her that it was only the Reserves and I also made sure that she knew that I still planned on going to college. I had further motivation to keep my grades up. I also applied to several colleges and decided to stay in Michigan and attend Eastern Michigan University. My determining factor was that Charlie was transferring to Eastern. The Marines kept me busy because I attended an early portion of the military program that committed high school seniors were to attend. Our activities included doing physical training and doing office work. I remember running three miles around Belle Isle. I think that I joined the Marine Corps because it was supposed to be the toughest branch of service and I was trying to fight my feelings of wanting to live as a female. I knew that society wouldn't accept me and I was scared to tell my parents. The older I got the more I felt that my father would have told me that as long as I was happy he would accept me with unconditional love. Derrick accepted me.

I know you are saying "Damn it took you until your senior year to stop fighting." Well, if you are thinking that you are wrong. Prior to one basketball game a couple of friends came up to Osborn. My cousin was visiting Coach Edwards in the boy's locker room. I was headed to my locker, which was in the hallway near what we called "Senior Corner." I walked up to a fight where five guys had ganged up on Howard. They had Howard against the lockers and were punching the hell out of him. I kind of panicked and went and jumped on two of them and knocked them down on the floor. I punched one of them and another guy from the crowd pulled a gun out on me and told me to get off his cousin. I said that I have a cousin too and ran to the locker room to get my cousin. It must have been God's grace but I did not get shot. (I'm still trying to figure that one out; but God saved me.) When my cousin and I got to Senior Corner the fight had broken up and no one was in sight. There were rumors that we had just engaged in a fight with one of Detroit's gangs called "The Young Boys Incorporated" (Y.B.I.). After we were at the game we were informed that the police were looking for Howard. They said that if he came back on Osborn's property again he would be arrested for trespassing. Needless to say, I was late for the game so I did not get a chance to setup the equipment needed to perform my duties as Public Address Announcer. After we arrived at Howard's house we spoke with him about the fight. Howard's eye was swollen with a huge bruise. He informed us that the fight occurred because The Y.B.I. had jumped his younger brother and was trying to take his Max Julian jacket. Max

Julian jackets were high profile items and people showed them off. That's something my parents would have never bought me. Howard expressed his thanks to me for saving his life. The problem was that I didn't have a description of the people that we were fighting and I was the only one on our side that went to Osborn. I remember telling my parents about the fight when I got home that day. My mother told me that she just figured that my role was just to fight. My cousin was home from the University of Toledo for break and he told me that I needed to lay low for a couple days until things calmed down. So without my parents knowing I would leave home in the mornings as though I was headed to school and then I'd sneak over to his house. Upon my return to school everyone told me to be careful and if I needed any help they had my back. Among my friends who said they had my back were the twins, Bill and Bob. These guys were damn cute and all the girls liked them. Again I kept the secret that I thought they were cute to myself. The twins were also good football players.

Another fight occurred during our Senior Picnic. The boys were playing football and a member from another high school got mad and jumped on one of the twins. Well when the fight broke out one of the twins got pistol whipped and got his jaw broken. I was a little buzzed and stayed out of the way. Other fights ensued during the Senior Hangout days. I remember a student from one of the other high schools; I think either Henry Ford High School or Cooley High School beat up another student from a different high school.

In terms of my academics I did very well my senior year. I received all "A's" and "B's" throughout the year. My courses included college preparatory writing, pre-calculus, American history, debate, and accounting. I loved the fact that I was getting out of school at around 12 o'clock noon. Of course I loved the debate class because as usual I loved talking and debating with others. I wasn't really fond of history (and go figure years later I received a degree in history). By year's end I became a member of the National Honor Society.

It was a struggle trying to go to the Senior Prom. My mother did not want me to use her car and I was too young to rent a car. This young lady from our church was going to let me use her car if all else was going to fail and I couldn't get access to a car. My father actually came through and agreed to let me use his car. I couldn't understand why Derrick was able to drive my parent's cars but I wasn't. Well Derrick had totaled my father's car a few years prior. In an attempt to fight my female feelings I called a girl named Tamara and asked her to go to the prom. She agreed but our prom experience wasn't like most dates. Other couples were hugged up and getting frisky. Tamara and I kind of kept a distance. We didn't even kiss or hug. I thought that her dress was beautiful though.

During the end of my senior year I started being friends with a couple of people who actually figured me out. This girl named Valerie and I started talking on the phone and shared certain things with each other. I remember that after we graduated she started calling me a girl and telling me that I needed to start wearing dresses. I guess she knew. There was also this white guy named

Ron. I spent the night over his house one evening. While we were in his bedroom about to go to sleep he shared his secret that he was gay and that his father was a retired Marine and didn't like gay people. I jokingly told him if he touched me I would knock his ass into the closet. I had no clue what "being in the closet meant." He informed me that I hurt his feelings and that "being in the closet was not letting anyone know that he was gay." I apologized for my ignorance and being so rude. Ronald and I hung out a little and talked on the telephone frequently. I actually shared my feelings of how I snuck and wore my mother's clothes and makeup when my parents weren't home. He and I actually went to a party that had a bunch of gay guys and lesbian girls.

My participation in church continued during my high school years. I was the president of the Youth Group, active in the Youth Choir, active on the Usher Board, a member of the Altar Boys, and active in other church organizations. I attended church basically every Sunday.

My days in high school were fun for I matured some and began to learn how to behave. I still, however, did not learn how to control my mouth. I figured that the discipline that I would get from the Marine Corps boot camp would help me become an adult. My graduation was on a very hot day in June and my Aunt Agnes came from Chicago to see me walk across the graduation stage. I was very happy because I really appreciated the support that she had always shown me. In fact my mother got mad at me because I didn't want to wear a suit under my graduation gown. She threatened to not go to my graduation. Aunt Agnes told her not to make those types of threats and told me not to worry that she definitely had come from Chicago to see me graduate. Once we got to the graduation ceremony I sat next to a friend of mine whom I called Momma Mia; her first name was Mia. Mr. Evans handed out the diplomas and announced me as "Dr. Burns" as I walked across the stage. After the graduation I took pictures with my friends. My father's hobby was photography. I took a picture with my friend, Valerie, and to this day I remember her red and white dress. Oh how I wished that I wore that dress. The one thing that I was always envious of was that my mother let Derrick have a graduation party when he graduated from the University of Detroit High School in 1981 but when it was my turn to graduate in 1983 I couldn't have a party. My thoughts were that my mother thought my friends were hoods and that she didn't want to have trouble in her house. Well when it was all over I was eager, but scared, to start basic training.

Marine Corps Boot Camp
Time to Grow Up Quickly

Since the Marine Corps is a type of training I will include a couple of chapters about my experience in boot camp and radio school. This training was a transition between high school and college. Warning. Some of these events will be funny. I actually was going to boot camp on the buddy system with a friend of mine named Jackson. He played high school football and always teased me by calling me a girl. Jackson was a real nice person and real freaky and he really liked his women. I remember the July morning that the recruiter came to take Jackson and me to the military building in Detroit. From there we flew out of the Metropolitan Airport to go to San Diego's Marine Corps Recruit Depot (known as M.C.R.D.). I was scared and throughout the flight I kept asking myself "what am I doing?" Again by joining the Marine Corps, I was thinking that my feelings about wanting to live as a girl would go away (they didn't).

Well we made it to San Diego and it was on. As soon as we got to the airport we were greeted and told to get on the bus and not to talk to anyone. I remember some marines, maybe some graduates (I'm not sure), told me and a couple other recruits to salute the mail box. Once we got on the bus we were told to sit up straight and place our hands on our knees. We were told to keep our traps shut.

Uh oh. Here we go. The yellow foot prints were imprinted on the deck at M.C.R.D. We were told to stand at a position of attention on the yellow footprints and we had to read a pledge that was placed on a sign that hung on the building. Once we read the pledge some marines started screaming at us. They told us not to put our hands in our pockets and to stand up straight and not to talk unless a marine spoke to us and asked for a response. These marines were yelling and scaring the shit out of me. I was thinking "What the hell have I done?" The line of recruits were taken through a barracks to get things that we needed for boot camp: things like our fatigues, our toiletries, beddings and linens, and a coupon book to use for supplies that we would need for the next twelve weeks. As the recruits formed a line we were told that we were worthless and we were the property of the United States Marine Corps. We were surrounded by barbed wired. If we tried to escape and got pass the barbed wired we would get shot. M.C.R.D. was right across from the San Diego Airport. Oops, I made a mistake. While waiting in line to get my hair cut, I accidentally (out of habit, I promise) put my hands in my pocket. This marine sergeant jumped in my face and started screaming at me. He told me that I better get my fucking hands out of pocket and asked me where I was from. After I told him that I was from Detroit, he asked me if I thought that I was a thug. He also asked if I had a pistol in my pocket and if so, did I plan on shooting him. As I stuttered the words "No Sir" he responded "Boy you are soft. Are you a boy or girl?" Things were getting worse. I had reached the barber's chair. The barber swiped his clippers across my head about three or four times and all my hair was gone. We were told to throw all of our contraband away and if we got caught with any contraband we would go to the Brigg. Candy, gum or anything that wasn't issued by the marines was considered contraband. One of the marines had gotten on one recruit because once he got his hair cut the recruit had dust in his head (yuk). The boy was so mad and apparently didn't like being yelled at so he punched the marine. Why the hell did he do that? Several marines came and wrestled the boy to the ground and took him to the Brigg.

Once we got to the barracks about 3 a.m. we were still getting yelled at and were told to take the razors and shave all the hair off of our face. If we had any hair on our faces we would really regret it once they got done with us. It appeared that no sooner than we were allowed to get in the rack (the bed) we heard a loud crash of a trash can being thrown on the squad bay deck. Oh my God. I was scared. This first day was hell and I was thinking that I messed up. I didn't think that I agreed to all of this.

Well my first full day of boot camp was really scary. It started at about 5 a.m. when we were awakened by the sound of a trash can being thrown across the middle of the squad bay and a lot of screaming and yelling from three marines. They were tall, thin and mean looking. They were scaring me. They told us that we had less than a heartbeat to get in the head (restroom) and to shit, shower, and shave. I was in such a rush that I cut my ear while shaving. One of the marines said "What the Fuck? This little punk from Detroit doesn't even know how to shave." Once we walked, and I can't say "marched" because we didn't know how, to the chow hall we were told that we were a "cluster fuck" and that we had 10 seconds to get in the chow hall, eat and get back into formation. Well, me being the shortest in the platoon, I was the last one in the formation (the formation went from tallest to shortest) so I was the last one to enter the chow hall and barely had time to get through the chow line and sit down before one of the marines told us to get the fuck out.

After I grabbed my tray from the chow line I proceeded to go sit at our designated table. Well, I made the mistake of walking past this marine. Oh my God. I was in trouble. He and three other marines all jumped up in my face and started hollering at me. They called me all kind of names and told me "Dirt bag, how about saying Sir, by your leave, sir." Recruits were to say this whenever we passed by a marine. My mind was kind of slow on that level because I was new to this and was never taught that procedure. My tray was shaking so bad that I dropped my orange juice glass and orange juice got on one of the marines. Oh hell. He really got up and personal. He was nose to nose with me screaming at the top of his lungs that I better get the fucking juice off of his trouser leg. I made the mistake of taking my napkin from my tray, while holding the tray, and wiped the marine's trouser leg. Oh boy, this thing is getting worse and worse. He called me "a faggot" and said that "We don't let fags in the Marine Corps." He then asked me "Are you Daddy and Mommy's little girl?" As I tried to answer, he and the other marines started yelling at me, telling me not to open my freaking trap. Wow, finally I was told to go sit down and swallow my chow. As soon as I sat down another marine told our group to get out and go get into formation. As we were placing our trays on the conveyer belt leading to the kitchen other recruits, which we thought were marines, were talking trash to us.

Once we got outside and got into formation we were told that our day would be spent processing. We had to sign more papers, get shots, see the dentist, and do other duties. I remember cleaning the heads and hallways. We had to varnish the brass with brass cleaner called Brasso; that stuff had a terrible smell. We spent most of the day grabbing mattresses and moving them to wherever we were told. The mattresses were too heavy for me and the marine in charge started picking on me, calling me all kinds of names. At the end of the day we were exhausted. The sun was hot and we were told to keep drinking water and eating salt. I hated salt but it was supposed to be good for you while standing in the heat. There were several recruits who passed out from heat exhaustion. I remember being told that we would be put in a tub of ice if we passed out. We were also told not to lock our knees after we got shots.

We spent a week processing and getting acclimated to the San Diego heat. During this week Jackson and I were told that we had a visitor at the Headquarters Building. We went down to the building and met our recruiter from Detroit. He was tripping on me because I was "like yes sir and no siring all over the place." He told me to relax and to chill. Jackson took it in stride and was cool as a cucumber. He was just so chill. Our recruiter told us that we would be alright and try to adjust as quickly as possible because the adjustment process will probably be the hardest part of boot camp. We spent about fifteen minutes with the recruiter and then walked back to our squad bay. Every moment of the day, every day of the week, we were told that the marines were our father and our mother. We were told that we were going to be taught how to breathe, eat, sleep, shit, shower and shave. We were going to be taught everything we needed to know in order to survive. At the end of the week we were told that we were in "Platoon 2078" and we were introduced to our senior drill instructor and drill instructors.

All three of these marines were introduced by our company commander. When introduced they came into our squad bay standing tall with their "Smokey the Bear" covers (hats) on. In my mind I said "How cute, they looked like Smokey the Bear, like on television." The minute they started screaming at us their cuteness disappeared. Marines are very particular in their appearance. These men were sparkling in their uniforms, from top to bottom. Their uniforms had creases in both their shirt and trousers; their boots were so shiny that they looked like mirrors; they had zero facial hair; and their shirts were firmly tucked into their trousers. These marines were going to teach us how to look like them. Senior Drill Instructor Staff Sergeant McLean, Drill Instructor Sergeant Walters, and Drill Instructor Sergeant Stevens owned us for the next eleven weeks. Senior Drill Instructor Staff Sergeant McLean was a tall, lean, and mean fighting machine. He was a black man that appeared to be taller than six feet. He was direct and we knew that he held us accountable for everything that we did. When he was introduced to us he told our platoon that he had been watching us for about a week. Some of us were acting properly; others weren't. Those that weren't would quickly learn the rules. We had better follow the rules or we would pay dearly for our mistakes. Overall, he was tough and strict, but he was only doing his job of developing us into marines. The rowdy, gung-ho ones were Drill Instructor Sergeant Walters and Drill Instructor Sergeant Stevens. When they were introduced to us they came into the squad bay deck classroom and started screaming at us; it was a terrified experience. I remember saying to myself, "Here we go again." This reminded me of the first night that we arrived at M.C.R.D. The drill instructors were like big brothers and the senior drill instructor was like a father-figure. They all stayed on us the entire time. They were responsible for our development into "lean and mean fighting machines." I believe that both Drill Instructor Sergeant Stevens and Sergeant Walters served in the Vietnam War. I know for sure that Drill Instructor Sergeant Stevens would always tell us that he served in that war and that his job was to prepare us for battle.

Boot camp consisted of physical training, grooming, drill, classroom training, rifle training, pistol training, mess duty, swimming survival, hand to hand combat, first aid training, inspection preparation, field training, and many other activities. Although at the time I didn't find these activities amusing, I did appreciate them as I matured through life. Some of my boot camp experiences were funny and some were not funny at all.

One of my early lessons, while in boot camp, was that neither racial nor ethnic harassment was tolerated. One of the drill instructors ordered Private Rodriquez and me to take a trash can out and empty it in the dumpster outside the barracks. At the time, Platoon 2078 was housed on the top deck of the barracks. As Private Rodriquez and I were trying to carry the trash can down the steps I was struggling because it was too heavy. The drill instructors were yelling to make Private Rodriquez and I hurry. Due to my lack of strength I became frustrated. Just as Senior Drill Instructor Staff Sergeant McLain was coming up the stairwell I opened my mouth and said something nasty to Private Rodriquez. I told him to help more and to hurry his Mexican ass up. Uh oh, my big mouth got me in trouble again. Private Rodriquez told me to shut up or that he would kick my ass. Well Senior Drill Instructor Staff Sergeant McLain heard the interaction and he started going off. He made Private Rodriquez and I run with the trash can to the dumpster, which by the way I was barely able to carry it while walking down the stairs. Once we finally made the dumpster and returned the trash can up to the squad bay we were ordered to run up and down the stairwell until we were told to stop. It seemed like an eternity. As soon as we were told to stop running, Drill Instructor Sergeant Stevens instructed our platoon that he was going to introduce to them what was called being "thrashed in the pit." Well here we go. Private Rodriquez and I were made to be examples of this exercise. When I say exercise, believe me, it truly was. Both Rodriquez and I entered a large area that was rectangular in shape and full of sand. Sergeant Stevens demanded "leg lifts, side straddle hops, run in place, sit ups, push-ups, mountain climbers…." This seemed to have gone on forever. Once we were done with the punishment we were ordered to run back up the steps and to our squad bay. We were ordered to stand at the position of attention by our racks (bunk beds). Apparently Sergeant Walters thought it was funny so he ordered the entire platoon to the classroom. Once we were in the classroom he started yelling out commands of thrashing the entire platoon, "Pushups, sit-ups…" I thought "damn is this shit ever going to end." Well the lesson here was that there is zero tolerance for discrimination towards race or ethnicity. We were either "Dark Green" or "Light Green" recruits. Marines were only "Dark Green" and "Light Green." My mistake never occurred again. Trust me I learned my lesson. Rodriquez and I became closer as boot camp progressed.

Physical training was pretty rigorous. The formation of the platoon was lined up from the tallest to the shortest. Since I was the shortest I was always in the back. This was quite a disadvantage. The taller recruits had long legs; while the shorter privates had shorter legs. That meant that whenever we ran anywhere the shorter recruits would have to work twice as hard to keep up. Our physical training consisted of running a few miles a day; we would march everywhere we went; our thrashing punishment was often; and we did other conditioning activities as well. We would sing different songs as we marched or ran. Some of the songs would not be what a lady wanted to hear. For example, the cadence would go like "I put my hand upon her twat…." Another song was about a "Yellow bird that landed on a window sill" and finally someone crushed his "Fucking head." I thought "Oh my, how gruesome?" We had the obstacle course, confidence course and other courses that we endured. There were several areas of the obstacle course that I could not master. One obstacle that I didn't perform well on consisted of a single bar that we had to jump and swing over. Apparently I had two problems. I didn't have the upper body strength to overcome the obstacle and therefore I couldn't master the technique. I never made it over the bar. By the end of boot camp the drill instructors would just laugh at me and tell me just run to the next obstacle. The other obstacle that I couldn't solve was the rope climbing. I don't understand because at the beginning of boot camp I was able to get partially up the rope. At the end of boot camp I couldn't make it even partially. We also participated with rifle pt. The M-16 was described as a light weight carrying machine. Well you never would have known it was light weight; especially when the drill instructors made us do exercises with the weapon. There were other privates that were sent to the "Fat Farm" during the beginning of boot camp because they weren't in physical shape. I remember at the end of boot camp I was told to stay back at the barracks, to stand "Fire Watch," while the platoon was completing the confidence course and the 5 mile "motivational run." During basic training we had several physical training examinations which consisted of pull ups, sit-ups, and the 3 mile run. The four platoons, within the company, would compete to see which platoon scored the highest. Senior Drill Instructor Staff Sergeant McLean was often upset with our platoon's performance for we often finished last or next to last.

In the third and final phase of boot camp we faced another physical activity that was very challenging; which included climbing "Mount Motherfucker." Well the name actually fit the description of the mountain. We had to march about 3 miles from our barracks and since the tallest recruits had the longer legs the privates in the front were stretching out and leaving us shorter privates behind. The shorter privates had to run in order to keep up with the rest of the platoon. Drill Instructor Sergeant Walters kept screaming at me, telling me to get my ass up there with the rest of the platoon. Well, it got worse. Once we got to Mount Motherfucker we were told to keep marching and that we were going to climb the mountain. I was thinking "hell I barely made it this far…how the hell am I going to get up there? Was somebody going to carry me?" The mountain was at least 3 miles high and very steep. Each recruit was fully dressed in fatigues; carrying our two canteens and our rifle; and carrying a backpack full of MREs, other fatigues, and lots of other items. We had to march through a sandy path that went straight up to the peak of the mountain. As I made my move forward I grew weary and I actually vomited a few times on the way to the top. The drill instructors kept yelling at me, telling me to catch up with the other privates. I kept thinking "Fuck this shit… I didn't agree to do this." The D.I.s kept asking if I were a man or a girl. I kept thinking "I'm a girl, what?" Finally we made it to the top of Mount Motherfucker and were told to stand at the position of attention. Hell we were tired. The next day we had to march down the mountain. Although it wasn't as bad as climbing up, it was still a challenge.

The conditioning was to prepare us for combat. We were to become "lean and mean fighting machines;" even little ole me. Well the truth of the matter was that once I completed basic training I was built so solid that Derrick would call me "Rock."

When it came to grooming and personal appearance we were taught how to shit, shower, and shave. No joke. For example, if a private was in the restroom the drill instructors would tell us when to stop using the head. We were taught how to iron our clothes with creases. We ironed our skivvies (underwear), covers (military hats), blouses (shirts), trousers, socks and anything else that we were instructed. We actually had to wash our clothes by hand. We would use the scrub boards in the rear of our barracks and wash our clothes in the sinks and on the cement counters. We learned how to thoroughly spit shine our boots. We also had inspections on a routine basis.

I remember my first inspection. The company officers and other drill instructors came into our barracks as we were in formation in the classroom.

This "Light Green" officer got in my face and started yelling at me. While he was inspecting my rifle, I accidentally hit him with the butt of my rifle. This was a direct result of my nervousness. As soon as the rifle touched him he started yelling at me that I assaulted him and that I was going to the Brigg. No matter how much he yelled at me I was not to flinch. I was only allowed to say "Sir yes sir" and "Sir no sir." Our knowledge base was thoroughly checked because we would get all sorts of questions about the Marine Corps history, weapons, first aide, or anything else that might come up. We were trained so that the first word out of our mouths was "Sir" and the last word out of our mouths was "Sir." We had many other inspections throughout basic training. Our final inspection was during "third phase" of boot camp. The commanding officer and many other high ranking officers, warrant officers and NCOs performed the inspection. We were so sharp you could actually hear the click and pop of the rifles. Our boots were so shiny that if you looked down at one of the other private's boots you might get blinded by the sun. We had many hours of classroom training and knew our information. Well I was impressed. You know what, we failed the inspection. One private had a button on his blouse unbuttoned. He actually missed the button. Another private had a thread of his uniform hanging from his trouser pocket. The thread was called an "Irish Pennant." Our drill instructors were yelling and going ballistic; we did not pass our Final Inspection. The purpose of the inspections were to make sure that we were prepared physically, mentally, and knowledge wise. These inspections were high intense and kind of scary. We had competition between each platoon to see which one had the best overall score. Our platoon normally finished third or fourth. Again there were only four platoons in each company.

I thought drill was fun because we marched to the cadence of our leaders. I often got picked on because I tried to do exactly what I was commanded and I always came up short. For example, I lacked rhythm and it showed every time I was out of step. I always tried leaning back when the drill instructor told us to lean back and strut our stuff. Well my nickname was "Frankenstein." The other privates would tease me and tell me to loosen the bolts in my neck. While standing in formation and doing drill with our rifles I would often have my elbows stuck out too far. Sometimes our drill instructors would make us stand still and hold the rifle still for a long period of time; it seemed like an eternity. My arms would get tired and I would move. Well Drill Instructor Sergeant Stevens would end up in my face screaming "Burns just wants to move his little combined body." I clearly remember him saying that and I used to have dreams about Sergeant Stevens yelling at me. He stayed on my case. We also had drill competition and were scored by the company officers. Of course, we never won that event either. In the final phase of boot camp we prepared for our graduation parade. Each graduation class would march in the parade once their graduation ceremony was completed. With all our practice and all of our getting yelled at, it rained during our graduation and our parade was cancelled.

Basic Training was comprised of physical, mental, and educational components. We spent many hours in the classroom. Some of the subjects that we were accountable for learning included: The United States Marine Corps history, first aid training, weapon concepts, and other topics. We learned that the Marine Corps was established on November 10, 1775. Wow my birthday is November 11, 1965. The Marines are a military operation that serves in the air, on land, and sea. During the Mexican War the Marines fought to the "Halls of Montezuma"; thus the Marine Corps Hymn "From the Halls of Montezuma to the Shores of Tripoli." Due to their war efforts during World War I the Germans began calling the marines by the name "Devil Dogs." We also studied about the history of all the wars which the marines took part. There were many other interesting historical facts relating to The Marines Corps.

We spent many hours learning first aide. We learned things from how to treat victims that are choking to methods of treating soldiers that were bleeding. One interested exercise that we took part of was learning the "Fireman Carry." The classroom instructors would laugh because it would seem that I was always partnered up with someone at least 50 to 100 pounds heavier than me. While my partner wouldn't have a problem picking me up and placing me on his back I often struggled carrying him on my back; but I did it.

We also spent many hours learning about weapons. At that time the M-16 was our best friend. Our lessons consisted of the procedure to disassemble the rifle, clean it, inspect it, and the history of it. We were introduced to the different types of rounds (bullets) that were used by the marines. Instruction also included the history of other weapons. We also learned about weapons used for hand to hand combat.

Imagine sitting in a hot classroom in the summer months in San Diego. Trash cans and other objects were thrown at the recruits that nodded off during class. The instructors would call you out in the middle of class. To be fair though, they would tell the recruits that if they felt sleepy to go to the rear of the classroom and put water on their faces. I often was one of the victims that were thrashed outside the classroom because I fell asleep. We would recite the information that we were taught while standing in formation. This repetitiveness became automatic. Our knowledge was tested during inspections.

Rifle and pistol training took place during the Second Phase of Basic Training. The drill instructors would joke with me because I was from Detroit. They would make remarks like "Burns thinks he's bad because he is a Hood Rat from Detroit." Then they would tell me to get my little ass up on the pistol range and fire my .45 at the target. I actually did fairly well firing the pistol.

The rifle range was the complete opposite. Rifle training was divided into classroom and rifle range instruction. The classroom instruction covered safety, setting rifle metrics (called sights), and rifle inspection. Although I thought that I was attentive during the rifle class I had problems setting my rifle's sights. The rifle range was setup at 100, 200 and 500 yards. After a week of messing up during rifle practice it was time for me to qualify on the rifle range. When I say messing up, well I kept shooting on someone else's target. The exercises included both slow fire and rapid fire of the rifle. We were taught how to shoot our rifles from the prone position (lying down), the kneeling position, the sitting position, and the standing position.

"All ready on the left... All ready on the right...All ready on the firing line... all shooters may commence firing when your dog targets appear," radiated over the rifle range loud speaker. Well my rifle qualifying started off pretty well. I scored a pretty decent score on the 100 yard line. My 200 yard shooting wasn't as good but the instructors were pretty excited about my score; thus far. Hey I was on my way to qualifying as a Sharp Shooter. Well once I got to the 500 yard mark I totally blew my score. Although I was lined up at target number 15, I was shooting on targets 16 and 17. As the sound of "Cease fire...Cease fire...Clear, unload, and lock" was announced over the loudspeaker my instructor announced my score. Guess what? Not only did I not qualify as a Sharp Shooter, I did not qualify at all. I flunked. Several recruits from my platoon qualified as Experts and Sharp Shooters. The majority qualified with what was called the "Toilet Seat," the Marksman. I was one of three privates, from our platoon, that did not qualify at all. As a penalty, myself and the other two recruits were singled out and couldn't stand in formation nor march with our platoon. We were being left behind while the remainder of our platoon progressed through boot camp. This was hard. We stayed at the barracks while the others boarded the bus and were taken back to M.C.R.D.

The instructors that were left with us kept reminding us how pathetic we were and that in order to graduate from boot camp we would have to qualify. For that entire weekend and the beginning of the next week we had to clean the barracks from top to bottom. This was the only activity that we had other that going to the rifle range. Well, I said enough of this shit. I was allowed to attempt to re-qualify on Tuesday. The rifle range instructor helped me reset my sights on my rifle. This time my qualifying started out poorly. I missed 8 out of 10 of my shots on the 100 yard slow fire while seated. The warrant officer came over to me and started joking about me and how well I shot the pistol. He was among those laughing and joking when I qualified on the pistol range. He kept calling me "The hood from the east side." Well Warrant Officer Mendoza told me that my problem was that I was too tight and that I needed to relax. My shots kept going into the bunker. As I continued to the 200 and 500 yard markers my shooting got much better. When my score was tallied and announced this time I had qualified with the "Toilet Seat"; I was a Marksman.

One thing stands out that I will remember for the rest of my life. Just as we had finished a long lecture about safety on the rifle range I broke one of the main rules. We were to be careful and to always point the rifle down range. Well an officer approached me while I was on the firing line, on my first day of actually firing my weapon, and I accidentally pulled my rifle back. It was pointed upwards and back as almost towards the officer. All hell broke loose. Not only was that officer in my face, there were several other drill instructors yelling at me. I learned a new type of thrashing. I got thrashed with my M-16. I had to do many exercises with my rifle. For example, I had to run in place while extending my arms with my rifle in hand. I also had to do squats with my arms extended while holding my rifle. I made sure that I would not repeat my offense.

Another mistake that I made included calling my rifle my gun. When I was first issued my rifle Drill Instructor Sergeant Walters asked me if I knew what I was holding in my hand. I excitedly stated "Sir, yes Sir. I'm holding my gun." Well my mouth got me into trouble again. Marines do not call their weapons guns. The D.I.s all gathered around and started calling me names like "faggot" and other derogatory names. One D.I. said "Burns is holding his penis in his hand" while the other D.I.s were laughing at me. Well I soon found out that marines call their penis' "guns" and their rifle either "M-16" or "rifle." I didn't make that mistake again either.

Well once I qualified I was surprisingly rejoined with my platoon. Upon being rejoined, Senior Drill Instructor Staff Sergeant McLain gave me a hard time. He kept calling me a wimp and told the other recruits that the "scared little girl" named Burns was joining our platoon. Well we were in the middle of Mess Week. I hated Mess Week because we had to wake up at 3 a.m. and march to the mess hall and work duty. Several of us were assigned to clean the kitchen; several were assigned to clean the mess hall; others were assigned on the serving line. It was pitch dark at 3 a.m. One morning I was in the kitchen clowning with some of the other recruits. I was actually talking about one of the instructors at the rifle range and saying that I thought that he was very funny. Well as soon as I started talking about him one of the D.I.s from Platoon 2079 walked into the kitchen and caught me in mid-stream. The next thing that I knew, I was outside being thrashed in the sandpit. It was a pitch black Wednesday morning that had already begun to get hot. I heard the drill instructor, "bend and thrust, push-ups, side straddle hops, push-ups, run in place, leg lifts, side straddle hops…." Man was I exhausted. My thoughts were that I didn't agree to this shit and that I wanted to get back in the bed and put the covers over my head. Mess Week was the initial week of our third and final phase of basic training.

The highlight of the following week was the swimming tank. The thought of being tested in the swimming pool took me back to Coach Thompson's 9th grade swimming class at Osborn High. I thought that I was a good swimmer. At least I did until I was told that we had to jump into the swimming pool with our fatigues and swim back and forth for several laps. I think that I made one lap and then I was done. I was told that I was a quitter. Damn right I was tired. Those that passed that test were put through other tests. Most of our platoon topped out at the first level. The peak level of the swimming tests was being fully dressed in military fatigues; with a backpack full of equipment and a M-16 strapped on the recruits back; with a helmet securely fastened to the private's head; and if my memory serves me correct the private's hands were tied behind his back. This was some sort of Houdini shit. Believe it or not, there were some recruits that passed this test. The remainder of that week was spent cleaning our barracks and working on other detail.

Hand to Hand and Close Combat Trainings were also instrumental parts of boot camp. Our Hand to Hand Instructor was a highly motivated marine who bragged about being able to kill people with his hands. He stated that he would teach us how to kill without using weapons. One exercise that I had mixed feelings about was teaching us how to choke people to death. I thought that it was fun when I was the aggressor. I had choked my partner until he turned beet red. I thought that was some funny shit. Well it wasn't so funny when it was my turn. My partner had choked me so bad I fell to the ground. I felt like I was going to die. My partner started laughing once he knew that I was alright. We also learned other karate moves. Also another component of Hand to Hand Combat included "The Smoker." Recruits would represent their perspective platoons and compete against each other in the boxing ring. Once the recruits were in the boxing ring they went blow to blow in an attempt to rip each other's head off. My participation included being in the cheering section in the bleachers. I didn't know how to box; nor did I want to know how.

The Close Combat Training included fighting with a pugil stick. This weapon resembled a large Q-tip that was about 3 feet long with pads on each end. I failed miserably at one exercise called "The Bridge over Troubled Waters." Two recruits were to battle each other on a narrow bridge; which had water on both sides. I thought that I heard the commanding officer instruct that we were to keep both hands on the pugil stick at all times and "If one of your hands comes off the pugil stick you lose and must jump in the water. Otherwise you are to fight until your opponent is knocked in the water." Well I got into my match with my opponent and I was knocking him around pretty good. Then all of a sudden one of my hands came loose from the stick. I thought that I was following orders so I jumped in the water. The commanding officer started yelling at me. He was telling me that I was a quitter and he didn't respect quitters. My answer was that I was merely following instructions.

Another Close Combat Training exercise included Bayonet Training. The bayonet was attached to the end of our M-16. We were instructed to attack these dummies that were completely padded. They kind of reminded me of the blocking dummies used during football practice. Upon attacking the dummies we were to make a loud "Hi-yah" noise. As I ran up to the dummy and attacked it I screamed what I thought was a motivational scream. Afterwards my drill instructor made fun of me saying that my voice screeched like a female. He asked me if I had a penis or a twat. At this point you know what I'm thinking. Of course I wished that I had the female organ.

The field exercises were pretty interesting. They included the gas chamber, camouflage training, night fire, mine and grenade training, helicopter perimeter training, and barbed wired field training. I will never forget the gas chamber training. We had to pack extra clothing so as soon as we got out of the gas chamber we were to strip and change clothing. As we stood in formation we watched the reactions of those recruits prior to us as they came out of the gas chamber. Some were coughing and gagging. When it was my turn I placed my gas mask on my face right before I went into the chamber. We were instructed that once in the chamber we would be told to take the mask off and leave it off until we were let out of the chamber. Once I heard the command to remove my mask I did as ordered. It seemed like an eternity until they unlocked the door. Once outside the chamber I placed my mask on the back of my head as I thought that I was instructed. Well, just like the pugil stick exercise, I must not have heard the directions properly. My drill instructor told me that I didn't follow directions and to get back in line so that I could go into the gas chamber again. He told me to make sure that I follow directions this time and not to place the mask on the back of my head. I came out of the gas chamber for the second time. This time I was gasping for air. The gas was burning and I immediately ripped my clothing off and placed it in the plastic bag. That was grueling. Needless to say I did not place the mask on the back of my head this time.

The camouflage training was pretty cool. We would take these chalk sticks and paint our face different shades of brown and green so that we would blend in with the brush in the fields. Then we would have to hide in the woods. The fact of hiding in the woods frightened me because of my phobia of snakes. Some of the instructors were so amazingly good at fixing up with camouflage that we did not know that they were hiding out. They blended perfectly with the trees. At the same time we were receiving camouflage training we were also being taught both light and noise discipline. We were told how important this was because many lives were lost in wars due to the lack of these disciplines.

It was fascinating to see the skies light up with night fire. It reminded me of watching the fireworks over the Detroit River during the 4th of July celebration. It was really an awesome experience. If you could imagine, the field was set up with rooftops to houses and buildings and there were targets that we had to shoot. Once I positioned myself on a rooftop and started firing at the targets I felt like I was a member of the S.W.A.T. team. The simulation was just like a scene from the movies. The night fire lasted for a couple of hours and was one of my most favorite events that took place during basic training.

Other field trainings included mine and hand grenade exercises. We were taught to walk very carefully so that we could avoid stepping on mines. The drill instructors that experienced Vietnam told us how they witnessed others being dismembered due to stepping on field mines. One story included how a person's body was blown in half; it was gruesome.

We also had the opportunity to pull the plug on hand grenades and throw them into vacant fields. We watched as they blew up. We were taught the art of getting down on the deck and covering certain body parts so they wouldn't get damaged. I remember one instructor asked us if we planned on having kids. There were many different types of grenades. Some were smoke grenades with different colors. There were red, green and yellow smoke grenades. The grenades also came in different sizes and shapes. This was a pretty cool training exercise.

Another interesting field event was building a perimeter around a chopper. We learned of many types of Marine Corps choppers. Several recruits would pile into a chopper and then jump out of the helicopter and build a perimeter around it while laid out in the prone position, with rifles in position to fire. For practice purposes the helicopters never took flight. As I lay on the ground I heard a private yell "Snake." I got word that a snake had crawled on his arm. That scared me terribly.

One of my most memorable events included the barbed wired course that we had to crawl through and over. Well the course appeared to be half the size of a football field. We were to step over and through some of the barbed wire; then we were to low crawl through some of the wire; then we would attack some dummies with a bayonet attached to our rifle. The memorable part was that the instructors were shooting live fire over the barbed wire that we were crawling through. The purpose was to teach us to stay low. I remember hearing the whistling of the rounds of ammunition as they fired passed my head. If you can picture the Three Stooges moving really fast you could imagine the speed in which I went through the exercise after hearing the shots. Overall, the field exercises were good lessons.

We spent the last few weeks of training preparing for graduation and our next tour of duty; which included Military Occupational School. During this time we were practicing for the graduation parade, making visits to the commissary so that we could purchase items to take with us to our next assignment, taking graduation pictures, and getting fitted for our Marine Corps uniforms. We did a lot of drill in our effort to prepare ourselves for perfection for graduation. As we marched past the grandstand I would smile thinking that this shit is almost over. Drill Instructor Sergeant Walters would make his comments about me smiling saying, "Burns you are still smiling you must be gay or something." I would think "female yes; gay not." Now when we talk about fine looking men, Honey, let me tell you. A man in the Marine Corps Dress Blues uniform is a site to see. Those Dress Blues make the ugliest man look like something that you might hang on your wall as wallpaper.

Wow. Finally, it was my last day of training. I was tired because I had stayed up all night with some other recruits doing things that we shouldn't had done. Let me say, I could have spent my night sleeping. Instead I was busy helping other recruits drag a private into the Whiskey Locker and locking the door with the padlock. We also taped one of the drill instructors in the duty hut. We took a roll of masking tape and taped the entrance so he couldn't get out. The next morning was hilarious because the entire platoon got thrashed in the sand pit outside the barracks. My big mouth got me in trouble again. This time it was extremely funny. There was a drill instructor from a different platoon who sounded like Popeye. Well, me being the clown that I was, I decided to mock him while standing in line waiting for breakfast chow. To my surprise I heard another voice that sounded like Popeye. Oops. It was him. He heard me mocking him and immediately took me out of the chow line and thrashed me in my graduation uniform. Other recruits thought that it was humorous.

It rained on our graduation day. Believe it or not, it was still hot on October 7, 1983. The rain felt good and so did graduating from The United

States Marine Corps. Our graduation was exciting but the parade that we had worked so hard to perfect was cancelled. Once the commanding officer made his remarks and congratulated us we were free to go. I remember Senior Drill Instructor Staff Sergeant McLain telling me how proud he was of me for the effort that I gave throughout training.

One final reflection of my Marine Corps boot camp experience is the mental capacity one had to have in order to successfully make it through. For one thing, our barracks was directly across from the San Diego Airport. For every airplane that took off we counted one less before it was our turn. I always found a way to do something funny. They had to separate Jackson and me because we clowned throughout. We figured that we would get into trouble anyway so why not give them a reason. For example, I normally slept on the top rack. Once we completed our nightly routine of singing the Marine Corps Hymn and being given the command to mount the rack I would mount it then continue to move. Well the problem was that we were supposed to lie at position of attention until we were told to relax. I would move prior to being told just for the hell of it. On a number of occasions the entire platoon had to practice getting in and out of the rack for an hour or so. Finally the drill instructors started thrashing me. I figured that the D.I.s would play games with us; why not play back. It was my way of getting through the difficult times of boot camp. Most of us enjoyed our Sunday mornings because it gave us a chance to attend church. Church was a way for many of us to release stress and ask God to help us make it through the process. I know that I definitely looked forward to Sunday Morning Worship. This helped me from a mental aspect as well.

Not only did boot camp make me grow up fast it also helped me develop other traits that would be useful throughout the remainder of my life. Although I always considered myself a leader I further developed my leadership skills. My mouth may still be an issue but, believe it or not, I became more disciplined in the way that I carried myself. I may still be silly but I am only trying to have fun and I want others to enjoy themselves whenever they are around me. For this reason once I adapted to boot camp I began doing things that I knew would get me in trouble, but at the same time everyone got a laugh. The laugh may have helped others get through this difficult time. Boot camp was a form of education because its purpose was to develop the troops into young adults. One reason that I joined the toughest military branch was to fight against my desire to be a female. My training did not, however, bring an end to my gender conflict. My next step after boot camp was Field Radio Operating Command School.

Field Radio Operating Command School

7-6-5-4-3-2-1-B00M. That's the life expectancy of a Field Radio Operator (F.R.O.C). "Well why the hell didn't someone tell me that." My next tour of duty included an arrangement in the middle of the Mojave Desert. We called it Twenty Nine Stumps, the real name being 29 Palms. Although Jackson and I arrived in the middle of October the weather was still pretty nice. He and I were used to the Detroit weather. It was a major contrast. We did, however, have more freedom than we enjoyed during the previous three months. When we arrived we were still locked at position of attention whenever we saw a marine. Both Jackson and I were promoted to Private First Class as we graduated from boot camp. Jackson was promoted because of his performance in boot camp. My promotion came due to the participation that I had prior to boot camp and for getting Jackson to join. Some marines called Military Occupational School the "4th Phase of Boot Camp."

F.R.O.C. school consisted of many hours of classroom instruction, hours of field exercises, a lot of physical training, a lot of field days (cleaning the barracks inside and outside), many hours of guard duty, and hours of standing in formation. We were issued several modules that we were to study so that we could be prepared for class. After we woke up around 5 a.m. we would go to formation and then proceed to the mess hall for breakfast. This time we did not have to march in formation because we were allowed our freedom to travel on our own. Once breakfast was completed, and believe me we didn't force down our food in less than a heartbeat like we were required while in boot camp, we would proceed to our class. We were nervous the initial time the instructor entered the classroom due to the fear of the unknown. The first instructor was funny and gross at the same time. He would crack many jokes in order to keep a relaxed environment. He would also tell the marines to let him know when we would have to fart. This man actually stated that he knew gas was a natural process so instead of being polite and holding it he actually had fart contests. He would allow the marine to stand and fart. Then the class would rate the fart in several categories such as origination, sound, quality, and effect. The sick ass marines enjoyed this.

The instructor was very interested and made sure that everyone understood the information that he delivered. In order to proceed to the next class we had to pass each module's exam. Each individual would progress at his own speed. Everyone passed Module One at the same time. The various modules covered types of radios, the equipment setup process, the different codes and languages used to communicate, and other materials. We would be threatened that if we divulged security information to anyone we would be sent to federal prison in Leavenworth, Kansas. We were told things about the inmates stirring shit with their hands. I think that some of these stories were told in order to scare us. We did earn a Security Clearance once we graduated from F.R.O.C. school.

We spent a lot of time in the field applying things that were learned in the class room. Most instructors would tell the marines to "Light em up if you got em." This meant that the marines that smoked cigarettes were allowed the freedom to smoke, one privilege not allowed during basic training. I was not a smoker so I didn't partake in the activity. While in the field we would set up antennas and other equipment. I would often get teased because some of the equipment was too heavy for me. Some of the antennas were very tall and I struggled in my attempt to raise those types of antennas. We were often reminded that we didn't have long to set up radio equipment because the life expectancy of a field radio operator was about 7 seconds. If you think about it, this would make sense because it would be a priority for the military to shut down their enemy's communication.

Every marine is considered infantry above all other duties. Therefore, we spent a lot of time doing PT. The physical training wasn't as intense as it was in boot camp because we were pretty much in good shape and didn't have a problem running several miles each morning. There were several marines that were motivated to attend jump school but this activity wasn't of my interest. My focus was to complete Radio School so that I could begin my college education at Eastern Michigan University. Jump School was not even a consideration for me.

Wow we actually had field days. My interpretation of a field day was not the same as the marines' idea. The field day would consist of cleaning the barracks from top to bottom. We even raked the sand that was outside around our barracks. We were to completely "police" the area, which meant pick up any piece of thrash including all cigarette butts. Marines would climb up on lockers or anything else they needed to in an effort to clean the barracks from the top to the bottom. I learned that the use of Listerine was not only for mouth wash. It was also for swabbing decks. While in boot camp we learned that we could make dust mops by assembling two marines and a couple of towels. One marine would hold the others legs and the other marine would place his elbows and arms on a couple of towels and be dragged throughout the barracks. We would divide into groups and assign work detail to each group. One group would clean the head from top to bottom. Another group would clean the main sleep area of the barracks. A third group would clean the outside. The field day would take a few hours. To be honest this wasn't my idea of a field day for I thought that we would be participating in track and field events. I guess that I was incorrect on this one.

Many hours were spent doing guard watch. We became familiar with "fire watch" while we were in boot camp. The watch was set up on four hour increments. I hated the graveyard shift (2 a.m.-6 a.m.). It seemed as though I frequently got assigned this shift. We were allowed to sleep a little during the morning if we worked the graveyard shift. I also had a dislike for working duty on the weekends. This happened once a month. Instead of being able to leave base for the weekend we would have to stay back and stand watch. We would guard several areas of the base. For example, we might be responsible for guarding the classrooms, several barracks (outside), our own barracks (inside), the commander's chopper, and other areas. We kept a log and had to write down any activity that we saw during our watch. Guards also could not leave their post until they were properly relieved. Both the old watch and the new watch would have to sign off in the log.

We also had many inspections of both our barracks and our person. Therefore we spent hours in formation being inspected to ensure that we looked like a marine. We would report to formation during the morning, lunch, and at the end of the day. Our day normally ended around 4 p.m.; unless we had watch. We would also have to stand in formation in order to receive our pay. We also had formation whenever special events took place on base. For example, we had to stand in formation when we were waiting on a ceremony for those lost in the Lebanon Bombing of 1983.

Now I would not be telling the complete truth if I said that all we did was work. We participated in many activities both on and off of base. We frequented the Enlisted Club on a nightly routine. Many marines thought that the E Club was a way to release stress and a way to forget about not being at home. Activities at the E Club included playing pool and arcade games, listening to music, and getting drunk. There was plenty of alcohol and I pretty much stayed drunk every night. Other activities included bowling, miniature golf, movies, and visiting the commissary. Marines also were motivated to participate in physical activities like doing extra physical training. For example some marines would jog an extra 2-3 miles a day. Others would participate in playing basketball, softball, or football. I spent time listening to music.

Activities off base took place during the weekends. We appreciated getting three day weekends whenever a holiday celebration took place. Groups of us would pile in a cab and ask the cab driver to take us to the Greyhound bus station so that we could get to our destination. Places that I travelled were my cousin's house in Oxnard, Disney Land, Las Vegas, and Tijuana. I visited my cousin Socrates in Oxnard. We listened to music and just enjoyed family time together. He introduced me to an alcohol called "151." I think that it got its name because of its proof. Well I thought that I could stump with the big dogs. Well, after taking a sip of the "151" I thought that my head would hit the ceiling. It was so strong that it could actually remove the paint from the walls. I visited Las Vegas for my 18th Birthday. This was an extended weekend because the marines celebrated their birthday on November 10th. At the time I wasn't of age so I wasn't able to gamble. I remember having fun at Disney Land. We also took a trip to Tijuana. After describing the events you would also say how would you forget? We went to a strip club in San Diego. A dancer stopped and stared at me, then smiled. I was basically frozen in my tracks looking at her and wondering "Damn why couldn't I have that body?" Jackson and other marines named me the "Barracks Slut" for they kept calling me a girl and teased me because I did a lot of reading and studying while they hung out. They would speak to me like I was a female. Actually, I never told anyone but I thought that the teasing was amusing. I never told anyone because I didn't want to get beat up. Once we got into Tijuana we saw some interesting things. Prostitution was legalized and many prostitutes would walk the streets and work business by soliciting action from the marines. One girl even had the audacity to have sex with a donkey. They set up a booth on the streets and the donkey was positioned so that he could have sex with the girl. I thought "How distasteful." I remember I tried to use my high school Spanish lessons to get by. While in one of the taverns a prostitute approached me and she was talking about "Suckie-Fuckie." My response was "My amigos –cinco dollares." I knew that she wouldn't deliver her services to my friends for $5. This was funny though; however I did not find any humor in the filthiness of Tijuana. Once we got to the hotel I felt sick because it was very unclean. It was so nasty that I slept on top of the comforter with my clothes on and I refused to drink any of the water or eat any of the food. I remember a few marines checked out of the hotel the next morning without paying. They said that they used fictitious names when they checked in and no one asked for their IDs. I thought that this was strange but I believed them anyway. I remember that due to my complexion and me sort of looking Mexican I was stopped at the border and the officials checked my identification several times. They finally let me through. The other marines laughed at me because Jackson called me "foreigner names" such as "Julio." Well we made sure that we met curfew and arrived back at our barracks in time for formation; for we did not want to face any punishment.

F.R.O.C. school lasted for several months and I graduated right before Christmas. I was concerned because I needed to get back home so I could register for my freshman classes at Eastern. My mother even called the company commander in her request to help make sure that I would be relieved from this assignment in plenty of time to attend college. Upon graduation from Field Radio School I received a promotion to Lance Corporal. Overall, my experience at 29 Stumps was pretty decent. My development continued and I was becoming a young adult. I thought that I was ready for college and due to my military training that I would do great. I became more disciplined and felt confident that I had taken another step in preparing for both life and my next step in my educational process. My original hope in my decision to join the marines was to help me battle my internal conflict regarding my gender. After all my rigorous training I continued to have a lot of thoughts about my gender identity. I did not know exactly how to express this to others because at that time I would not be accepted by society; even worse if I would have told others

I may have put myself in danger. Therefore my feelings and my experiences had prepared me for the next big step in my education.

From Huron to Eagle
My College Days

I can't believe this. I'm walking up this huge hill to attend an 8 a.m. class at the Mark Jefferson building. The hawk was definitely out and it was a really cold morning. I had just left sunny California and now I find myself hustling to class in the Michigan cold. When I finally made it to class I was huffing and puffing and definitely awaken by the cold air.

January 1984 was the beginning of a long college experience. It actually took me 14 years to complete my undergraduate degree. During this time I gained valuable experience in both my educational and everyday life adventures. Through this time frame I withdrew from many classes, sat out of school for several years, went to school on a part time basis, and changed my major several times. I also gained valuable experience in the "real world."

Eastern Michigan University was known as "the party" school. Yes, this was great I found myself partying and drinking more than actually studying and attending class. It appeared that there was a party every weekend, either at McKenny Union or the Suds Factory. I had many friends due to staying at a local college. My best friend at the time, Charlie, had transferred from Alabama State. He played football there so I hung out with him and many of the football players. My first party experience was at The Suds Factory. Dr. Burns had arrived. Well, I had just completed training with the marines and was used to drinking, so I thought. I decided to prove myself to others by drinking anyone under the table. Beer was on special for 25 cents per glass. I used some of the money that I earned from the marines to buy myself and others alcohol. I drank more than I should have and couldn't properly handle myself. I went into the restroom and threw up everywhere. After I woke up in my dorm room I was told how my friend, Charlie, had to rescue me and bring me to my room. He had to undress me and put me in my bunk. I had a terrible hangover for the rest of that weekend. From that point forward my friends and acquaintances reminded me of how Charlie had to save me.

During my first semester I lived in Walton Hall. College life had just begun and I was in the process of learning how to adjust to it. I quickly became familiar with the sound of a train travelling through Ypsilanti at the wee hours of the morning. It woke me up on a consistent basis. If it wasn't the train whistle, it was the noise that fraternities and sororities made during their pledge periods. I remember waking up to the sound of the Sigmas stepping in front of

Walton Hall. It must have been around two in the morning. I was so angry I opened my window and started yelling to them to shut the heck up. That caused a problem with my roommate. Our argument led to us not talking to each other the rest of that semester. Not only would the fraternities and sororities step, they would haze those that were trying to make it into their exclusive organizations. I remember looking out the window and one of the pledges had just been hit in the head with a snowball. The Alphas line would wear all black and would be stepping and enthusiastically chanting. I would think "Why couldn't they do this stuff during the daytime. Some of us were trying to do simple things, like sleep." On other occasions some of the fraternities and sororities would gather in front of The Hide-A-Way during the day.

Although I did a lot of hanging out and partying during my first semester I attempted to focus on my reason for being in college. I took four classes during my first semester: Psychology 101, English comp, government, and biology. I soon found out that the wiser students refrained from taking 8 o'clock classes. I often found myself playing hooky and missing my early Psychology class. I would often go to Dr. Flagg's office to make up exams that I missed. I struggled trying to adapt to school during my first semester. If English would have been my only class I would have done well; however that wasn't the case. I did pretty well in the lecture portion of my biology class. I soon found out that lab was a very crucial part of my biology class and I despised the lab section because I thought that there were portions of lab that were gross. As a result, I refused to cut on the fetal pig and I couldn't remember how certain cell slides looked under the microscope. Due to my poor performance in lab I received my lowest college grade, a "D+." My grade for the lecture was a "B," but I flunked the lab. Biology was my only four credit course. So in my first semester I had a 2.3 G.P.A.

During my first visit to Ned's Bookstore on Washtenaw Avenue I stumbled across someone that was very ignorant. After purchasing my books I headed back to my dorm. No sooner had I walked outside than I was greeted by this white-trashy looking man in his early 20s. He told me that he hated me because I was a "nigga." I was kind of scared because he looked like he may have a knife or a sharp object. It was getting dark outside and I didn't know exactly what to do so I started to run. My books were heavy and I did my best not to drop them. When I went home I told my father and brother about the experience. My brother's response was that I should have responded by saying "I love you too." Derrick was home from Princeton University, a mostly Caucasian school where he also experienced racial tensions.

Since I missed the fall semester I decided to stay at school during the spring and summer. I moved to Putnam Hall during these semesters but instead of having one roommate I had two. I took two classes in each semester and did a little better. I played in the Intramural Softball League. I hung out with Charlie and his girlfriend Ruthie a whole lot. We frequently travelled to Lansing. Since I was in the Marine Reserves I had to attend monthly meetings and complete a two week tour of duty during the summer. My spring and summer semester grades were pretty decent.

I also met this friend from Virginia, by the name of Angie, who stayed down the hall from me. I would often go to her Dance and Aerobics classes with her. The girls would wear their tights and leotards and I would sit and wait for Angie thinking "Dang I wish that I could participate." Angie was into painting nails for both girls and guys. One evening she painted mine blue and I joked with her that her color was prettier than mine. We would often play a game of Gin Rummy and throughout the game I talked much thrash. I won the first game and then she decided to bet me on the second game. The bet was that if I lost I would allow Angie to paint my nails pink and if she lost she would do something that I decided (I can't remember exactly what). So in order to get my nails painted pink, I messed up and kept playing the wrong card. Angie won the game and I had to let her paint my nails pink. While she was in the middle of painting my nails a friend of hers, who we called Zoid, knocked on her door. He stood about 6 feet 3 inches tall and was very athletic. He was also cute and very nice. Zoid made a comment that went something like this "I didn't know that Dr. Burns was into getting his nails painted pink…wow I hope you girls have fun tonight." Angie explained the bet and Zoid left the conversation where it was at. Zoid was a pretty cool guy who stayed to himself but both he and Angie liked each other. Angie would definitely share her feelings about him to me. During the spring, Angie told me that she was moving back to Virginia. I was really sad because she and I became good friends.

During the summer I completed a two week tour of duty with the reserves. We did a re-enactment of a beach landing. Several ships were used for the exercise and I was on the USS Raleigh. Our ship ported out of Norfolk, Virginia and landed in North Carolina. We were stationed on a ship for a few days and were dropped in the ocean about 20 to 30 yards out from the beach. We walked ashore with our M-16s in hand and took over the beach. In order to make this simulation as real as possible the marines flew jets over our heads.

While on tour I realized the life that military men experienced while on ships. The living quarters were really small and extremely hot. The bunk beds were stacked three high. In the tight quarters we bumped and jostled each other like the Three Stooges. The stairwells were really steep and we had to be careful not to fall down the steps. I definitely learned how to use my "sea legs." There was an incident where everybody got excited because a black Russian Ship appeared to be circling our ships. The mess hall was smaller than what we were accustomed to. One day it stormed and our ship rocked from side to side and the movement was so heavy that it appeared that we were almost walking on the walls. Some of the marines made fun of some of the naval personal on ships because they said that they were wearing mascara and other makeup. We also were assigned guard watch and as it seemed I always ended up getting the "grave yard" shift. We were to stand watch over the waters and report anything that we thought was moving. My eyes got tired during the wee hours of the morning and they started playing tricks on me. I thought that I saw some people swimming towards our ship so I called my reporting officer and informed him. I think that he was pretty pissed at me for waking him up during the early morning hours.

Well once we made it ashore we had to set up a perimeter and set up our radio communications area. I was lucky because my company gunnery sergeant and company officers wanted me to be the company runner. I think that I may have gained favor with them because while I was on ship I would buy cigars and passed them out. Well I got teased by many of the marines and was called the "Company Bitch." My responsibilities included running errands for the company officer and gunny sergeant. Every time I was sent on an errand marines from my platoon would say things like, "There she goes again. The bitch is on the move...." I would think that the jokes were funny. When I got back to my reserve station in Detroit I was up for a promotion to corporal but my superiors, in my platoon, didn't feel that I was ready for one.

I sat out the Fall Semester of 1984 because I failed to handle my business right and didn't have a dorm room. I tried to talk my mother into allowing me the opportunity to move into an apartment but she refused and sent my student loan back to the bank. So I moved back home for that period of time. My mother was adamant about me getting up and going to work so every morning she would wake me and make me leave the house. I didn't have a car so I had to walk to find employment. One day I was walking on Van Dyke Road and I saw a huge snake crawling on the inside of a window in an abandoned building. I felt myself become sick and I wanted to drop to the ground. My body shivered and I really picked up my pace. One day I ran into my cousin's friend who was named JoJo and I told him that I was looking for a job. He referred me to the Kentucky Fried Chicken on Van Dyke and 7 Mile Road. I went directly there and saw another one of our friends, Cordell, and he introduced me to the manager. The manager hired me and I began working that next week. JoJo and Cordell were my cousin's teammates on the football team at Osborn. I worked at KFC for a few weeks and didn't like the way that the manager would treat us. He spoke to us in a very rude manner and he always stayed on our backs. One day I was breading some chicken and I had just had enough. I couldn't take the abuse anymore. The manager said something that was very rude and I threw a bag of flour at him and walked out. I was done. I thought I deserved to be treated better than I was being treated. My mother asked why I was home so early and I just said that the manager told me that he no longer needed me.

My mother began riding me about not having a job and made sure that I woke up early every morning and went out to find a job. I finally found one at Burger King on Mound Road and this time I really liked the management team and I enjoyed working for them. My hours consisted of the closing shift and I was responsible for cleaning up the equipment and store. I would also work the broiler by placing burgers and buns on a rack and sending them through it. I would then place them in a steamer and write the times on the steamer. There was a time table for the expiration of the burgers so once the burgers expired I would throw them away. I worked this job until I returned to school at Eastern.

Once I returned to campus at E.M.U. I applied for employment at the Burger King on Washtenaw Avenue. I would either take the bus or walk three miles to work. This Burger King was set up in zones which included the front cashiers, the drive thru, the burger side, the whopper side, the specialty board, the fry station, and the broiler. I would normally work either the broiler or the burger side. One day while I was working the burger side, I saw a flame coming up through the broiler and I ran and told the manager. She must have been inexperienced with grease fires because she threw water on the fire. The next thing I knew we were standing outside on a cold February evening. The flames had gone right through the roof. I remember customers getting angry and requesting their money back. We kept telling them that the building was on fire and they had to evacuate. People appeared more concerned about their money than their safety. Well the Burger King was shut down for a few months.

I returned to Walton Hall during the Winter Semester of 1985. Charlie and Ruthie moved into some apartments across the bridge and I would often visit and spend the night. It was a break from dorm life. I wanted to hang with Charlie all the time. We went to an event where a fraternity was sponsoring a function for those that wanted to join their organization. Charlie's grade point average met the requirement; but mine didn't. I had a 2.47 grade point average and the requirement was 2.5. Charlie pledged and I had to sit out. So I would hang out with his girlfriend. I called Charlie and Ruthie "Daddy" and "Mom." I had referred to Charlie as "Daddy" since our time at Osborn. Now if you stop and think about a guy calling another guy "Daddy" you would think that was kind of strange but I didn't think so back then. He would often tease me by asking me if I needed to sit down to pee so in my mind I always thought that maybe he knew about my gender conflict. I attended events with Ruthie and hung out with her. We went to Charlie's football games and traveled together to his road games. I remember going to a slave auction with her in Walton Hall's lobby. Ruthie would tell me that she thought certain guys were cute and in my mind I would agree. I didn't speak my mind though for fear that it would end my relationship with Charlie.

I kept busy with campus activities while Charlie was pledging on line. I would spend a lot of time in the Hide-A-Way playing Ms. Pac Man and would often score over 100,000 points. I also became active on the Dormitory Government Board. This student government body was designed to make dorm life better for the students. I also continued my party life.

Once Charlie crossed his fraternity's line we started to hang out again. I remember going to the book store and purchasing paraphernalia for him as a gift. My boy looked good in his frat's garb. We partied at Michigan State and other universities. We hung so tough that one of my roommates told me that Charlie was "Scooby Doo" and I was "Scrappy Doo." Charlie, Ruthie and I were one happy family. To this day I think the world of them.

I continued to hang with Charlie and his friends; most were on the football team. Instead of calling me "Dr. Burns" they started calling me "Nurse Burns."

I guess they figured out something that I didn't have to reveal. Well my semester went on and I attended my classes more regularly than I did my first semester. I met a couple more friends that were in class with me. One girl I met was one of Charlie's friends and she had planned on pledging Delta (which to this day I wish that I could pledge). She was in my College Algebra class and we became good friends. I also met Big Mac; he was in a newer fraternity, Phi Etta Psi. I met Big Mac through Charlie. They both played for Eastern Michigan's Football Team. Big Mac and I took a Bowling class together. Once the semester concluded I moved back to Putnam Hall.

Of all my classes that I took I remember my accounting course. It was one of my four classes that I took that semester and my results were pretty poor. I earned a "C-." I couldn't grasp the concepts because they seemed very different from what I studied in high school. My accounting class was held in a huge auditorium in Pray Harold and due to the class size I was intimidated and didn't seek the necessary help that I needed to understand the materials. Even though I pulled an "all-nighter" studying for the final exam I scored a "D" on the test. As a result I made a major decision to change my course of study. During the semester I came to a realization that I enjoyed numbers, however I did not want to be stuck behind some desk doing accounting. Thus I changed my major to mathematics. Little did I know that my lack of attention in my high school geometry class would come back to haunt me.

I took two communications courses during the spring semester and I did fairly well. A couple of football players, from Detroit Cooley High School, were in my classes. They would always give Charlie and me a rough time because they beat Osborn in the city championship. These guys were also on our spring intramural softball team and they were good athletes.

I spent the spring semester preparing myself for the Marine Corps officer's training. I would take my morning jog along the trail leading to the football stadium; I would run on the inside track at the Intramural Building; I would work out with Charlie and a couple of his friends; and I would also work out in the Slimnastics Room. I wasn't as strong as Charlie and his friends so I would have to lift half the amount of weights that they would. Charlie and his friends would pick on me because I worked out in the Slimnastics Room. Girls worked out in there, but I needed the machines for cardio exercises. The guys would always tease me but again I kept my thoughts to myself for fear of losing my friendships. The guys always told me that "Babes hung out in the Slimnastics Room and men were in the weight room." Hey I must have been a "Babe" but I wasn't telling anyone. The Officer's Candidate School was divided into two parts which lasted six weeks each. Both parts were split over two summers and were held in Quantico, Virginia.

This time I was greeted by the platoon sergeant when I got off the bus. He was more pleasant by comparison to my first night at M.C.R.D. in 1983. This time I was a marine. But I still wasn't prepared for the dry heat in Quantico. I thought that California was hot. We had to drink plenty of water and we were told to pour our salt packets into our canteens.

My first segment of O.C.S. was supposed to last six weeks. However, due to an injury I received a Medical Discharge. Like Marine Corps boot camp there was a lot of physical training, class room training, field training, and other types of training. I was in better shape going into O.C.S. than I was when I went to boot camp. Our physical training consisted of a lot of running, obstacle course training, and a lot of marching. I don't remember getting thrashed like I did in boot camp because the main punishment was receiving chits and write-ups. If a candidate received too many of these then the candidate would be dismissed from the program. One of my main goals was to overcome the single bar obstacle that I couldn't master in boot camp. There was a bar outside of our barracks and I would practice with the guidance of one of our sergeant instructors.

Well long story short, the obstacle course led to my demise of Officer Candidate's School and my military career. Although our obstacle course had the same obstacles as the one we trained on in boot camp, it was different from the perspective that candidates raced against each other. I was off to a fast start and I actually made it over the single bar; then over the double bars; then all of a sudden it happened. As I climbed the wall and jumped off, I fell to the ground clutching my knee. The damn thing gave out again. I had pretty much recovered from my prior ACL tear, my football injury. This time it was my medial meniscus. I tried to get up and continue running but I was ordered to the ground by my sergeant instructor. He gave me a lot of credit for trying to continue but he also told me that it wasn't smart. They noticed a sever limp in my march and I couldn't run. My injury resulted in surgery at the Army Dewitt Hospital in Maryland.

Prior to my injury I had class room training in subjects like Marine Corps history, leadership training, and other items. These classrooms were hot and the instructors would often make us stand up and stretch. The candidates would get written up if they fell asleep so I often found myself standing up in the rear of the classroom. During my free time I studied so I would be prepared for class. I wanted to successfully complete my officer's training for a couple reasons. First it would help me pay for school and second the officer's quality of life was a whole lot better than the enlisted.

Other courses at O.C.S. included survival training, first aide, and weapon training. The survival training led us to the field where we learned how to setup our unit out in the open. We survived by eating M.R.E.s and using our water in our canteens to heat our M.R.E.s, bathe, drink, and for other reasons. Our lessons also included methods of taking care of the wounded and applying first aide techniques. We studied the history of the weapons. We had plenty of inspections so that we were properly developed into Marine Corps officers.

O.C.S. had its advantages over boot camp. First of all, we weren't getting yelled at all the time. Although we were disciplined the punishment wasn't as physical. If we didn't follow rules we would just be kicked out with a Dishonorable Discharge. The mess hall was a better quality facility and the food tasted much better. The overall atmosphere was designed to treat us more like leaders than followers.

My platoon sergeant and sergeant instructor appeared to take a liking to me because I displayed my leadership skills from day one. For instance, I taught the other candidates the Marine Corps Hymn and I shared with them the practice of singing it prior to going to sleep at the end of the day. I was respected so much that when I got Medically Discharged the platoon wanted to thank me and wished me well. We had different names for the platoons and we named ourselves the "Cabbage Patched Candidates." At my discharge, the platoon wanted me to have a shirt. I wanted to cry and I remember the sergeant instructor told me to keep my bearings. I had shared with both the sergeant instructor and platoon sergeant that they were the type of men that I would take a bullet for. I also was in pretty good condition compared to others and this was proven as I completed my first Physical Training Exam. I timed very well in the 3 mile run; I maxed out on the sit-ups and pull-ups. I also asked for assistance in areas where I needed help. For example, I admitted that I struggled with the single bar on the obstacle course and the sergeant instructor coached me until I did better.

Unlike boot camp we had more free time. Whenever we were on free time and we weren't assigned watch we were allowed to go to the Candidate's Club. We listened to music and ate healthy foods but were instructed to stay away from alcohol and greasy foods. We were allowed to leave base during the weekends but would be in trouble if we didn't report back on time. I made sure that I reported in a timely fashion. One weekend I travelled to Crystal City in D.C. and I did a lot of shopping and partying. I went with a couple other candidates. Two of them were Omegas and the third reminded me of Eddie Murphy. While we were at Crystal City we went to a club called the Underground. The other three candidates were impressed with the women and I was really impressed with the environment. The atmosphere was enhanced by the strobe lights, a spiral staircase, and a balcony. We enjoyed the variety of music as we partied until about 3 a.m. While in D.C. we also visited the Veteran Wall and saw many names of our deceased military men. We also visited and shopped in Georgetown. Overall, I had an amazing time.

Once my surgery was completed at Army Dewitt Hospital I was sent to the Discharge Unit. I spent a couple weeks there prior to being discharged. While other candidates were being discharged for disciplinary reasons or because of their desire to not be there I was being sent home for medical reasons. While the other candidates would march to the mess hall I would be driven there. I felt like I hit the lowest point in my life. When I returned home, my father told me that I would be okay and that I was taking things too hard. It was truly a difficult time.

Upon my return to Eastern Michigan University in the Fall Semester of 1985, I lived in room 327 in Walton Hall. I also applied for re-hire at the Burger King on Washtenaw Avenue. After my father dropped me off at the dorm, I decided to go down the back stairwell to get outside. Wow, what did I do that for? I ran into a girl who had the most beautiful smile and her warm personality showed all over her face. She was helping her roommate, Susie, carry some wood upstairs so that Susie's dad could build her a loft. I thought "Why aren't any of these so called men helping them carry the wood up the steps?" I felt for both of the girls and decided to put my crutches down and assist them. I only needed my crutches for support because it had been several weeks since I had surgery.

After helping the two women, I introduced myself and found out their names. Denise was the African-American girl with the beautiful smile and Susie was her roommate. Susie was Caucasian. Both girls thanked me. Denise started leaving little cute notes on my door. It was convenient because her room was diagonal from mine; she stayed in Room 323. After she left so many notes I decided to figure out who this girl was. Besides I hadn't quite given up on fighting my gender issue. I figured that "I might as well keep trying." I never told anyone of my desire to live different from what my appearance was. One afternoon, after class I decided to knock on Denise's door. From that point we became close friends. Although we didn't really go out on dates, we became boyfriend-girlfriend after about 30 days.

On many nights after work I would end up in Denise's dorm room. She would tell me that she could smell me coming. I asked her what exactly did she mean by that. Was she implying that I had bad hygiene? She would say, "No Silly, I smelled Burger King all the way from the other end of the hallway." I remember a couple of instances early in our relationship where Denise should have picked up clues that I had gender issues, what she now calls "serious issues." One Sunday night I was lying in Denise's bed wearing some of her panties and nightie and Susie and her father returned from the weekend earlier than anticipated. Denise and I heard a key in the door and we both replied "Oh shit." Well, Susie and her father must have seen me in the nightgown, but I don't remember either saying anything. Another instance occurred during the Halloween when I was in Denise's bathroom putting on makeup. Walton Hall's dorm rooms were designed so a bathroom separated two dorm rooms. The person in the next room was called the suitemate. Well I had put one of Denise's dresses on and was trying to put makeup on when all of a sudden I heard a loud squeaky laugh. It was her suitemate, Tori. I must not have locked the door. Although I thought I had, I must have been in a rush to get dressed. These times reminded me of when I was living at my parents' house and heard a car in the driveway. Often times I would sneak and wear my mother's clothes and makeup. After hearing my parent's car pull into the driveway I would rush to undress and get back into my male clothing. They had no clue, or at least I don't think they did. When I ask Denise about these situations she says that she must have blocked these things out because she thought that I was just being silly. No, I guess that I had "issues."

That semester I took the minimum number of credits to ensure that I maintained my full time status. My English class stands firm in my memory because I enjoyed writing papers and did very well in this class. Denise liked writing too but she was more of a creative writer and she had one of her poems published. After writing a paper on "Dr. Martin Luther King, Jr. and the Civil Rights Movement" my professor told me that I should change my major to English because I was a good writer. I changed my major several times and I ended up with history as my major. History majors are required to write many papers.

Several African-American fraternities and sororities and other African-American student organizations formed the P.R.E.S.S. Club and organized an Anti-Apartheid March. My Resident Advisor, who also was my next door neighbor, invited me to attend the rally and march. Little did I know that I would end up leading a crowd of about 300 or more through the city of Ypsilanti. As I lead the chants, the crowd behind me repeated the chants. I was making up sayings as we marched. Chants of "Divest Now" rang loudly through the city and we also sung "We Shall Overcome." I vividly remember police cars escorting us through the city and it was a non-violent protest where we were urging universities and companies to withdraw their investments from South Africa. This was the largest march since the Vietnam War and the biggest movement since the Civil Rights Movement. Pray-Harold was historical for being a building where Civil Rights demonstrations took place during the 1960s. After the Anti-Apartheid March I decided to write an editorial called "My Turn" for the college newspaper called the "Eastern Michigan University Echo." This article urged both the black and the white students to stand up for their rights. As a result of my involvement in the march I met several activists and was invited to speak at the University of Michigan. Little did I know that the group that I was addressing was a Socialist organization. I spoke proudly about bringing an end to racism and that we all should celebrate Democracy. I was also invited to attend a forum at the University of Chicago.

During the Winter Semester of 1986, I attempted to follow in the steps of Charlie. I had hoped to pledge the year prior with him but due to my grade point average I did not met the requirements. Therefore I was privileged to have two personals. Both Charlie and Robert were my personals. Charlie was the Dean of the line; Robert was also my personal because he was the lead pledge on the previous line. Due to my height and size I was the lead pledge on this current line and I caught hell. Without giving details of the program or naming the fraternity I will give only a brief synopsis of my experience.

Our line began with six pledges and once I got kicked off line only four remained. We were placed on line before we knew it. We met over at one of the Big Brother's apartments and were sitting around joking with a couple of the brothers who crossed line the previous year. All of a sudden I was told to stand in the corner with a potato chip bowl on my head. Guess what? My big mouth got me in trouble as usual. I told those guys that I wasn't going to be made fun of and refused to follow their order. Next thing that I knew I was asked to leave and that I would not be allowed to pledge. After I was asked to leave I continued to knock on the door and apologized and asked permission to rejoin the brothers who wanted to pledge. After my persistence I was invited back to the line. Our line would have to run almost everywhere we went in Ypsilanti. Our line experience included learning the fraternity's history, familiarizing ourselves with the Greek Alphabet, learning poetry, doing a lot of physical activity, getting physically abused, drinking, and anything else that the Big Brothers bestowed on us.

We visited Frog Island often so that we could get paddled. My first experience with "the wood" resulted in me crying with tears dripping down my face. Once the Big Brothers noticed that I was crying they all jumped on me and starting slapping me and calling me a "Bitch." I was told that the Frat only accepted men and wasn't an organization for girls. The effects of getting hit on my rear end with paddles were that my butt became crusty and purple in color. We often joined with the pledges from U of M and went to a nearby cemetery for pledging activities. "The wood" resulted in me getting kicked off line. While my boy, Charlie, was having fun in Florida (winter break), some visiting Brothers came up and wanted to deliver "some wood." Before I knew it one of the brothers hit me with a table leg in the back of my knee that I just had surgery on. I turned around and asked him what the hell he was doing. I tried to explain that I just had surgery on my knee. Before I could get the words out of my mouth I was lying on my back on the ground and about 10 or so Brothers were standing over me singing "Somebody's trying to sneak in the frat." They beat us with hangers "like the pimps used to beat their prostitutes." The Big Brothers would tape the end of the hangers and beat us on the back of our legs. After I resisted the physical punishment the Big Brothers and the line had supposedly "held court" on me and decided to kick me off line permanently. They ruled that my mouth would get the whole line hurt or killed and I thought that it was a bunch of bullshit and that they took advantage of kicking me off line while Charlie was gone.

I later found out that the original plan was to reduce the line from six to four pledges. The first pledge that actually dropped line jumped out of a car at a red light on Huron River Drive. We called him "Jimmy Weak Back." I was told by a reliable source that the person overheard the Big Brothers and knew that I was going to be kicked off line for two reasons. One was because they wanted four pledges because four brothers had crossed on the previous line. The other was because my mouth and attitude were too dangerous.

Some of my memories of pledging are now funny, but weren't at the time. One cold February night we had to run and meet one of our Big Brothers who had just had a flat tire. Once we met up with him we had to drink a couple bottles of Mad Dog 20-20 and then we were to change his tire. Unknown to us, we were to complete the tire change by lifting his car up without the jack. Since I wasn't as strong as the other line brothers I had the privilege of actually changing the tire while the other four pledges lifted the car by hand. We were ordered to sing old Negro Spirituals while we were changing the tire.

There was another instance where the Big Brothers wanted to play C.I.A. This was a very dangerous activity because while our line was running beside a car that one Big Brother was driving, another Big Brother would reach out the window and pull me along with the car. I was running at the same speed that the automobile was travelling. One of the pledges yelled that it was dangerous and that I could have gotten killed. So finally, the Big Brother let me loose.

I had a weed connection and there was a Big Brother from U of M that was hooked on the stuff. In order to stay on his good side I would often purchase some and give it to him. We would ride in a car whenever we would go to Ann Arbor. Since we all piled in the car I had to sit on someone's lap like "a bitch." One time we were riding with the Big Brothers from U of M and I was sitting on the lap of the Big Brother whom I supplied the weed to and he told me not to worry that he had my back and he wouldn't let me get hurt. He told me once things got kind of rough he would yell "Break" and the pledges were to haul ass as far and fast as we could go. I actually liked the U of M Big Brothers better than the Big Brothers at Eastern.

There were visiting brothers from Western Michigan and Oakland University that came to town for the weekend. While in the cemetery one of the Brothers started whispering in my ear like I was a girl. He told me that he could see a vision of me wearing a red dress and red pumps. He also told me that I was dressed up real pretty with red lip stick. He ordered me to talk to my line brothers like I was "A Babe." I was told that if he heard me and I wasn't talking "real sexy" to my line brothers that he would kick my ass. He told me to tell them how I would let them get a piece of tail if they treated me right. So I did exactly what I was told. Other Big Brothers heard me and circled me and slapped me and treated me very disrespectful. Needless to say I envisioned this mentally (and enjoyed talking to my line brothers in my most feminine voice) but I never let any of the Brothers know my true feelings for the fear of bodily damage.

Another memory took place in my dorm room. The Big Brothers were trying to teach us how to step. Due to the problem that I had my entire life (remember the lack of rhythm) I ended up getting kicked in the chest and almost fell out my third floor window. I was teased and told that Charlie must be my Daddy because I was like him and had no rhythm. They also told me that pledges often get their legs broken when they can't step because they don't want the organization to look bad. The incident where I got hit with the wood in my knee occurred a few days after.

Once I got kicked off line I felt really bad and I felt embarrassed and didn't want to face my friends. I sort of hung low and hung out with Denise and her friends. My grades suffered as a result of me pledging. There were three main reasons that I pledged that particular fraternity. First I knew that it was a great organization that was active in the community. Secondly, Charlie was in the frat and I wanted to be like him. Finally, I thought that by joining this tough fraternity I would fight my gender issues. My pledging experience further enhanced my inner feelings. As usual, I kept my secrets to myself.

Due to spending the majority of my time pledging, my grades for the Winter Semester were pretty low. I earned a 2.3 grade point average for that semester. Among my classes that I most remembered for the winter 1986 semester was Play Production. The class wasn't hard to comprehend, but it was difficult for me to stay awake in the class due to spending most nights pledging. I was merely going through the motions and kept nodding off during lectures. I saved my grade, which wasn't much of a save, by manufacturing a small scale model stage as my project and by working at the Quirk Auditorium. Denise was very talented at using her hands and putting things together and she was instrumental in putting my model together. At the very end of the semester I worked for extra-credit by cleaning up the stage after a play. My job was to take down the stage lights and other materials. This work gave me hands on experience and I really enjoyed learning about the materials used for play production. I remember telling my mother that I wanted to major in Drama and was heavily discouraged by her. She stated that I would not be able to get a good job in the acting field. In my humble opinion I was very good at drama. Besides I spent most of my life pretending to be someone I didn't want to be. I also took African-American literature, a history course, and a communications course.

After the Winter-1986 semester ended I called home to see if I might be welcomed home for the spring and summer. My mother had taken my house key a few years earlier when I first joined the Marine Corps and she rejected my request to spend my summer at home. In fact she told me that I had to find a new place to call home because I was an adult. Wow I felt that was harsh. Since I had nowhere to go I continued to stay in Room 327 in Walton Hall. Daily notes were posted on my door reminding me that I had a deadline to move out. I had nowhere to go, meaning that I was homeless. My friend Charlie advised me to stay calm and that he would help find me a place; in fact he did. Charlie went around campus collecting advertisements for roommates and he found a posting for a sublet for the spring and summer terms. I moved into a basement apartment on Jarvis Street, one block away from campus. Two lesbians rented me the apartment, with the agreement that I would let them continue to stay there during the summer on a part-time basis. It wasn't a problem for me.

Since I felt that I had my own place I could pretty much do as I pleased. I continued to work the morning shift at Burger King and had a little cash that would help me survive. After paying my agreed portion of rent and bills I had a little extra money to buy beer, stockings, and women's underwear. Whenever I made purchases of female items I would say they were for my sister. I actually remember sitting on the toilet while one of my roommate's fathers walked in on me. I didn't lock the door because I was the only one at the apartment at that particular time and didn't expect any visitors. Little did I know that the girls were coming back that day for a brief visit. While sitting on the toilet and urinating, I heard the bathroom door open and a deep voice said "I'm sorry sweetie." My thoughts were "Oh shit, I got caught…what shall say?" I didn't hear anything further about the incident.

During this time a friend of mine hooked me up with a job at Naked Furniture. My responsibilities as Finishing Supervisor were finishing furniture, scheduling the finishing process, creating a store schedule for the finishers, inventory, and sales. Our store was located at the end of the strip at Arbor Land Mall. My job was further than Burger King so instead of walking I caught the bus. The finishing process took place in the store's basement or outside behind the store. Due to some of the products being flammable we couldn't work in extreme heat because the product would turn out poorly and the chemicals could cause a fire. We used women's nylons to finish some of the furniture. The use of nylons became a perk for me because I would often take some of the pantyhose home for my use.

I had to ask for a vacation once I was hired because my brother was graduating from Princeton University. I spent a week in New Jersey with Derrick. He treated me to pizza, Philly Steak Cheese Hoagies, and ice cream. I even drove to the mall so that I could buy some stockings. Neither Derrick nor my parents were aware of what I went to buy. Hey it was my money and my business. I also visited Princeton's campus and enjoyed the scenery. Ivy grew on the sides of the buildings and was very picturesque. I was so proud of my big brother because not only was he graduating from one of the most prestigious schools in America, he was graduating with honors. He earned a full-ride scholarship from Bell Labs and he spent his summers working his way through college.

Denise would visit me often during that summer. In fact one time she came up from Inkster for a couple of days; these few days turned into a week. We had planned to barbeque but it rained for several days so we extended her stay. Our outdoor barbeque turned into making barbeque in the oven. We loved pets and I had two kittens: Kitty and Baby. I remember walking Denise to the Greyhound Bus Station one morning. I also attached a leash to the kittens and attempted to walk them. After dragging them half a block Denise decided we'd carry them.

In another attempt to fight against my gender issues I dated Denise. Later in life she would tell me that I never told her, prior to our dating, about my issues but I reminded her of the things that I would do. For example, I did something that I would not dare tolerate from my man. While having intimacy I would often wear panties and stockings and ask her to role play with me as though I was a girl. I also would ask to wear her makeup. One day I was sick and she agreed to help make my face up if I took some Castor Oil for my illness. Although the medicine was nasty I took it anyway because I wanted her to do my makeup. During our frequent walks I would always tell her that I wasn't like other guys. Obviously, I wasn't. I didn't know too many guys that acted in the manner in which I did.

There were several reasons for me dating Denise. She was a very warm person with a wonderful personality and had a way in which she made those around her happy. I loved her as a true friend and wanted to reciprocate and make her happy as well. As mentioned I thought that by dating Denise I would be able to fight against my issues and with her I could overcome these battles. She often reminded me of how she would watch me walk across campus when she first met me and I looked "pitiful" and sad. My friendship with her made me happy because I was making her happy and she truly deserved it.

I decided to stay in the apartment on Jarvis Street during the Fall Semester. Denise moved back on the third floor of Walton Hall. The two girls moved out of the apartment and the landlord arranged where this boy from Saginaw was going to share the apartment with me. There was a major problem. When the landlord presented the apartment to him I was still in the small bedroom so she showed him and his mother the huge master bedroom. I wasn't aware of any deals that were made where he was taking over the master bedroom so once the girls vacated I moved my belongings from the small bedroom to the master. He kept threatening to beat me up and in my opinion kept shit stirred. I objected to the company that he kept because he would always bring his boy to the apartment and gang up on me. The two often reminded me that I got kicked off line because of my "bitch-like" tendencies. I'm not sure if Mr. Saginaw was aware that his friend had a warrant for his arrest but the word spread. I would often end up in Denise's dorm room in an effort to avoid conflict and not get in fights.

My parents made a surprise trip from Detroit during one weekend and Denise was actually at my apartment. Not only did I have to explain the reason for her being at my apartment, I also explained that we were moving in together during the next semester. I couldn't understand why my mother was so upset with Denise and me moving together. After all, I owed her thanks that I was living at Jarvis Apartments because I was almost homeless after she refused to allow me to move home during the past summer. Denise and I talked about getting married and living with each other in our efforts to make sure that our relationship would last. As a matter-of-fact, we got engaged on her mother's birthday. On October 14, 1986, I called my boy Charlie and told him of my plans. He and Ruthie had been living at Maplewood Apartments for a while.

The story of our engagement goes something like this: my day started with me working at the furniture store and I informed all the employees of my plans for the evening. Everyone was so excited and the girls kept asking me what kind of flowers I planned to get Denise. I ordered pink and white carnations. After I got off work, around 6 p.m., I called Charlie and asked him to pick up a couple bottles of Champale. We all were poor college students and couldn't afford Champagne. I arrived at Denise's dorm room around 7 o'clock or so. I had a pair of handcuffs that I had bought from a gag store and I talked her into letting me handcuff her. I'm not too sure why she let me, but I figured maybe she thought that it was sort of kinky. I called Charlie and asked him to come pick me up. Once I left the dorm room I called Denise and told her that I stepped out with Charlie to run to the Hide-A-Way, which was adjacent to her dorm hall. About 9 o'clock I called her from Charlie and Ruthie's apartment. She was pissed at me and sounded like she was going to cry and she asked me what I was doing. Denise was able to reach the phone because she was not handcuffed to a fixture so she could move around freely. I told her that we were on the way back to her room. Once we got to her room Charlie went upstairs and picked her up and told her that we were going back to his apartment for a little while. I purposely stayed in the car so I wouldn't have to take the handcuffs off of her. Once she got into the car with Charlie, she asked me to free her. I thought quickly on my feet and said that I accidentally left the keys at Charlie's apartment and we would be there within a few minutes. Once we got to Charlie's place we let Denise walk in first. The apartment was dark and all of a sudden from nowhere Ruthie had turned the lights on and sitting on the table was a vase of flowers with a sign that read "Congratulations Denise." She still demanded that I take the handcuffs off of her immediately. So I took my time to look for the key and then all of a sudden I reached in my pocket and pulled out a grey box and dropped to one knee. I gave her the box and took the key and freed her from the handcuffs. She opened the box and began to cry her tears of happiness. When she opened the box she saw the marquis diamond ring that was handed down from her grandmother to her mother. Charlie and Ruthie told her that there was more and they brought the Champale from the refrigerator. Denise asked if she could use the house phone to call her mother and deliver her the news. Her mother said that it was one of her best birthdays because of the joy that her daughter experienced. Well, damn, why couldn't I have been that lucky girl?

Denise and I moved together into Sunnyside Apartments and we both were working so we were able to afford the rent and bills. Our apartment was spare but we had a television and some furniture. Denise worked at American Bulk Foods and I was working at both Burger King and Naked Furniture. During this time my classes were scaling back. I took two classes and had slowed down in my efforts to graduate. Actually, the so called "real education" was just beginning. Both of my classes were evening classes.

I received a call from Miosha, asking me if I wanted to work for her at the University Women's Hospital and I was hired on March 17, 1987. Denise also received a call and was offered employment at U of M's Hospital and began her employment the following week. At this point academic progress slowed for both of us. I ended up leaving Burger King and reduced my schedule to part-time at Naked Furniture. Denise resigned from American Bulk Foods. The university was a good job for young folks that had just turned twenty-one years of age. We both worked through the summer and applied for jobs on campus. After working on campus for Building Services we both said that it was the dumbest thing that we ever did and regretted it for almost a year. The University of Michigan's Building Service Department was quite a different animal from the hospital. During the Fall Semester of 1987, I attempted to take a calculus course; and like I said "I attempted." Due to me being a clown in the 10th grade and not properly learning geometry I struggled with my calculus class. After a few weeks I decided to withdraw from the class. By the way I had already dropped several classes prior. This was a turning point in my college education. I ended up changing my major again to early elementary education. I later changed my major a couple more times.

The Big Day was June 11, 1988. Wedding bells were ringing for Denise and me. My mother adamantly opposed us getting married because, "She didn't want Denise and her mother to have a 'Big Show.'" My mother told me in a direct way not to invite any of her family nor friends. She also hid in a hotel during the weekend. That was alright because my father and brother both were a very strong supporting cast for "The Big Show." After Derrick took me out on Friday we went home. He had a friend who was also getting married on June 11th. His friend was an Alpha and therefore we had a party for both of us at the Alpha House. The Alpha was interested in girls but I was more interested in getting drunk. As normal, I kept my thoughts to myself. There was some fine ass "Alphas in the House." After we left the Alpha House, Derrick took me to meet some of his friends; one was a television newscaster. After that we went home.

Due to my nerves I couldn't sleep the night before our wedding. I was nervous about our big day and I was more nervous and kept thinking "What if Denise called me out in front of everybody?" I was thinking how to figure out my method of escape in case she spoke up during the vows and said that she refused to marry me because of me doing a lot of girlie things like wearing female clothes and make up. Well the wedding went well except when the director played the wrong song, as Denise walked down the aisle. Our plan was to have Luther Vandross' "So Amazing" play while she made her walk. Oops, instead "Let Your Body Do the Talking" played in her uncle's church.

After being married for a little while we were having some financial struggles, which is normal for young couples so Denise's mother let us move into her house on Carlisle. We both took classes on a part-time basis. I changed my major to business education and enjoyed several classes. One of my favorite classes was a business class for secretaries. I thought "Wow wouldn't it be something if I became an executive secretary." I enjoyed Dr. Ogden's keyboarding class and his personal finance class. He actually took the finance class on a field trip to a pub in Toledo. The pub was infamous for being on the television show "M.A.S.H.." Other than taking a few classes at Washtenaw Community College, and withdrawing from them too, my college education became stagnant.

I remained out of school for a few years but I finally restarted my classes in 1993 after I had become active in the labor movement. I gained knowledge about politics and the labor movement while away from the classroom. I walked several informational picket lines, attended State and International Union Conventions, held several union positions, helped the local union negotiate a contract with the university, and became active in local politics. So while I sat out of class I was still becoming educated. I met my good friends LeRoy and Mary. Mary became another mother and helped me with adjusting my attitude. I travelled to Miami and Las Vegas as a delegate for A.F.S.C.M.E. Local 1583. I witnessed the speaking of Bishop Tutu and Presidential Candidate Bill Clinton. (I will cover more details later in the book.) I ended up getting suspended from union leadership for a four year period and therefore was afforded the opportunity to return to school.

Our son, Ace, was born on February 17, 1991. Denise and I both wanted a baby and I wanted to give her the gift that she deeply wanted. After years of trying and many trips to the doctor's office we were finally successful. Denise's inability to get pregnant was not her fault because the doctors found that my sperm cells were swimming backwards. Depression and frustration sat in for us both. We shed many tears over our unsuccessful attempts and Denise took many pregnancy tests and finally the test was positive. We made a doctor's appointment and learned the good news. I was ecstatic to see the joy this baby would bring us both.

I took advantage of my suspension from union leadership and returned to Eastern Michigan in 1993. Once again I changed my major and this time my major was related to something that I was passionate about. Due to political involvement my career goal changed from accountant, to math teacher, to elementary teacher, to executive secretary, to United States senator. I figured that in order to become an effective politician that I would need to know history. Therefore I turned my studies to history and political science; this time without withdrawing from any classes. When I left school, several years prior, I carried a 2.5 G.P.A. That wasn't nearly good enough if I wanted to reach my ultimate goal. Therefore with Denise's financial help and mental support I turned up the heat. My last eighteen classes yielded success: 15 "A's," two "A-'s" and one "B." The lowest grade was my most prized grade.

I received a "B" in historical research. Remember the discussion about my papers at the beginning of this book? The course started with at least 25 students and ended with less than 10. It didn't start off very well for the first half of the course covered "Historiography." I still get a headache just thinking about the subject matter. Well, we studied linear history, from the beginning of time. Most of the class scored poorly on the quizzes and the mid-term. I flunked most of my quizzes and received a "D" on my mid-term; there was hope for me but other students dropped the class like flies.

The second part of the semester was my strength and I looked forward to the challenge. The second part of the class dealt with a lot of reading and writing. So most of you think that you know how to write a book review, well so did I until I ran into Dr. Goff. We learned that a book report didn't only cover the material inside the book. It covered information about the author's background and the critics and supporter's opinions of the book. The book reviews were about 6 to 10 pages in detail. In teaching us well, Dr. Goff ripped our writings into shreds with a fine tooth comb. In the end he was preparing us for our term paper, which was like no other. I also wrote a very motivational paper about my brother, entitled "Derrick R. Burns –The Most Influential Person in My Life." I proudly described in my paper how he influenced me to become a better student. Derrick had been a serious student from the very beginning. It was not a chore for him to pick up a book and read. Once he read something he could recite it forwards, backwards and forward again. He received high honors throughout school, from the beginning through his college graduation. As I wrote this paper, I felt Derrick's energy and the results showed. I produced an "A" paper with high remarks from Dr. Goff. I also received "A's" on all the book reviews that I wrote. Finally, was the big one; when I say big one I mean B-I-G one. It was time for the term paper titled, "The Philosophical Difference between Dr. Martin Luther King, Jr., Malcolm X, The Black Panthers and, The Student Non-Violent Coordinating Committee." We had major work even prior to writing the paper. We had to create a Theme Statement in which we had to prove. Time and time again I would take my statement to my professor for him to reject it and have me reform it. Once I developed my intended statement the research began. In gathering my research, I spent hour after hour in more than a dozen libraries throughout Michigan. We were required to present our note cards; these cards were checked for grammatical errors. We had to re-write these cards several times. Once the presentation of cards was approved then it was time to write the paper. I presented my rough draft to Dr. Goff on several occasions and each time I realized that I had to make changes. We received a grade on the draft, which I received a "B+." Our End Notes and Bibliography were also graded for proper syntax. Once I rewrote my paper several more times my final grade was an "A." As you may imagine this paper was heavily graded. It resulted in my receiving my most prized college grade. I always made the statement that I should have had this paper published. Despite earning a "D-" on my mid-term I received an overall grade of "B" in the class and I was one of six students still standing.

I had several other history classes which included United States history, Greek history, Native American history, military history, the Old West, the comparison of women between the U.S. and Great Britain, and other courses. I was forever grateful to Dr. Goff for he built my foundation for both my reading and writing skills. I mentioned prior that during my early stages of college I was applauded by an English professor for my writing skills. History students also do a lot of writing. The tests are even essay exams. I took an early liking to Dr. Boyer for he was a Native American who taught my second part of U.S. history. I enjoyed his style so much and I enjoyed learning about the Native American culture that I took his Native American history course. We studied how different Nations had different beliefs and cultural activities that separated them from others. I thoroughly enjoyed Greek history for we studied about the great philosophers and Socrates'. We were taught the famous statement that "Socrates' said that only a fool knows everything." I also enjoyed studying the Greek topography and landmarks. We studied how the young Greek boys who took a liking to older males were treated like young girls. Whenever the older men wanted to date the younger boys the older men would be gentlemen and seek permission from the younger's father to date. The older men would often present the younger with gifts like flowers. The young boys would dress up very pretty and use gaffs to hide their male organs. Of course I was fascinated by this. I also enjoyed studying about Annie Oakley and Calamity Jane and the

Buffalo Girls in my Old Western U.S. history course. After studying the country and western music and understanding the words I took a liking to it. I also wrote a paper in honor of my favorite U.S. congresswoman, Maxine Waters. She was my hero in her handling of the Rodney King incident. My dedication resulted in me earning a 3.74 grade point average in my major, history.

My political science courses included studies of public administration, introduction to American law, international relations, international law, a couple political analysis courses, and an internship for U.S. Congresswoman Lynn Rivers. Although I didn't write as many papers in this concentration I had many essay exams and wanted to clearly demonstrate my writing abilities. I thoroughly enjoyed writing a paper in my introduction to political analysis course, which compared the labor unions in Europe to the organizations here in the United States. One finding showed that there was more apathy towards the labor organizations here in the U.S. I studied about many conflicts that took place in the Middle East and soon learned of the severity of Holy Wars. "Power tends to corrupt, and absolute power corrupts absolutely. Great men are almost always bad men" was a phrase that I learned early on in my political science studies. This quote came from historian Lord Acton. If you think about this you can see the validity, even in today's society. I learned a valuable lesson in my Introduction to the American legal system course, which included speaking up in order to ensure that I didn't get overlooked. I had difficulty understanding a particular lecture and I asked my professor several questions. He soon became irritated and directed a rude comment at me in front of our class. I decided to stand my ground and I visited him in his office and I questioned my professor on his rudeness. His statement was that he had 100 students in the class and he didn't have time to answer my questions. I advised him that it was my job to ask questions and make certain that I understood my lessons in which I was paying for. I thought that because I was so adamant with my directness that I was going to flunk this course. My grade was an "A." My last dance included an internship, during my final semester, for United States Congresswoman Lynn Rivers; another favorite leader whom I met through the labor movement. I later was on her escort committee as she addressed an A.F.S.C.M.E. State Convention for Council 25. I earned a 3.9 grade point average in my political science courses.

Finally, my big day was here. April 26, 1997, was graduation day from Eastern Michigan University; ten years later than I was originally supposed to graduate. I earned honors and was inducted into the Phi Alpha Theta (history) and Pi Sigma Alpha (political science) National Honor Societies. Although neither my father nor mother was at my graduation, my brother and my hero was there. My father had fallen sick in 1995, with a major stroke that paralyzed him. My mother had a speaking engagement with her Zeta Sorority organization. Derrick who had always supported me once again was there for me. He had a lot to do with my drastic improvement in grades. I admired his motivation throughout his school years and I applied that same motivation towards my studies at the end of my undergraduate years. So again I offer many thanks to him.

Bringing It All Together
Education

As I said in the beginning, my primary reason for writing this book is to help others overcome situations that may seem difficult. In my quest to accomplish this I will tell my autobiography throughout the book and at the end of each section give a brief discussion on the key points in which I think will help others. In including this chapter it is not my purpose to insult anyone's intelligence. I am only trying to highlight some of the facts that were important to me. Please continue to enjoy.

One typically thinks of classroom instruction when speaking of education. I'm here to tell you that education is far more than classroom activities. I am a firm believer that a human begins learning at birth. For example, a baby learns to cry when it's hungry or needs its diaper changed. My memories took us back to my pre-adoption age before I began grade school. I learned to stand up for what I believed to be right through learning about the Civil Rights Movement and Dr. Martin Luther King, Jr. while sitting on the floor watching the news with my foster family. I may not have actually understood the events at the time but as I grew older I could reflect on what I saw from the television. These early teachings travelled with me throughout my life. My foster family would often get into arguments and physical fights and as a toddler I picked up on these things. Through many altercations during my early school days I learned that there were other ways of dealing with disagreements other than physical encounters. I was taught that things should be worked out in a more civil manner. I also learned that it was alright to stand up for what I believed, but it was important to understand the correct way in which to stand my ground. For example, I learned that pouting and stomping my feet were not acceptable and would not be tolerated; but if I calmly spoke my opinion I could more effectively be heard.

I learned many valuable lessons in the military and work environments. For example, I learned how to temper my attitude and control my mouth when respecting authority. This has sometimes been a challenge because I had to learn how to balance what I thought was standing up for my beliefs and learning how to address my superiors when I felt violated. I am still in the process of learning to control my mouth. This, for me, has been a continued process. I became more disciplined throughout my experiences in the military. Although I did not immediately begin using this discipline once I entered college, the discipline was instilled in me for future purposes. The work environment further educated me on how to become a professional and how to properly represent myself and others. I learned proper dress and behavioral for professional environments.

My education also taught me that life would bring many obstacles, but I had to somehow find a way to overcome them. Several examples of obstacles that I faced included racial, gender, and financial concerns. As mentioned earlier both my brother and I were harassed because of skin tone. Derrick learned how to walk away from altercations where I usually ended up in fights. I often acted out in class in my efforts to gain attention and to try to make others like me. I thought acting out in class would make others think that I was cool. However, Derrick's approach was much better and resulted in far more educational success. He would study and not allow the interactions with others to distract him from his learning. I was often called names like "Peckerwood" or "Honky" and took exception and resorted to handling these distractions in my own way. When I became distracted I often missed important lessons that could have taken me much further in life. I was further educated by my experiences through my relationships with others. Racial tensions were still intense during the early 1970s. By me being a biracial child I witnessed the aggression from both black and white children of my own age. My eagerness to be friends with others and in becoming the class clown that I was resulted in me bringing three "D's" home on my 10th grade report card. This, my friend, was not acceptable. Through my interactions with my peers I further learned to appreciate and value others no matter what background they arrived. This experience taught me to treat others in a fair manner and in a manner in which I wanted to be treated as well. Although times are much better in today's age I truly appreciate the relations that I have with all nationalities.

Although I have always felt that I was part of the female persuasion, I kept things internal. I was scared to address my feelings to others due to either being beat up or ostracized. As a child, my foster father used to call me a "sissy" because of my continual crying and playing with my female cousins. Although I truly believe that Gender Identity Disorder, which I devoted an entire section of this book, is innate I also believe that one learns gender behaviors through interacting with others. For example, I attempted to hide my feelings due to knowing that they wouldn't be accepted during my early ages. Although I may have done things that others could have questioned I was still learning and developing my personality and ways of dealing with my emotions. In my adult years I often questioned whether it would have been worth it if I would have just let everyone know my thoughts of my gender at an early age instead of waiting until I was grown. I sometimes reflect on my college experiences and ask myself "Why would my friends call me Nurse Burns instead of Dr. Burns?" Maybe they knew more than I offered them credit for. How should I have reacted when I was ordered by a visiting brother to speak to my line brothers in my most feminine sexy manner? Why was I turned on by this? These are questions that I ask and often wonder if it was worth trying to fight my inner conflicts. This obstacle did not prevent me from gaining a valuable education. It did, however, teach me that there could have been an easier method of dealing with my issue. For example, I kept my thoughts internal until my adult years and further deepened my depression. This will also be discussed later in my book.

Financial matters were another obstacle that I overcame in earning my college education. My mother and I had conflict about my student loans during the beginning stages of my college education. Therefore I had to work my way through college. With the help of Denise, I continued to press forward until I earned my degree. I sat out of school for several years and I went to school part time. In all it took me 14 years to gain a four year college degree. My perseverance paid dividends with a bachelor's of science degree. Denise and I worked hard and made many sacrifices in order for me to afford my education. In the end, I overcame obstacles of race, gender, and financial matters and still became educated. You too, my friends, can accomplish the same. Like the older people say, "Once you earn it, no one can take your education from you." Education is a very important aspect of life.

In addressing the principle of "Perseverance" I would say that you are the driving force to your own success. Things may appear that they will block you from reaching your goal but the truth is that you can only block yourself. No matter what comes your way, if you continue to press forward and work towards your goals you would achieve them. One of my political science professors, Dr. Kinney, shared a story with our class about a method of attacking huge obstacles when trying to accomplish a goal. She told us that she understood the pressure that we had with all the classes, papers, exams, and other school work that we were responsible for. However, she also told us a story of a mouse and a huge block of cheese. She said that a mouse nibbles on the cheese, one bite at a time, until the cheese is gone. She equated that big block of cheese to all the tasks that we were assigned as students and told us to nibble one piece of our assignments at a time. This process worked for me because it allowed me to focus on my immediate task at hand and allowed me to complete everything at a high quality. I say this to you, through proper planning and focus you can achieve your hardest task. I firmly believe in God and know that He will help me accomplish my successes. He has already brought me through and due to my faith I have persevered. It may have taken 14 years to accomplish my degree, but I have it and "No one can take it away from me."

Another important lesson that I learned was that everyone advances in life at their own pace. Not every student graduating from high school is ready for college. I knew that I had some maturing to do once I graduated from Osborn High, so I decided to go into the Marine Corps Reserves. As mentioned before, I thought that this was another method for battling my gender conflict but it also was a method in which I would mature and prepare myself for college. Once I enrolled in college I changed my major several times. I went to school part time, dropped many classes, and sat out of school for several years. My grades started out with a sub "B" grade point average. My father would tell me that I would wake up when the rock fell from the sky and hit me in my head. Once that happened I was on my way to success. The success was measured with the results of my last 18 classes. I raised my grade point average from a 2.57 to a 3.18. My grade point average for my history courses was a 3.74 and for my political science courses I held a 3.9 grade point average. It took time for me to become focused on how I might proceed in life. Now please don't take me the wrong way. I'm not saying sit idle and don't try to accomplish anything. I am saying get focused and prepare to proceed in your progress of accomplishing your goals. Life is indeed short and time does not stand still. My experiences showed that although my wheels may have appeared to be spinning in mud I was still trying to accomplish my mission.

Do it for yourself. You are your main support. Others may support you, but you must do it. Choose a mentor and follow the things learned. You must apply yourself 100% in order to maximize your results. Many people may say positive things in support of you but there is a song that says "Don't depend on anyone except yourself." You have some people who truly care and want you to succeed and then you have others that become obstacles. No matter what you face your ultimate success comes from your own desire. My big brother and my mentor, Derrick, took a different path to his college success. He studied hard, read a lot, and learned quickly. He earned the life that he now enjoys. I, on the other hand, took a longer path to gain my education and success. While I sat out of college for several years I asked myself, "What did Derrick do that was so different from me? Why is he so successful and I have not accomplished anything?" After I stepped back and reflected on his dedication to education I decided to be more like him. I remember sitting at my kitchen table studying, hour after hour, until I understood and had a grasp of my studies. Denise and Ace would both think that it was funny but while preparing for my exams I would do silly things like stand up in the middle of my bed and recite information that I had learned in class. I remember reciting things from Socrates' that I gathered from my Greek history course. There it is. I became focused like my brother but I can't say that he did weird things; but he was focused. My father told me, "No matter what you do give 100%." In today's society there are many workers that stand on the roadside carrying signs for various companies. I say to them be the best sign carrier that you can be. I tell my sister and friend, Blythe, that I can see who will be more successful by the way the person carries the sign. Some people haphazardly carry the street signs, as though they don't appreciate the privilege to have the job. Another sign carrier may be on the street dancing while holding the sign. The latter person is the one giving 100% to the job. As a former manager I would be more apt to hire that person than the first sign holder. Again, success is simple. Trust in God; give 100% at whatever do you decide to do; and stick with what you do.

Education, both in the classroom and in everyday life should be valuable to everyone. It is indeed a solid block to your foundation and the results can lead you to climbing many mountains. Like Socrates' says, "Only a fool knows everything." It was my hope to demonstrate in this section that an education is valuable and sometimes we have to make sacrifices in order to maximize our efforts of learning. Lessons come in many shapes, forms and experiences. Please enjoy the rest of my book. In the next section I will tell you how I furthered my education through political activities and community involvement.

Derrick R. Burns
Princeton University
Graduation
1986

David B. Burns
AKA Jala A. McKenzie Burns
Eastern Michigan University
Graduation 1997

David B. Burns
immediately after radio school
December 1983

SECTION 2

COMMUNITY INVOLVEMENT

Making Changes in the Community

"Gas prices are too high. The cost of living is going up. I hate my job because my boss is mean. The crime rate is ridiculous. Drugs have taken over our neighborhoods." Have you heard any of these complaints? If so, I ask you, what have you done about it? In fact, what are you going to do about these issues?

I learned at a very young age that if something wasn't right one should get involved and make it right. As a toddler I watched many riots and peaceful marches during the Civil Rights Movement. These protestors were standing up for what they believed to be right. Now I am not suggesting that you rise up and become a revolutionary or that you start a riot on your job. This would be, in my humble opinion, nonsense. Maxine Waters, the U.S. congresswoman who represents California's 35^{Th} Congressional District described riots as "Being unorganized chaos." She was speaking of the actions that many took following the Rodney King verdict in the 1990s. She was absolutely right: there is an orderly way to get your message across without burning or pillaging places. Congresswoman Waters is my all-time favorite political figure and therefore I wrote a paper on her during my senior year at E.M.U.

My mother and my Aunt Net taught my brother and me to stand up and get active in the work place. I have fond memories of both my mother and Aunt Net discussing their teacher union. Every year, it seemed like there was a threat of a strike that would delay school openings in the fall. They both worked for the Detroit Board of Education. My dear friend, whom I call Mother Mary, taught me that "Right was Might" and to stand up for what's right. Both Derrick and I learned how to become active in our neighborhood. For our mother was the founder and first president of the Shields Street Block Club. She also taught us how to stand at the polls and make a difference at the voting sites by passing out literature. I also have fond memories of a picture that included my uncle, which was taken in 1968. He was seeking office for The House of Representatives for the State of North Carolina. By him being an African-American this was unheard of. This picture has also stood firm in my mind and I would always think of how proud I was to see it. These individuals taught and practiced the art of becoming involved.

This following section will discuss my involvement with the labor movement and my political activity. Readers will see that I got involved and attempted to change the things that I didn't agree with. Please enjoy and understand that in order to make a difference one must not only voice an opinion but one must be active.

My Political and Community Involvement as a Child

In 1973, soon after my adoption into the Burns' family, I began my experience in community activities. My mother, Willa Burns, decided to bring her community together by organizing The Shields Street Block Club. My mother would instruct Derrick and me to pass flyers out on Shields Street. Derrick passed flyers out on one side of the block and I the other side. The announcement that Shields Street was having its first block club meeting spread rapidly. The meeting was scheduled for a Saturday night. The basement was filled with neighbors. My mother loved to make her "party foods" and deserts for events. The neighbors all came together and nominated the officers for the Shield Street Block Club. Mrs. Willa Martha Burns was the first elected president. Some people who are elected for office would just appreciate the title. Oh, not my mother. She had better plans and great ideas. She was successful in getting support and getting the neighbors united. Services such as snow removal, curb painting, tree planting, Halloween Block Parties, and other events took place. My mother successfully encouraged the Shields Street Block Club to get organized with the Krainz Woods Association. The Block Club picnic was held at Mayor Coleman A. Young Park, which is a couple blocks from our home. Throughout my mother's life she organized many protests, including one against the Ryan Road Prison and a long standing unlicensed business that polluted our neighborhood. Throughout the years my mother was very active in the NAACP, several church committees, and other organizations. I witnessed her work for the Stork's Nest, which lent support to single mothers. My mother affected me nearly every year because she kept me wondering if the Detroit teachers would strike and if school would open on time. My mother's political and community involvement helped shape me into the woman that I am today.

Dr. Charles E. Morton, our pastor of Metropolitan Baptist Church, ran for Detroit City Council during my 6th grade year. I proudly wore the "I Love Charlie" button to school and almost everywhere I went because I was ecstatic to help my pastor with his campaign. Due to the encouragement of Dr. Morton and others in our church I became active on many church committees. During the campaign time our family would go from door to door and circulate Dr. Morton's campaign materials. I stood with excitement at the election site and passed out his campaign literature and asked the voters to vote for my pastor. He deserved a seat on the City Council. Although Dr. Morton did not get elected to the Detroit City Council, he won a special place in my heart. I always thought the world of him.

There were other years that I would stand at the election polls and pass information out in an attempt to get the voters to support the millage so that the Detroit Public Schools could continue to have extracurricular activities. These activities would encourage children to stay active in school. Other students that participated in sports and other activities would also pass out literature.

Another community project that I participated in while growing up was the Detroit Beautification Project. School children travelled around the city and helped clean up the city. We did things like pick up trash, plant flowers, paint objects, and other activities that would make Detroit look like a more attractive city. As a child, I enjoyed doing things that allowed me to be with other children my age who enjoyed helping Detroit look nice too. The other kids and I would often talk and have fun while we were doing our part for the city.

Throughout my younger years I was very active in our church. I proudly served on several committees and wanted to make others proud of me. Many adults would often praise my efforts at doing good deeds at church. Committees that I served include the Youth Usher Board, the Altar Circle, the Youth Choir (I couldn't sing a lick. Remember my lack of rhythm?), the Laymen Committee, and the Youth Group. I served as an officer on many of these committees. While serving as the president of the Youth Committee in 1983 I helped organized a field trip to Boblo Island. I also served as the Co -Chairman of the Youth Day Program in 1983. Through these church activities I developed leadership skills that would follow me through the rest of my life.

My political and extracurricular activities during my middle school years were plentiful. For example, I enjoyed serving on the Student Senate because I was empowered to help make some decisions for other students. I was surprised that my peers had elected me to serve, but I think that it was more of a lack of interest from others than my popularity. My lessons included becoming acquainted with political procedures during the Student Senate meetings. For example, I learned how to present a proposal to the floor. The leadership learned how to successfully debate both sides of issues. We also learned how to vote on different proposals. One proposal that I sponsored was for a School Bake Sale in an effort to raise money so our Equations Team could have money to travel to the State Competition. We also voted and spoke on behalf of students who wanted to have an After School Basketball Program. Mr. Wynn would stay after school to supervise and play with the boys. Therefore these activities that took place early in my life helped shaped my political and community awareness.

As mentioned earlier in the book, I was also the vice president of my Junior Achievement Organization during my eighth grade school year. While in this position I learned how to become accountable for other people's money. (I don't manage my money well, but I can manage others'. Go figure.) During our process we learned both business procedures and how to get involved with the community. We had to present our projects to organizations in the community.

I remember presenting our vases to the Hamtramck Chamber of Commerce. Not only were we trying to make money for our organization we also wanted to raise money in order to help others participate in Junior Achievement.

My political socialization began at an early age. Through these many activities and being around others that encouraged these activities, I became shaped into an active member of society. Many scholars teach that babies are born with innate behaviors. Others teach that people developed learned behaviors. I can proudly say that I believed that both behaviors have shaped the person that I am today. I love helping others and therefore have been active politically at work, school, and the community.

Labor Union and Political Activity

My labor union participation started in 1990 when the University of Michigan wanted to cut jobs in the Housekeeping Department. The layoffs would affect the livelihoods of many workers. I didn't agree with job cuts and therefore wanted to voice my opinion. After our Housekeeping Department informed us of the upcoming job cuts I became upset and called my A.F.S.C.M.E. Local 1583 union hall. I had heard many negative things about our local president and soon after becoming involved found out that the rumors were false. The propaganda that was spread throughout the membership had begun to divide our members.

As a result of our meeting with President Carter we organized an Informational Picket. This was bad timing for the University of Michigan because the Nurses' Union was also in a fight with them. Our local had over 2500 members and the Nurses' Union also had many members. The nurses went on strike and our local picketed. Within the first hour of setting up our picket lines we could feel the unity of both unions fighting for what we believed to be right. The nurses were fighting for their wages and we were fighting for our jobs. I thought, "So this was what my mother experienced while she fought for her employee's rights as a school teacher." I proudly stood on the picket line and walked the pavement in front of 1500 East Medical Center Drive.

With both unions being very organized we were able to deliver our message to the community that we were standing up for our rights. There was turmoil at the university. I remember a car that was decorated with labor signs had stalled in front of the picket lines and backed up traffic. People started honking their horns and yelling that the university was unfair to its workers. Union members from both picket lines were carrying signs that displayed messages. The Nurses' union signs displayed messages that suggested that the Nurses were fighting for their wages. The signs that the Local 1583 members carried described how unfair the university was in cutting jobs. Many people from other unions and from the community joined both picket lines. Things became so intense for U of M that the university's Board of Regents wanted to meet with our local leadership. President Carter was good friends with former Bargaining Chairman Anderson and they communicated with each other. Former Bargaining Chair Anderson had served the local for many years and knew the history of the labor contract and also had established rapport with several of the Regents. Mr. Anderson also served Council 25 as a staff member. After a couple days of picketing and several hours of meeting with the Regents our local was gaining ground. The Regents agreed to ask some former Regents about the history of the wording of the R.I.F. language. In the end, the university eliminated some jobs that were vacant instead of cutting hours and laying employees off. The housekeeping staff celebrated the victory and thanked President Carter for his assistance. In terms of our impact on the nurses' strike, they returned to work a few days after our picket ended and they received a decent pay raise.

In the aftermath of my initial Informational Picket I decided to bring our local union back together by meeting with various employees. I gained the utmost respect for our local president. He was constantly under attack by The M.A.C. and other individuals that sought personal gains. I decided to take this fight on myself by printing my own literature and passing it out to the local membership. In my quest to reach the entire 2500 members I walked the entire University of Michigan campus, both campus and medical center. I reached out to the entire membership in my effort to unite them. Carter was really about his business of protecting the local membership and I wanted the employees to be informed. He would often state that those that were out for personal gain did not realize the impact that they had on the livelihoods of its members. Many supporters backed me in saying that others should stop attacking our local leaders and build a united front. After all, a strong union is one that stands together.

The local leadership approached me several months after the picket and suggested that I seek election for the medical center executive board. I was nominated for the medical center executive board representative position, a district steward's position, and a delegate to the International Convention that was held in Miami, Florida. Mary, the recording secretary, introduced herself to me and gave me her overwhelming support. The election of the international delegates was held at the membership meeting and Mother Mary and I won the vote by a landslide. I finished second behind her by two votes. There were six delegates elected.

The political campaigns kicked off immediately following the union meeting. I didn't take my nomination lightly although I was on the slate with the majority of the incumbents. Therefore I marched the entire medical center during the morning, afternoon and mid-night shifts because I wanted my voice heard. I also campaigned with our president in an effort to get him re-elected. There were five other candidates that were vying for the executive spot.

After a hard fought campaign Election Day had arrived. The day began at 6 a.m. when the polls opened. Election Day had brought very long hours both day and night. The polls opened at 6 a.m. and closed at 6 p.m. Our slate decided to meet at the local hall around 10 p.m. We attempted to listen in on the count. As my votes were being tallied people started chuckling due to the overwhelming support that I had received. Everyone thought that meant success for our entire slate. Mother Mary and I each won by a landslide; I captured 83%

of the votes for my executive board seat and I also won the steward position by a landslide. I now represented 1500 members from the medical center. Our slate won every position outright except for president, bargaining chairman, and sergeant at arms. The incumbent bargaining chairperson won outright. She was the leader of M.A.C. The primary election resulted in two run-off elections that were to be held within a couple of weeks. President Carter had more votes than the other five candidates that he was facing but he did not have enough votes to win the election outright. Therefore he and the sergeant at arms were both in the upcoming run-off elections. The battle for the run-off election for president got kind of nasty because the other candidates gained up against Carter and supported the M.A.C.'s presidential candidate. Local 1583 had a newly elected president and the fight was on between the majority of the Executive Board and M.A.C. I remember breaking down and crying because my mentor lost his election. Therefore our slate won every position except for the president and bargaining chairman. The fight was on for the next few years.

My first experience as a delegate to the International Union taught me the procedures in which a convention was organized. There were many delegates from across the nation. Our order of business included discussion of various resolutions presented by the union committees. One vital resolution included A.F.S.C.M.E.'s endorsement of Miami's offer to give Bishop Tutu the Key to Miami City. A great controversy surrounded our endorsement of him and the conflict between Miami and Fidel Castro. Miami City did not offer a Key to the City nor welcome Castro, however the city welcomed Tutu with opened arms. As I walked through the corridor, during a break, chills went down my spine as I witnessed a huge standoff between African-Americans and Cubans. African-Americans lined up on one side of the street and the Cubans were on the other side. The block was a long stretch and I could tell strong emotions were in the air. The last time that I witnessed anything close to this was when I led the Anti-Apartheid March through the streets of Ypsilanti, Michigan. I was so proud of our African-American friends because they stood strong for what they believed, which was that Bishop Tutu was to receive a Key to the City of Miami. As I watched the site from the corridor, I saw and heard the crowd chant "Mandela." Wow, this was truly history in the making and I was so proud to be part of this moment. Bishop Tutu addressed the delegates once we resumed our convention. He was well received by our A.F.S.C.M.E. union.

The Miami Convention was very successful due to a lot of business being completed. It was a wonderful experience for me because it taught me many lessons regarding the political arena. This experience led me to think further about my college education and I now found my niche and knew exactly in which discipline I wanted to earn my degree. I now realized that I wanted to become a United States senator. In order to be an effective politician I would need to know my history. I turned my attention to earning my degree in history and political science.

As the convention business wrapped up I met several important leaders from Council 25 such as Council President Glass and Council Secretary-

Treasurer Larry Roehrig. Both gentlemen were very polished and articulate. They both told me of how proud they were to see a young person such as I get involved and I was also told that the Council had heard great things about me and how I helped organize the Housekeeping Informational Picket. President Glass welcomed me to his team and advised me that my future in A.F.S.C.M.E was bright. I became a strong supporter of both officers upon meeting them. President Carter had previously spoken to several Council 25 leaders about me and I was seen as a strong union activist.

After returning from the convention the new officers were sworn in. My passion for becoming the best union representative ever inspired me to work hard. I would find myself busy with grievances during the day shift. I spent a lot of time walking the entire medical center and meeting with the members during the evening shift. Executive board and membership meetings were held during the evenings and weekends. I didn't find myself spending time at home and although I was gaining support from the membership I was losing support from Denise.

The membership voted for me to represent them as a delegate to our Council 25 State Convention in 1991. The convention was held at the Hyatt Regency in Dearborn, Michigan. Although this was my first Council 25 Convention I could participate more because of my experience that I had in Miami. I had previously met with Council President Glass and Secretary-Treasurer Roehrig and understood their main items for their agenda and I agreed with their stance on many topics and therefore continued to support them. I would speak in favor of various resolutions that I supported. Many other delegates would approach me during the hospitality parties and often tell me that I spoke like a Southern Baptist preacher because I normally had a hum to my voice when I addressed the public. I guess that was from being really passionate about my topics. The Council 25 Convention had a similar tone as the International Convention that I had attended the previous year. Several state leaders addressed our convention. Overall, I thoroughly enjoyed my experience at my first Council 25 Convention.

The membership had elected me as part of the Bargaining Committee and since this was my first experience at the table and I trusted the Council 25 representatives. I agreed with using their expertise because we were negotiating for 2500 other members. The Council negotiated contracts for many locals throughout the state and they would bring polished attorneys down to our local to bargain against the university's attorneys. In my opinion it created a level playing field. The bargaining chairman was anti-Council 25 and had a major dislike for the council president. After many days of negotiating the university and A.F.S.C.M.E. Local 1583 had reached a tentative agreement. The membership met at the Michigan Union in the attempt to ratify the contract. However, the membership thought that we could get a better contract and voted against the tentative agreement. After returning to the negotiating table the university offered a better contract with higher wages. This time the membership voted to accept the contract.

Campaign season for the International and Council positions was among us in 1992. Council 25 President Glass was one of the longest tenured members on the International Board and he had come under fire due to propaganda from groups like M.A.C. The elections were to be held at the International Convention in June and it was being held in Las Vegas. Opponents circulated information calling Mr. Glass "A crook" and mentioning that "Baby Face Burns supports a crook at the Council Level." My opposition made every attempt to keep me from being elected as a delegate for the International Convention for 1992. However, Mother Mary and I were always seen together and her support was so overwhelming that people supported her and me together as one. The turnout for the vote at the local membership meeting was overwhelming. As in previous elections, Mother Mary and I carried the vast majority of the votes once again. We were among the six members elected as delegates for the 1992 International Convention. As a matter of fact, five of the six members elected were supporters of President Glass. The issue was that the delegation had six of the eight members that supported Glass and two members that didn't. The bargaining chairman won a seat as a delegate and the local president received an automatic bid. As a result our vote would be split during the International Election. Since our local was the largest in the state our vote counted heavier. In the past, Council 25 could count on Local 1583 for the full vote. This proved to be devastating because President Glass had lost his election.

An exciting and most memorable thing occurred for me while at the convention. I had the privilege to hear Presidential Candidate Bill Clinton address our delegation as he was seeking his first term in office as United States President. A.F.S.C.M.E. was the first union to support Bill Clinton's bid for the White House. I was a huge Clinton fan and was really impressed with how articulate he spoke, with his Arkansas twang. (I will discuss later on in this section where I was allowed to attend President Clinton's speech at Eastern Michigan University during his 2nd term in office.)

While at the convention I spoke on several resolutions that covered various topics. My public speaking skills were on the incline and I really enjoyed speaking in public forums. The main focus on the convention included both our union elections and the upcoming national elections. Many politicians addressed the delegates in seeking the support from the labor movement due to politicians relying heavily on union support. We also discussed the location for our next convention.

After returning from Las Vegas, I received a letter from the International Union that advised me that charges were filed against me and several other union officials for "Supporting outside influences directed against the Union." I questioned what the hell was going on. The Local 1583 president and bargaining chairman had filed charges against me and a couple other officers with the International Union. These charges were in reference to the affidavit that we signed stating the "Local Executive Board was the highest body of the union whenever the membership meetings were not in session. The local executive board had the right to initiate and terminate the employment of the office secretary." I told the International Court, I stood for what was right and the constitution read "The Executive Board is the supreme being of the local union, unless when the membership convenes." Therefore our argument was that the local constitution allowed us to make the hiring decision. Not only were we found guilty of the charges, the International Union suspended several officers from leadership roles for the next four years.

Overall, I accomplished many things during my time in office. I sat on the University of Michigan Medical Center's Profit Sharing Committee and helped our employees gain an additional bonus for their contributions to their jobs. I fought back the challenges that I received from The Membership Action Committee, who deemed me as a "Money Hungry Gangster." I gained the support of the membership, even after we were suspended. I also walked several picket lines for other unions. For example, I supported the Teamsters' Union and enjoyed walking their line and building union solidarity. I became politically involved and as a result became more focused on my goals in life. My dream was to become an U.S. senator. In having this dream I could now shift my college studies towards history and political science. In the final analysis, I accomplished my mission of being the best representative possible. Many people respected me for this accomplishment. While I sat my four years out of office as directed I became active in local politics and I earned my bachelor's degree. There was a change in administration for the next term because a new president and bargaining chairman were elected.

During my suspension I became active in local politics. Former Bargaining Chairman Anderson's nephew, Jerome Ralston, was running for mayor for the city of Inkster, Michigan. Jerome was 28 years old and we shared a common goal of wanting to become a U.S. senator. After meeting with Jerome and his wife, Kitty, we agreed that I would serve as his campaign manager. Jerome was a young African-American businessman who owned a quarter of a million dollar cleaning service. He was always neatly dressed and was a very attractive male. Kitty was a very attractive businesswoman as well.

There were six candidates that were seeking the position of mayor. Of the candidates the former mayor, from the 1970s, decided to seek the position. There was the incumbent, the former mayor, Jerome Ralston, and three others that would face off in a tough campaign season. Therefore with this fight upon us we knew that a change had to be made. There were also elections for the City Council and School Board. The tension grew throughout the city because many jobs were up in the air and the entire community would be affected by the election results.

Inkster, Michigan had approximately 25,000 citizens, which were predominantly African-American. The citizens were mostly deemed as hard working citizens whom were trying to raise their families. Crime was on the rise and there were many Drugs Lords running their drug dealings on the city's streets. The quality of education was on the decline. Overall, the city was crying for a change in local government, where the residents could take back their city.

Jerome Ralston had some brilliant ideas that he wanted to bring to Inkster. He was a very successful business owner and had supplied jobs to members of the community. Our platform included items such as creating more jobs for the citizens, bringing the community together to place pressure on the School Board so that the quality of education would be better, pressuring the legal department and enhancing neighborhood watch programs in our efforts to bring a halt to drugs and other crimes, repairing and rebuilding the city by forming a Community Project Committee, and creating a "Think Tank" so that the community would be able to generate ideas that would bring the city back together.

Although our potential for winning this election was very strong there were a couple concerns that we desperately needed to address. Jerome Ralston had moved to Inkster in the last year and the other candidates were trying to influence the voters that he was a "Carpetbagger." Jerome had been a resident of Inkster but moved to Farmington Hills in an effort to get his business off the ground. Although we acknowledged that he relocated within the last year we also set out to prove that he was born and raised locally. Our thoughts were that the opposition had to find things to demoralize the character of Mr. Ralston because our campaign was so strong. The other issue that the old school politicians tried to sway voters against supporting Jerome was his inexperience. Both the incumbent and the candidate whom was the former mayor were at least in their late sixties. The other four candidates were 40 years old or younger; Jerome being 28 years of age.

I often met with Kitty and discussed activities that she and her husband had planned. Kitty and I organized things such as phone bank campaigns, public speaking engagements, door to door campaigns, advertising and sign postings, and other activities. We setup a phone bank in the basement of the Ralston's home. We normally had about 10 or so members of the campaign committee who would make phones calls to the residents of Inkster. We made many phone calls to the various churches in Inkster so that we could address the many different congregations. Ralston participated in some very intense debates. Issues such as the approach to reduce crime, improvement of education, unification of the city, and other issues would be debated. Several debates involved the mayoral candidates teaming up against Ralston. I would always advise Jerome to keep his cool and that we must be winning the voters' confidence or the other candidates would not have focused on him. We also strategically performed the door to door campaign and we would use the phone bank to call a particular area of the city in which we planned to visit that week. We also were invited to several functions that other candidates sponsored. We hosted our own function at the Stardust Lounge on Inkster Road. Our committee decorated the lounge with "Make a Change...Vote for Ralston" signs. Overall, we put a pretty well organized campaign together.

The demise of our campaign occurred on the last two nights before the primary election. We were involved in a debate on each night and it was truly our time to shine. Well, on the first night the incumbent's campaign manager stepped to the microphone and he spoke directly to Candidate Ralston. He asked, "Please tell us the difference between a City Ordinance and a Law?" Mr. Ralston looked at me and smiled and then he spoke his answer. He stated that an ordinance was a rule established by the City and a law is enacted by the State. Jerome then smiled at the incumbent and his campaign manager. The supporters asked questions of the various candidates and we felt that things went fairly well.

The final night didn't go as well as the night before. Prior to the debate I advised Jerome to keep his cool and that the opposition would try to paint him as a "hot headed and inexperienced" candidate. I was merely relying on my past experience when I was a union leader. This debate was huge. This would leave a lasting impression on the voters and we knew that many voters were still undecided. The debate was held at the Inkster City Recreational Center. There were more than 500 voters in attendance. These voters included both business owners and private citizens.

As the debate opened, the campaign manager of the former mayor stepped to the microphone and looked at the audience; then paused and looked at me; then turned and looked at my candidate. He asked, "Please tell us the difference between a City Ordinance and a Law?" Ralston sat straight up in his chair and his face turned bright red. He proceeded to go off on the campaign manager. He stated that he didn't respect stupidity and that he was smart enough to understand the strategy that both the incumbent and former Mayors were trying to accomplish. Jerome spoke directly to both mayoral candidates for about five minutes. Once he was done he faced the audience and said that his opponents were trying to show that he was inexperienced and he stated that he had answered the question the previous night and would not repeat his answer that night. In my opinion I thought that this was the dramatic decline of our campaign. Many members from the staffs of the other mayoral candidates continued to pound on Ralston in trying to show his inexperience. Jerome was asked to discuss his political history on many occasions throughout the night.

Finally election time had come and it was time for the voters to place their ballots. After we placed our votes we called all of our campaign committee members to ensure that everyone was at their designated location. I used Jerome's van, which we had decorated the night before, and drove throughout the city encouraging voters to vote for Candidate Ralston. I actually used a speaker system to announce, "Get out and vote today… Make a change… Jerome Ralston for Mayor." Well this seemed to be going quite well because a lot of people were honking their car horns in support. After doing this for a couple of hours, I was pulled over by a city official and was told that I was breaking the noise ordinance and that we would be ticketed if I continued to use the sound system. I contacted Jerome and he encouraged me to stop what I was doing and to drive to the various poll sites and make sure everything was turning out okay. The voter turnout at several of the polls was very slow. We worked the poll sites throughout the day and the polls closed at 6 o'clock that evening.

Once the polls closed the poll workers started forwarding the results. Initially it showed that we were doing pretty well and that we were going to advance to the November elections. Once the results were in we found that it was in fact a low voter turnout. There were a total of 25,000 residents. As the votes were tallied we found out that although we ran a good campaign we lost the primary. My memory serves me that we finished a close 3rd. This was a disappointment because we surely thought that we would win this election. Both the Incumbent and the Former Mayor would face off in the November elections. Jerome Ralston and I each received phone calls from both of the remaining mayoral candidates whom wanted to express their congratulations on running a good campaign. Both candidates stated that they respected our enthusiasm and that we had great ideas which each would place in practice once the elections were over and the new term was in effect. The former mayor from the 1970s won the November election and was sworn into office at the beginning of the next calendar year. In the aftermath of our campaign we realized that as new comers to Inkster Politics we ran a very effective campaign. The city officials would improve their focus for the betterment of the city.

After the city election I continued my participation with the local union but I began to pull my support from President Collie because I felt that he was distancing himself from me. Therefore I approached one of my strongest supporters and asked him to run for local president. Michael Edwards agreed to pursue office as long as I was his campaign manager. He also wanted me to serve as his consultant in case he won the election. My support was definitely there because he was a good person and seemed like he wanted to help others. As I did for former President Carter, I created and circulated literature in support of Candidate Edwards. Collie was shocked as he mentioned, "It was like you spit in my face…with all that I did for you." My response was that he pushed me away when I was trying to help him. Well Edwards and I walked the entire university on many occasions. We would campaign "Change is in the air" throughout all three shifts. I thought that I had a lot of energy. Well Edwards was like the energizer bunny for he was always on the run. He had many family members and friends that supported him. Mary urged her supporters to back him as well. The campaign was so fierce that Collie got his father involved on campaign day. Collie's father was an old school politician and kept trying to weaken my candidate's appearance by degrading me about my suspension. Voters throughout strongly supported Edwards and weren't listening to Collie nor his father. Once the election results were in Edwards had won the election.

As Edward's consultant, I would walk with him hand and hand making sure that he learned on the job. I sat in his first meeting with the Human Resource Department representatives. We organized several informational pickets both for the medical center and for the campus. Our picket line on campus was so long that our supporters wrapped around the building that we were picketing. I helped organize a union field trip to the Detroit Pistons' basketball game. Mr. Edward's biggest accomplishment was the agreement to use a bigger and better union hall for the members.

The closest that I came to reaching my goal, becoming an U.S. senator, was serving as an intern for United States Congresswoman Lynn Rivers. I completed this internship during my final semester of undergraduate studies in 1997. She effectively served in Congress from 1995-2003. Lynn resided in Ann Arbor, Michigan which was the same city that the University of Michigan (my employer) was located. I met her several times at several labor functions. Due to her wonderful personality and professionalism she became one of my favorite politicians.

Congresswoman Rivers staffed an office in Ann Arbor and one in Westland. I served in Westland. My duties were divided into both inner office and field tasks. As an intern I served at the entry level where I reported to the office manager and I was also supervised by her staff members. I respected her staff because they were very professional, outgoing, and accomplished a lot. They prided themselves on building a very good rapport with their constituents and they taught me well.

My inner office tasks included items such as developing a database which included contact information for all of the labor unions within Lynn's District, emailing her a weekly summary of the current events that took place in Michigan, shadowing her staff members and becoming educated on the tasks that an United States congresswoman was responsible for, scheduling some appointments for several functions, and answering the phone calls from the citizens which she represented. Overall, I learned many lessons in the activities that a U.S. congresswoman was responsible.

A final opportunity presented to me included the chance to be in attendance for one of President Bill Clinton's speeches which was held at Bowen Field House at Eastern Michigan University. President Clinton was one of my favorite presidents of all time; the other being Franklin D. Roosevelt. I appreciated his shrewd manner in which he handled himself during the Presidential Debates. He is a very educated man who did a lot for minorities during his service as President. Clinton addressed his support towards minorities in terms of being business owners. He spoke of the many items that he supported in order to help women become small business owners. President Clinton had the full attention of his audience at Bowen's Field House and we all continued to stand and cheer him on as he addressed many issues including tuition, healthcare, social security, and other issues.

After sitting out my four year suspension I again became active in Local 1583 and Council 25. I served as a district steward and delegate to The Council 25 State Convention in 1997. Again I stepped to the plate as a representative who stood up for what was right. M.A.C. had died down and therefore I was not under continuous attacks like I was in my previous leadership role. In fact,

President Edwards tried to encourage me to run as the next bargaining chairperson. My focus had previously been to campaign for bargaining chair prior to my suspension but due to my completion of my education and plans for relocating to North Carolina I declined the invitation. I did, however, accept the invitation to seek the position of delegate at the Council 25 State Convention in 1997. As a delegate and serving as an Intern for U.S. Congresswoman Lynn Rivers I had the honor to escort her to the podium so she could address the delegation. That was my last hooray in terms of labor politics. Although I relocated to North Carolina I continued to give advice to Edwards.

In the end, I gained valuable experience as a labor leader and in local politics. I learned how to properly represent others. Again the main theme was to maintain my creditability as well as the organization in which I represented. I thoroughly believe in standing up for what I believe is right; no matter what the consequences may be. I may have been suspended from office but in my heart I know that I did what I believed was right. Jerome Ralston may not have won his election but our campaign made a difference in the fact that it made local politicians more accountable for their roles in the city. My lessons as an intern for a U.S. congresswoman helped me maintain my interest in politics. Not only did my leadership skills improve, but my public speaking skills also advanced.

Bringing It All Together
Community Involvement

In this final chapter of this section I will share on some of my experiences in my community involvement and then I will speak about the importance of participating in the work environment. My involvement in the community has not been what I anticipated once I relocated to North Carolina but I have participated with a couple organizations and I do have visions of doing some greater things. My community participation lessened over the past 10 years due to my bouts with depression. (I will further discuss in Section 3 Overcoming Depression.) The following paragraphs will discuss my involvement with The Transgendered Community and the Winston-Salem African-American Chamber of Commerce. I strongly encourage others to become active in their communities in order to better them.

In 2004, I decided to live my life as the female that I am and started participating in Kimball Jane Sargent's Transgender Women's Group. (I will discuss more in Section 4 Gender Identity Disorder.) I lived in Fayetteville, North Carolina and therefore was able to make the monthly meetings which Kimball sponsored. I looked forward to these meetings because I had an opportunity to share my views with others and they were able to share with me. During the early stages of my transition I had many questions and could rely on the experiences of others. We would discuss things such as properly presenting ourselves as the females that we were and other items such as makeup tips and our inner most feelings. As I became more comfortable with society and as my transition progressed I felt the need to share my experiences with others. In 2005, I relocated back to Charlotte and therefore my attendance to these meetings was limited due to the long distance to Raleigh.

In 2011, while I was working at Verizon Wireless, one of my customers advised me that he was the Chairman of the Winston-Salem African-American Chamber of Commerce. I was very much interested in joining this organization because I am a strong believer in networking. Part of my education at E.M.U taught me that in order to accomplish many goals people had to network with each other. Due to my heavy work load and rotating schedule I wasn't able to attend many meetings but the ones that I attended I found great satisfaction. The chamber consisted of African-American business owners and other people who provided services. Although I could not join the organization officially representing Verizon, I could join as an individual that worked for Verizon. I often tried to get other friends that I knew to join the chamber.

The meetings that I attended were held at the North Point Grill where the food is awesome. There would normally be around 8-10 members in attendance for each meeting. The chairman would advise each of us to connect with one another in order to grow our businesses. I met several people that helped me with my sales. I also supported several companies in an effort to help generate business. I remember purchasing pocketbooks and jewelry from two African-American owned companies in my support of the companies.

In my opinion if people network and do business with each other their clientele base would grow. This was one of my secrets as a highly successful sales person with my wireless company. I had the highest clientele base in our University Parkway Store because of my networking with others. I am not saying that I only network with African-Americans because I network with anyone that has anything in common with me. A function that I attended in 2011 was a celebration at the Huff House. This celebration involved people of all ages. The older folks celebrated the talents of the younger people. There was a lot of poetry, dancing, singing, and playing of musical instruments. Several community leaders were in attendance at the event. I met North Carolina State Representative Larry Womble, whom I was very impressed with. Representative Womble was a former educator that was very intelligent and one who served his people well. I thoroughly enjoyed this event and looked forward to other Huff House events.

As mentioned earlier, my community involvement had not been what I have hoped due to my battle with depression. Now that I have overcome my battle I have several things that I plan on becoming involved with. I have a couple friends that help the homeless. One of my friends who is also a sales representative for Verizon volunteers his time to serve dinner to the homeless during Thanksgiving and Christmas Holidays. I often expressed to him that I treasured his efforts in serving the homeless and I was going to volunteer to help out for the Christmas Holiday in 2010. I didn't get a chance to volunteer though due to the passing of my mother on December 19, 2010. I had several health issues throughout the 2011 calendar year and therefore could not volunteer as I had hoped. I do however plan on donating my time in the near future. I have another friend who does missionary work for the homeless. She often expressed to me that it is a real experience in helping the homeless because she often has to decode who really needs her help. Overall, she also gets great joy helping those truly in need. Once I become healthy my plans are to help the needy.

I also want to become more involved with the N.A.A.C.P. While growing up I witnessed my mother's involvement with the N.A.A.C.P. and often said that I wanted to become involved with the organization. My mother would often sell tickets for the annual dinner. The recent news relating to both President Obama and the N.A.A.C.P. endorsing same-sex marriages have caught my eye. I am a very strong supporter of Barack Obama and really appreciate his efforts in trying to bring the economy back. My plans are to contact the N.A.A.C.P. and become active in the organization.

I also plan on contacting several local politicians and becoming more involved than I have been during the past few years. As mentioned prior I was very active in local politics while in Michigan and have recently gained interest in becoming active again. The citizens must be heard and in order to make this a better society I must do my part and get involved again.

In bringing this section together I asked that you find a way to become active in your community. If you are struggling with issues at work or in your community I challenge you to do something about it. Instead of saying that you are tired of gas prices going up or you are tired of issues on your job or that you are simply tired of this and that I challenge you to take a stance. If you have been passive before push yourself to take a stance and fight for what is right. Understand that we as older folks can teach our youth the method in which they can become vital parts of society. Let's groom our younger folks in becoming leaders for they will have the same challenges in the future that we face today.

As I mentioned earlier my mother was very active in serving her community, both work and outside work. My witnessing of her activities helped shape me for the person that I am today. My mother fought for her rights on the job, rights in her community, and rights at the polls. My mother's zest rubbed off on me and led me to becoming active in the union and participating in politics and community activities. Therefore parents help educate and groom your children for their future endeavors.

When I reflect back on my union activities I learned several things. I learned that instead of always being fiery I could express myself in a more professional manner. I could also channel negative energy into things more positive. I also realized that when a leader becomes so powerful the leader will come under attack so that leader must be on guard and continue to do the things that are right. I was heavily scrutinized by the M.A.C. but I kept doing my job at representing my 1500 members. I was so powerful that I had both state and international members pulling at me in order to sway me to join their factions. The International Court ruled that I violated the local constitution and therefore suspended me from office. I often wonder that if I wasn't as powerful would I have only received a slap on the hand like the president and bargaining chairperson or would I have still been suspended. I also discovered that many connections can be made through organizations such as unions. My reflection of my role in politics shows me that I became appreciated for serving as campaign manager and as intern. Some people rely on others in order to fight for their rights. I say that we all must be heard and decide what our role is going to be. If we sit back and become idle we will not be able to enjoy a good quality of life. In both roles I became more polished and more capable of expressing myself in a way that others would appreciate. By doing so I gained both the respect and the support of those that I wanted to influence.

In closing this section I say that if things are not what you expect in your community then take a stance. If drugs are on the rise in your neighbor don't just sit back and allow it. Take action. Become active in your community and organize against the crime. This action is important in an attempt to bring order to your society. Make a change.

I thank you for your reading of this section of my book. My hope was to bring awareness to my readers so that you know that you are an important figure in making changes if things are not as you would like. I encourage you to take a position and become active so that your environment becomes much better. I encourage my readers to press forward to the next section in this book. My ultimate goal in writing this book was to help others. My experience with depression can now be a testimony to others to overcome. Please enjoy the reading ahead for it is special.

Anti-Apartheid March
October 3, 1985
Ypsilanti, Michigan
Used by permission-The Eastern Echo

A.F.S.C.M.E Convention 1990
Miami, Florida
Photo credit: Courtesy of A.F.S.C.M.E.

A.F.S.C.M.E Convention 1990
Miami, Florida
Photo credit: Courtesy of A.F.S.C.M.E.

Mary D. Clark
Former Recording Secretary
for A.F.S.C.M.E Local 1583
Representing the employees
at the University of
Michigan

SECTION 3

OVERCOMING DEPRESSION

Howard Lausen Burns
Jala's Dad
June 23, 1921 to May 6, 2000

Aunt Mae and
Uncle John Walker

Depression
How Deep Is It?

In my decision to write this book I wanted to help those in need. My purpose of this book is to share my experiences with people so that they too can know that they can overcome mountains. In my humble opinion I think that this section is the apex of this book. The things that I say here in this section must be heard. I am a strong believer in doctors; for my sister Gina is a doctor. I do believe in science and the medical field. However, what I present to you is real life experiences and I think is deeper than what one might find in a text book or a study. I have experienced more than 10 years of depression and have finally overcome. You may be surprised in what you read in the upcoming pages. Some people will call me crazy or other names, but the actions that I took were for reasons to help me deal with my pain. If I made it through, you shall also. The following section of my book is special in that it shares my life story of my issues.

I have several members of both my adopted and biological families who suffer through depression. Several family members cope with their pain by hiding it with alcohol consumption. Others try to keep their pain internal. Some of my family members hurt so bad that they just think that it is part of life. I'm here to tell you that depression can be beat.

The "Great Depression" occurred during the 1930s. "Major Depression" is something that people fight every day. Pain and suffering is not fair to the living human being; but it exists. Why must we hurt? How do we cope with pain? Are others effected when love ones are suffering through depression? What must we do to make other people's lives more enjoyable? Why does misery love company? How do we face tomorrow when we feel like we can't make it through today? These, my friend, are real questions that we face and that affect our society as a whole.

I am not a pastor of a church, nor am I a doctor, but I am here to present something very real that can help you conquer your pain. In this following section I will share 10 years of my life whereas I suffered through depression. You will learn of my four in patient hospitalizations and four partial hospitalizations. I will describe what it feels like to be at rock bottom. For on August 6, 2002, I was suicidal and was admitted to The University of North Carolina Hospital's Psych Ward. I will describe the pain that I was told that others faced while I was suffering. My life did not stand still but I did because I couldn't move forward. It was like I was sinking in quick sand. I felt as though a shade was pulled over my eyes and everything was pitch-black. I tell you, this was no fun at all. Many of the readers are blessed enough to read the following information. Others are in so much pain they are not in a position to read this. I know that during my early stages of depression I did not want to do anything but lie in my bed and face the wall. I pray that if you are a love one of someone suffering from depression please share my story in efforts to help them overcome.

Three sisters that I give special thanks to are Gina, Blythe, and Jamie. Gina, my sister-in-law, and I are so close that I only consider her my sister. (We break the bond of in-laws.) I refer to Gina as my "mother-figure." Blythe is a real person but choose to keep her real name private. So that I can protect her identity and conform to her wishes we both created a name which she perfectly fits. Blythe and I first became acquainted with each other while working for Cingular Wireless. She was an employee of mine and we soon became the best of friends. During my early stages of depression she adopted me as her sister. Her family and I are very close and I am included as part of her family. Jamie and Blythe both share a commonality; they both we former co-workers of mine. Jamie and I met immediately after my third hospitalization (Mecklenburg County) in 2005. We were on the same team while working in The Sales Action Center for Alltel. Shortly after, Jamie also adopted me as her little sister. They say that blood is thicker than water. Others say that you can't pick your family. I have a wonderful family but during the many years of depression I gravitated towards my three sisters. By the way, my brother Derrick, is also awesome. Throughout this section you will read about the influences and roles that each person played during my depression.

I am not a preacher, nor a pastor, and I am not going to force religion on my readers. I am a Christian and a true believer in God, Jesus, and Grace. I have recently completed a lot of reading. My Cousin Irene suggested that I read a book that was written by Pastor Joel Osteen called "Every Day a Friday: How to Be happier 7 Days A Week." The reading of this book helped me refocus on my life. Although I am a Christian, I realize that not everyone is a believer. I respect the opinions of everyone. After reading Osteen's first book I began reading another book that he wrote entitled "Become A Better You." At the same time Sam, a friend of mine who also adopted me into his family, suggested that I read Pastor Joseph Prince's "Destined to Reign." These three books have continued to strengthen me and help me stay over the mountain of depression. I was also flicking through the TV channels one Sunday morning and a certain pastor was delivering a message that "Even Christians Struggle with Depression." I truly believe that we all can learn from everyone no matter what we think of them.

People suffer pain due to relationships, financial stability, careers, family issues, deaths, gender and sexual orientation, and other reasons. Throughout this section you will discover the many issues that led and kept me in depression for years. Those in pain use both healthy and non-healthy activities to cope with their depression. Some people, such as me, become suicidal. Pain gets so bad that you do not wish to go forward in life. Say what you will, but different people cope various ways with depression. You will find in this section that I used many coping skills throughout my depression. I didn't have the will to live.

Prior to proceeding in this section I ask, and again I'm not trying to force religion on anyone, that God bless this section dealing with depression. Please help those that are hurt find healthy ways to overcome their suffering. Please allow for my experiences to help those in need. As a small child I learned the song "Do Something for somebody every day. Go scatter a blessing along life's way. Be watchful and pray. Do something for somebody every day." My friends, I offer my life's experiences to you in order for you to fight the battle of depression. Please enjoy the reading and hopefully you will find my experiences helpful. If I can climb the mountain, you shall also.

My Early Stages of Depression

My biological mother, Carla, conceived me while she was institutionalized for depression. Some people say that depression is hereditary, I say that it is real. After birth, I was left at the hospital by my mother and would soon be placed in the foster care system. This is where I believe my pain began and where I developed my issue of trust. I have memories of going through several foster homes. People say that much abuse takes place while children are in foster care. I can't say that I was necessarily abused but I can say that I have some memories that place pain in my heart. I remember being beat with a brush by one of my foster family members. I remember my last foster father would often become drunk and fights would break out between him and my foster mother. I also have a vivid memory of him placing a gun on the floor and him telling me to shoot whomever I desired: he, my foster mother, or myself. I have memories of crying and hiding whenever the agent from the Children's Aid Society would come to take me on visitations. These are truly hurtful experiences and are reasons for not trusting others.

These experiences during my toddler days affected the result of who I am today. I probably developed more trust issues because of the feelings that I had because I was taken from family to family. I can see why I was considered a "Special Needs" child. I can also see why I have always struggled with my socialization skills. I have learned to cope with my socialization skills while performing my professional duties but I still have issues while I am in a group setting. I often find myself sitting alone when others are gathered. I may have also developed anger management issues during my stay in my last foster home. Certain things are so painful that I lash out in anger. By lashing out in anger I hurt those around me and often these same people begin to withdraw from me; which causes me more pain.

While I grew up in my adopted home I witnessed my adopted mother's actions of trying to control everything. It was discovered that she felt much pain and anxiety due to not being able to control decisions that I made. I have memories of some remarks that were made at my mother's Home Going ceremony, where the speaker stated that she was probably up in heaven directing Paul to move furniture where she wanted and trying to reorganize heaven. The officiating pastor of my father's services stated, "Willa is known as the General because she directs things in her own way." In being molded by her I also developed controlling behavior. As an adult I would often catch myself trying to control the actions of others and would immediately bring a halt to my behavior. Many of my friends would tell me that they did not want to be around me because of my controlling behavior. This is a cause for more depression. I remember Denise, Ace, and I riding in our Mazda MPV van and I started yelling at the top of my voice because Denise would not do what I had asked. Ace began crying because he was scared by my actions. This behavior would also shape Ace's behavior. He also has many reasons for the depression that is in his life.

During my early elementary education I struggled with making friendships. Others would call me names and often pick fights. I would act out in class in my efforts to release my anger and in an attempt to make friends. Gender was another obstacle in my life which led to my depression. It was difficult living a gender which I would not accept as being mine. I participated in several events in order to fight my conflict of gender. I played football, joined the Marines, attempted to join a fraternity, and even got married. Still my thoughts of my gender revealed that I am female. Many transgender and gay people become suicidal because of not knowing the proper manner in which to deal with their identity. Deeper into this chapter you will read about my suicide attempts.

My first experience that I encountered that involved death was the passing of my Aunt Mae. She fell ill of breast cancer and spent several months at her house prior to her final days. Aunt Mae was admitted into Henry Ford Hospital a few days prior to her death. I remember watching The United States Hockey team win the Gold Medal in the Olympics around 4 p.m. on that cold Sunday in 1980. Within minutes I received a call from my mother informing me that Aunt Mae just passed. As was the norm I spent the weekend at her house. Aunt Mae was like a surrogate mother to her sisters and she treated Derrick and me as her grandchildren. Whenever my mother and I had spats I would call Aunt Mae and ask if I might come spend some time at her house. I loved my Aunt Mae so much. She was deeply rooted in Christianity and taught us "Oh how Jesus loves me." Aunt Mae would spoil us during Christmas time by bringing us huge trash bags of toys. She would often buy me teddy bears and other stuffed animals. She and my dad were two awesome people that impacted my life. When I lost Aunt Mae I felt like a friend, a grandmother, and an aunt were gone. I remember my crying fit as I left her funeral services. My God Parents had to escort me to their car and to the gravesite. This was on a cold February day.

My father would often tell me "Dave, you worry about too much. You can't control everything. You should worry only about the things in which you have control." He was right because I would always tell him how I was upset with the way people were treated because of their race. I would also worry about my results of my citizenship grades whenever my report card was due. I knew that I acted out in class in my efforts to release frustration. My father and I were very close and I became majorly depressed after his passing.

My many failures and the fact that I couldn't accomplish some of the things that my peers would achieve often led to my depression. For instance many of my friends were excellent athletes and although I enjoyed sports I wasn't as gifted as them. I also did not complete Officer Candidate School due to injuring my knee. During college I became interested in becoming a member of a certain fraternity. My best friend crossed the line the year prior to my attempt but I wasn't good enough to make it into the organization. The brothers dismissed me from the line while they sung "Somebody is trying to sneak into our frat." These are examples of my failures that also led to early stages of my depression.

Another factor in my early stage of depression would involve the normal sibling rivalry. Derrick was a gifted student and I was a "Special Needs" child. He worked hard and earned the grades that were rewarded. I, on the other hand, was interested in being a class clown and still received decent grades all except for the first semester of my tenth grade year. After all, my high school course of study was "College Prep." Although I don't remember directly expressing my jealousy to Derrick it was only natural that I had my feelings due to his grades being far better than mine. I regretfully remember making a statement to him as he departed for Princeton University. I said something probably out of frustration and anger that I wished I never would have said. It was sad that I felt the way in which I did, but it was even worse that I let the hurtful words come from my mouth. I told him, "Good I'm glad you are leaving home…and I don't care if you come back." I was indeed jealous of my brother's talents, and even worse, my pain was actually due to me not being as successful. Obviously I did not mean the words that I stated and as I grew older Derrick became my mentor. I developed the same dedication that he had towards education. The readers know my pattern, from earlier reading, that the lack of control of my mouth kept me in trouble.

During the time where I worked at the University of Michigan Stores Department I attempted to find my biological mother and was only successful at getting her non-identifying information. I also almost lost my job due to the betrayal of a person whom I thought I was very close to. As a requirement I had to take a psychological exam and complete therapy. My friend, Mother Mary, drove me to Dearborn, Michigan to visit a mental health facility so that I could take the Minnesota Multiphasic Personality Inventory (MMPI) test. The exam consisted of more than 500 questions and was deemed to determine a person's mental state. The MMPI is designed to tell many things about a person and it also determines the validity of a person's answers.

My results of the MMPI revealed several things about my personality. The exam is designed to ask so many questions in a variety of ways so that the results would reveal if the person is telling the truth. Therefore certain questions were asked in different ways, but should have had the same result. It was deemed that I was telling the complete truth and that there were not any discrepancies in my answers. Results also showed that I was deeply depressed about my past experiences. Further results deemed that I had many effeminate traits. Relationship problems between my mother and I were revealed. Test results showed that I had a good relationship with my father. The findings also showed that I was very immature for my age. In my earlier days I had always wanted to either be a baby or be a girl. Trust issues were also found in my study. Overall, The MMPI discovered enough about me that I could go forward with counseling. Some of the results led me to a further depression. For example, I did not want my union leadership knowing about my gender issues because I felt that the results could further separate me from my union supporters.

Furthermore, in order to keep my job I had to complete the recommended treatment. I was extremely scared because if I had lost my job I did not know how I could take care of my two-year-old son. I felt that my bigger issue was that of trust due to being betrayed by my supervisor. Mother Mary and I both transferred over to the university store's location and had established a relationship where I saw her as a maternal figure. She was 20 years my elder and due to not having a good relationship with my adopted mother coupled with the fact that I was yearning for my biological mother I drew to Mother Mary. My supervisor, whom I will not mention her name due to protecting her privacy, expressed to me that she would also be a mother figure. I called her "Mommie." I often called my supervisor after work so that we could discuss my issues. I wrote several letters to my supervisor expressing my pain that I experienced and that I really wanted to find my biological mother. In the letter I addressed my supervisor as "Mommie." I also told her that I often felt like a lost child that was taken away from its mother for unfair reasons. The supervisor used the letter to set me up and I almost lost my job. My supervisor told the department head that I was stalking her. She described me as driving a black truck and that I followed her to her house. This was very far from the truth because I did not own a truck, nor did I drive one. One day the department head called me in the office and stated that I was being warned because of my behavior. I was warned, "Do not call your supervisor at her house. Leave her alone. Do not follow her to her house." She advised me to take the remainder of the day off in order to avoid tension that may have resulted from the meeting. I advised her that Mother Mary gave me a ride to work and that I didn't have a way home. Therefore the university security was called and gave me a ride home. As I left the building I saw my immediate supervisor and she appeared teary eyed. During the night time hours I received a call on my house phone and as I answered there was silence on the other end. I figured that I knew exactly who might be calling. My thoughts were that it was my supervisor. I called my supervisor because I thought that I was returning her call and that she was too scared to say anything. I merely was going to apologize for whatever happened between us and planned on telling her that I would keep our work relationship strictly professional. As soon as she heard my voice she immediately hung up the phone. On the very next day I was called in the department head's office and issued a letter calling for my discharge. Mother Mary was allowed to leave her job and take me to my apartment.

After haggling with the local union president about getting proper representation I had to call the Council 25 President. Several of my friends suggested that the local president didn't want to help me because he was afraid that if I maintained my job I would team up with Mother Mary to get him out of office. Word had it that Mother Mary was running for president and I was running for bargaining chair. Flora Walker, the Council 25 President, and my Aunt Mildred had formed a union many years prior in Detroit. She also had much respect for me because as a younger person I effectively represented my members up until my suspension. The council president met with the Human Resource Department and agreed to issue me a Final Chance Agreement which stated that I would take a psychiatric evaluation and that I would complete therapy. The agreement also called for relocating me to the Stadium Warehouse area. The final detail showed that if I were to establish relationships with my supervisors outside of work that I would be immediately discharged.

Much of the counseling discussed my mistrust and betrayal that I had just experienced. I also discussed the fact that I missed not having a biological mother and that I was hurt because I did not have good relations with my adopted mother. My therapist would often tell me that she knew that I hurt and that I was depressed. I didn't really understand the depth of my depression at that time. I continued with many therapy sessions for about six months. During that time I had started working in a more relaxed area and had a wonderful supervisor. He often told me that unfair things happened both at work and in life in general. He also told me that as I aged I would understand the battles that I experienced. Overall, I had a wonderful supervisor and several great employees whom I worked with. After a year, I transferred back to familiar territory, the University Medical Center.

Things had seemed to calm down and I continued to focus on my education and was drawing closer to my final year in college. I guess I suppressed my depression by focusing on my goals of receiving my degree. I continued my employment at the university hospital while working in the Material Services Department and then transferring to the Environmental Services Department. While working in the Material Service Department, in 1995, my father had fallen ill to a major stroke. My mother was out of town at a family member's funeral. I had just completed my Winter Semester and received my report card, which I can proudly say were straight "A's." Upon receiving my report I called my father so that I could deliver the outstanding news. My memory serves that I called him and after getting the answering machine I joking left a message telling my dad to sit down because I had some news that might knock him to the floor. I received my report card and I got all "A's." I didn't receive a call back from him prior to my time to report to work. I worked the midnight shift Thursday through Monday as a stock keeper. After returning from work, I attempted to go to sleep. I normally had trouble sleeping during the daytime because of my normal routine of trying to accomplish things during those hours. As I tried to go to sleep my Aunt Net called me and informed me that the hospital was trying to get in touch with my father's brother, Uncle Tom. Aunt Net told me that my father had a major stroke the night before and that he was in the hospital in the outer Detroit area. All I remember is being in my car crying and driving nearly 100 miles per hour. I had to get to my father. I was greeted at the hospital by my Aunt Mildred and I remember telling her that if anything had happened to my father and he passed away I would be devastated and wouldn't want to continue my life. My father was everything to me for he supported me in every aspect of my life. Once I saw my father and accompanied him for several tests I called my brother, Derrick, and told him that I was worried about our dad. Once my mother returned from out of town, she scolded me for not getting a hold of her first. My response was that she was in some airport and I did not know her flight arrangements and therefore I did not know how to get a hold of her.

After a couple days at the hospital he was transferred to Henry Ford Hospital in Detroit. One of my most feared moments was when I saw him wrapped up like a mummy. My mother saw me cringe at that site and comforted me by telling me that the doctors were only trying to control his body temperature. He stayed at Henry Ford Hospital for quite some time. During his stay at the hospital Uncle Tom was also admitted due to health problems that he was having with his legs.

After being discharged from the hospital my father was sent to Bortz Nursing Home. The nursing home was short staffed and I felt like my father was not getting the best treatment. After driving down from Ypsilanti and entering his room I would often smell urine where my father had sat in a wet diaper for long periods of time. I would also notice that his food would be sitting on a bedside tray on the opposite side of the room. My father was paralyzed and needed assistance with his daily activities. I remember voicing my concern about my father's care and my mother instructed me to shut my mouth and tend to my own business. She also stated that "He is my husband." I felt that I had a right to speak up because he was my father and I was very close to him. I remember being in so much pain from seeing my father and the care that he was receiving that I received my first speeding ticket. I was leaving Bortz and was driving 45 miles per hour in a 30 mile zone. I saw blue lights flashing in my mirror for it was the Warren Police Department pulling me over.

My father travelled back and forth between Bortz Nursing Home and a nearby hospital due to complications that he was suffering. I would travel from Ypsilanti to Detroit several times a week because I struggled with the fact that my father became ill. My mother showed her determination by bringing my father home to their house on Shields Street. It costs my mother over twenty thousand dollars for renovations in order to make their home handicap friendly. She turned the den into my father's bedroom and she added a restroom onto his room. A handicap ramp was added to the back of our house. My mother accomplished her goal by hiring a nursing staff that tended to my father throughout the day and evening hours.

Both of my father's brothers passed during his illness. Uncle Russell lived in Chicago and Uncle Tom resided on the East Side of Detroit. Another hurtful event occurred as we were going to Uncle Tom's services. My mother gave my father's caregiver the car keys after he placed my father in the back seat of the car. My mother sat in the back of the car and instructed me to sit in the passenger seat in the front. Both the caregiver and I thought that since I was the child and actual family member that I should have driven to the funeral. As I expressed, this was very hurtful.

As time passed I continued my education and work. On April 26, 1997, I graduated from Eastern Michigan University. Several important people attended my graduation. My brother, who had always supported me, flew in from California. Mother Mary, President Edwards, Denise, Ace, Uncle Bubba, and Aunt Mildred were all in attendance at my college graduation. Missing in action was my mother because she had a speaking engagement for her sorority. Her absence was another painful memory that I experienced.

Once I graduated from college, I turned my resignation in at the university and worked a couple other jobs before we moved to Charlotte, North Carolina in 1998. Both Denise and I stepped out on faith and relocated to Charlotte while neither of us had employment. We were just ready for a change. I remember driving through the mountains on our way to North Carolina. I was scared of heights and being in the mountains was no help. Denise told me that I was holding onto the steering wheel so tight that I looked like I was constipated. However, as we rode through the West Virginia Mountains, I felt like we were leaving all of our problems on the other side of the mountains and that we were starting out a new life that would be fulfilled with joy and happiness.

After working several temporary jobs I was hired at BellSouth Mobility DCS and began a long career in the cell phone industry. My employment at BellSouth began as a finance collector. Wow, I was actually on the other side of things. I was used to collectors calling me and harassing me about my bills. This time it was my turn to handle collection issues. I worked in a call center that handled both inbound and outbound calls. My department handled soft collections so we had to provide exceptional customer service. Throughout my time as a financial representative I received many awards for my performance. I received several Fabulous Five Monthly Awards and won the Fab Five Annual Award. However, I found it difficult in my wanting to move into a manger's role. I felt that because I had a bachelor's degree and I had experience as a manager I deserved the right to become a manager. The department manager felt different. For some reason she did not support me moving into management. As a matter of fact, I was sent through many hoops in an effort to be promoted. I had to take an exam that was similar to the college G.R.E exam and I was one of two people that passed the written exam. More than 100 people took the exam. After passing that exam I had to take a phone role play practical exam. Although I passed that exam, as well, I ended up interviewing five different times before becoming an acting manager. My manager at the time would encourage me and just tell me to play the game and that upper management wanted to see how I reacted to rejection. Well little did they know but rejection had been a big part of my past and was very painful. My final interview seemed the toughest because I had to interview in front of a panel of my close friends who all were team leaders. I was very confident in my abilities but I was sort of uncomfortable interviewing in front of my peers. The interview went very well for the next day I was called into the department manager's office and was given a choice of either becoming a team leader or an acting manager. The position that I interviewed for was team manager. I was informed that the acting manager position would last six months and that if I did not perform a satisfactory job I would be placed back on the phones as a finance collector. I looked the office manager directly in her eye and replied that not only do I accept the acting manager's role I would be the best manager on her staff. From the things that other managers stated to me this particular office manager was threatened by educated African-Americans. My thoughts were that "This white lady doesn't like me for whatever reason."

Within a month of being promoted to manager, I received a call from my mother telling me that I needed to come to Detroit because my father had been placed in hospice and didn't have long to live. I arrived in Detroit and went to check on my dad. For the first time I was allowed to sleep in the guest bedroom in the back of the house adjacent to my father's room. I had become accustomed to sleeping in the basement. My father would often call my name during the night and ask me to rub his legs because they were painful. He would listen to his radio during the night for he listened to WCHB and Martha Jean the Queen. This was a Christian broadcast which we enjoyed a lot.

My most painful memory came on a Wednesday evening. I spoke to my father for the very last time. I was standing at his bedside and we were talking about how I loved him and that if my biological father ever came into my life it wouldn't mean a hill of beans because I had a father. I also told my father that I would one day become successful in life. Oh how I loved my father. He told me that he was proud of me and that whatever I do make sure that I give 100%. I explained to my father that I wanted to take F.M.L.A. so that I could spend time with him. He instructed me to return to work due to the financial struggles that I faced. I assured him that I would make it through financially and that I really wanted to spend the next 30 days with him. For some reason I thought that God was telling me that my father would pass in 30 days. After our conversation I kissed my daddy on the forehead and headed to the basement where I normally slept. I did not want to disturb anyone when I left for Charlotte at 4 a.m. the next day. I had made many trips from Charlotte to visit my father but I painfully knew that this was my last time seeing him alive. I had trouble sleeping that night and cried throughout the night. I did not want my father to die.

After returning to Charlotte I was greeted by many BellSouth employees. They all showed their support and love and wanted to help me make it through my difficult times. No doubt, within 30 days after leaving my father's bedside, my brother called me with the news that our father had died. Now I will show you how I see that God works. My mother needed some support at home during my father's passing hour. I followed my father's direction and returned to North Carolina. My mother would have struggled being alone during my father's passing hour. I also would not have been strong enough to witness the passing of my father. Derrick's flight was delayed a couple of hours and five minutes after midnight on May 6, 2000, my brother called with the news of Daddy's passing. Derrick stated that no sooner had he entered the house he received the call from the Hospice Center where my father had transcended above to heaven. This, my friends, is the power of God. He placed Derrick in the household directly at the time of our father's passing in order to comfort our mother. I would not have been strong enough to stand the moment. My father had passed due to the effects of prostate cancer. He first was diagnosed with prostate cancer in 1986 and with proper treatment it went into remissions for 14 years. Once it resurfaced in 2000 it wasn't long before the Lord called my father Home to be with Him. I remember thinking that when I received the news I was in the bathroom putting on makeup. I thought internal thoughts that this would be for the rest of my life.

After receiving the call from Derrick, I gave Denise the news and I left the apartment to go for a long walk. I remember walking the streets from North Sharon Amity and Central Avenue for many miles. As I walked the long road before me I continued to cry. I would ask the Lord "Why God must this happen?" After returning home I lay down in the bed and just thought "How much I miss my daddy." Around 7 a.m. I called my supervisor and close friend whom we called the "Rock" to tell him the news. We had just paid our rent and did not have extra money for gas. He calmed me and told me that everything would be alright. My department manager called me within the next 30 minutes. She advised me that I could use her Amex credit card if I needed help getting to Detroit. I declined and just called my bank and placed a stop payment on my check that I used to pay rent. Denise, Ace, and I loaded the car and headed to Detroit. It was a long drive through the mountains. As my drive started I started to shed many tears. This was the hardest thing that I ever experienced before. My daddy was gone and I would not ever see him again.

Once at home in Detroit, I called several team members and asked that they give their best while I was gone. I was assured they would and they asked me to just think about my family because it was my time of need. My mother and I took the news very hard. My brother stood strong as he could as he was close as well. If not for Derrick I don't know how I would have made it through. While Derrick helped our mother set the arrangements I was instructed to take our father's suit to the funeral home so that they could prepare him for his final services. This was also a hard drive because all I could think about was completing a task which I didn't want to do.

Once my father's body was ready for the family to view we headed to the funeral home. I remember the eerie feeling that I had when we entered the funeral home. I tried to stand strong for my mother and my brother was by both of our sides. Now don't get me wrong Derrick was close to our dad but I felt like I was closer. For I always felt that Derrick and our mom were closer. Anyway Derrick stood like a rock and comforted both my mother and me. Once my mother viewed her husband's body she instructed Derrick to let me have my time. They both headed to the car and once they cleared the room I broke.

My memory for some reason serves me that we were in two separate cars (I'm not exactly sure). I do know that I bawled like never before because my friend and my father, the one who originally took me in was gone forever more.

Wow, suddenly the funeral services were upon us. The funeral director met us at the house. There were two family cars. Derrick and Gina gathered their kids and accompanied our mother. Denise and Ace travelled with me. My memory serves that we travelled in two smaller limousines. Once we arrived at the church we lined up at the front entrance. Our walk to the front seat seemed like it took forever. I looked at my father as he lay in his casket and then I had to take a final look. This was harder than I could ever imagine. As tears rolled down my face I took my seat. I became more emotional as "His Eye Is on the Sparrow" was sung by a soloist. This was my father's favorite song. My pain increased as they closed our father's casket for the last time. Once the service ended we gathered back at the family cars and headed towards Woodlawn Cemetery, his final place of rest; the same resting place of Rosa Parks. I struggled watching them lower him in the ground. As the words, "Ashes to Ashes; Dust to Dust..." were announced my heart sank as low as I could ever remember. Our father is gone to be with God.

My father was truly a Christian man. He reminded me of my sweet Aunt Mae. Dad served on the Board of Trustees and would often attend the "Fathers and Sons" Banquet. He was honored as "Man of The Year" by the Metropolitan Church. Howard was a great family man who spent a lot of time playing cards and board games, travelling, and playing ping pong with us. He was a dedicated team member of his bowling team. Dad was truly an awesome father and we miss him much.

As I returned to my job at Charlotte I was greeted by co-workers with several plants and cards. They shared their love with me for they all knew how much I loved my father. Things went on as normal for a few months and then finally the announcement that BellSouth Mobility DCS was merging with Southwestern Bell. These two companies formed Cingular Wireless. As a ramification of the merger our call center in Charlotte was closing and I had to make a decision between moving to Ocala, Florida; Johnson City, Tennessee; or Fayetteville, North Carolina. I didn't want to move to Ocala because I had heard that it was in the middle of nowhere. So I decided to choose between Johnson City and Fayetteville. After I made a trip to Johnson City I decided that I did not want to live in a rural area. My thoughts were, "It is too country for me." After all, I was from Detroit. I made the choice to work in Fayetteville. I did not want to live in Fayetteville because it seemed like an old town with not much to do. Therefore I purchased a house in Raleigh and decided to make the hour and a half commute. I put more on myself than I thought. My daily drive included three hours of travel.

Once I agreed to work in the Fayetteville Call Center I requested to be in the first group of managers. Groups of ten managers were moved at a time. I was on the first wave of managers to open the Fayetteville, North Carolina Call Center. One hundred employees were appointed to the ten managers and once a two week training class had concluded we were open for business. The same office manager that made it hard for me to be promoted advised me that I was close to being promoted to area manager but she wanted me to wait a little longer before I moved up. Most of the managers detested their moves to Fayetteville and contemplated breaking their agreements and moving back to their former cities. In lieu of a relocation package we agreed to serve two years at our new location. As time went on I saw different political games that were played. For example, a representative moved from Alabama and was promoted to team manager. Within a few weeks that same team manager was promoted to area manager. I thought that this was awkward but did not make my complaint known. This area manager had headed the Save Team and since her position became vacant she asked me if I was interested in becoming the manager of the Save Team. I agreed to take that leadership role. I informed her that my birthday was coming up and I had planned a trip to see my friends in Johnson City. When I returned she advised me that she wanted to meet with me so I could interview for the job. My response was that I thought that I had the job and that I would need time to update my resume'. She expressed to me that I didn't need a resume' for our meeting. I proceeded with my interview and upon conclusion was informed that her close friend whom also relocated from Alabama was given the save manager position.

Another factor in my depression was my drive to climb the corporate ladder and become a company executive. Derrick had served as a vice president for several corporations that were located in Silicon Valley. I was very proud of him and also thought that I had potential to become a corporate officer. I developed my hope from back when I was vice president of my Junior Achievement Organization. It appeared that with all the games that were played that my advancement would be limited; at least if I continued to work for the same person who tried to prevent me from moving into management in the first place. This person had been promoted to Call Center Director and her husband was given a job to direct the technical team. However, she wasn't willing to help me advance. I must have been a threat to her.

The Fayetteville Call Center scheduled managers and team members to work "block schedules." This allowed for managers to work similar shifts that their employees worked. I had a young lady that was a Captain in the Air Force who also became personally affected by 911. Her sister was on one of the airplanes that crashed into one of the Twin Towers. After our Human Resource Department was notified I was instructed that as her manager I had to speak with her. At the time this was the most devastated task that I ever had to do. So I took the young lady into one of the conference rooms and had to have the discussion with her. She and I cried and I held her in my arms and let her know that God will pull her through. She took a personal leave of absence. To my knowledge she was eventually called up to active duty from her reserve unit.

After a few months our teams and schedules changed. This is where I met my friend, Blythe, who later adopted me as her sister. Blythe was going through some challenges because her one-year-old son was often sick due to a congenital condition and she had other family matters that concerned her. I would counsel her often in order to help her get through her tough times. My area manager would often tell me that I couldn't show favoritism and needed to write her up when needed. She would also say that our work relationship was priority over our friendship and if I needed to write her up then I should. Several team members became jealous of Blythe because she was at my desk either getting counseling or coached about an opportunity that presented itself. My thoughts were that the team members should not have become jealous because I gave them all equal share of my time. My area manager would often tell me that I fought harder for my team than I did for myself. Well I guess that it was in my bloodline because I stood up for what I believed to be right.

After working long hours I had lost a balance at home. Upon purchasing my house I advised both my mother-in-law and her boyfriend that I would relocate them from Michigan. My thoughts were that Denise would be happy. My finances started to become a bigger issue than it had prior to moving from Michigan. I struggled with the fact that Ace's schoolwork was heading downhill. My gender issue was becoming a bigger concern because I truly wanted to be the "real" me and I was tired of pretending to be someone that I wasn't. The fact that my father was deceased finally hit me because things had started to slow down because I had been really busy during the first two years after his death with my promotion to team manager and with my relocation to the Fayetteville Call Center. My career had seemed stagnant and I wasn't happy because I had a vision of becoming an executive. These in my opinion were a lot of issues that could put me over the edge; in fact it did.

Blythe had discussed my issues with me and expressed that I needed help because she could tell that I was suffering from depression. I decided to take her advice and I went to see Dr. McFarlane, the psychologist in Chapel, North Carolina. Prior to my first consultation Dr. McFarlane needed me to complete the Minnesota Multiphasic Personality Inventory (MMPI) test. This was the same test that was required of me back in 1989, 13 years ago. Although I remembered that it was a long test, I did not remember how long nor could I remember what was asked on the exam. I sat for a few hours while completing this survey. Many questions were phrased in different ways so that the tester's answers could be validated. The findings were very similar to the findings in 1989. Dr. McFarlane explained that the results showed me being, "dead in the middle of the circle" which meant that I answered the questions honestly and could not have been more honest. Results showed that it appeared that a female took the exam and therefore I had the personality of a girl. It was determined that I was in a deep clinical depression. Further results showed that I was very immature for my age. After reviewing the MMPI results Dr. McFarlane placed me on FMLA and Short Term Disability. She set up appointments for the immediate future and wanted me to have my thyroid checked.

Dr. Dee was my Primary Care Physician and had just begun treating me for Diabetes. I thought, "How bad could things really get?" For many years I ignored my Diabetes and denied having the illness. Prior to being placed on leave I had issues with kidney stones. Test results showed that my thyroid was inflamed. I soon found out that being ill was expensive.

As time passed I became more and more depressed. I was so depressed that I would lock myself in my bedroom and lay in the bed facing the wall. My mother-in-law would make comments like, "You can come out from your room" or "You can unlock your door because we aren't going to hurt you." My thoughts were that she should keep her mouth shut and stop making condescending remarks to me. Many friends and co-workers would call my cell phone but I would not answer. In fact I had locked my cell phone in our computer desk in the living room; my bedroom was upstairs.

I remember a visit that I made to my psychiatrist. She asked me all sort of stupid questions but I held my peace. I wanted to smack the crap out of her. She asked me things like, "Do you see monsters and aliens? Do you hear voices?" I told her that I was depressed, not crazy. She prescribed medications for me that did not work for me. Throughout our sessions we tried several different medications but I seem to be sinking lower and lower. Medicine is not always the answer; at least that is what I thought.

I asked Denise to join me for one of my sessions with Dr. McFarlane. After declining several requests she finally agreed to come to one of my sessions. At our initial meeting Dr. McFarlane and I agreed that she would address me by my preferred name, Jala McKenzie. Once Denise and I entered Dr. McFarlane's office I decided that I would let Denise do most of the talking. That was a difficult task for me because I was used to talking. Denise discussed the fact that she witnessed my depression and that she saw that I began smoking and drinking every day. I never really smoked on a regular basis until this moment. She described the manner in which I locked myself in my room and withdrew from the family. She described our financial burdens and how she felt when I voiced my opinion about my career. Then the moment came when all hell broke loose. It was Denise's turn to address my gender issue. She described the manner in which I wanted her to talk to me and touch me while we were having intimacy. She told Dr. McFarlane that I wanted her to treat me as a female when we were making out. Denise also told Dr. McFarlane how she felt when I made the most feminine sound that I could make when I was about to climax during intercourse. I knew that this was hard for her and I apologized to her for making her feel the way she did but I felt that I was a female and wanted to be treated as such. As a female I wouldn't want my so called husband acting like a woman and requesting that I treat him in such a manner. Denise and I (and I think even Dr. McFarlane) were in tears when the session ended.

A few days went by and I kept telling Denise that I needed help and that I was at my breaking point. One day Ace kept knocking on the bedroom door because he wanted to spend time with me. After opening the door and hearing him complain I got upset and started banging my head against the wall. At that point I had it and didn't want to take it anymore. By the way, Denise tried everything that she knew to help me. For example, since I was off work she directed me to take her to work at Chapel Hill and to pick her up. I couldn't understand at that time and thought that she was just being a burden. She was actually trying to keep me moving and not allowing me to sit there and wallow in pain. On August 5th I had decided to take extra Zoloft pills prior to my appointment with Dr. Dee. I took about six or seven. Once I arrived at my appointment I informed Dr. Dee of my actions. She made me lay on the bed and didn’t allow me to leave until she contacted Dr. McFarlane. Once she spoke to Dr. McFarlane, I was informed that if I felt like I wanted to hurt myself or anyone else that I needed to take myself to the emergency center. I told Dr. Dee that I needed help and that I was going to head home because Denise should had arrived from work because she drove separate due to my appointment. Dr. Dee said that she would not let me leave until she called and spoke with Denise. Once they both spoke I was free to go home. Once at home I continued to tell Denise of how I needed help because I wanted to die and that I was tired of the pain that I was in. I had enough and didn’t want to take it anymore. The next day became the lowest day of my life.

August 6, 2002
I Want to Die

When people hurt they can truly be in pain. I know that I was lower than one could ever get. I was in so much pain that I wanted to end it all. I didn't care about going on. I was tired of dealing with financial issues, gender issues, career issues, family issues, deceased family member issues, medical issues, and just plain old issues. Do you get the picture? I was in pain and suicide would bring a halt to my pain.

I continued to tell Denise that I needed help and I felt as though she was brushing me off. She kept saying that she never knew me as being happy. On my drive to drop her off at work I told her that I needed help. All I remember is her telling me that my tirade was making things hard on her and that she didn't want to deal with my issues before she reported to work. I became so furious that I lost my voice. I was trying to talk and nothing was coming out of my mouth. I repeatedly kept trying to say, "I'm tired…I'm tired of all this… I'm sick and tired of the B.S.… I don't want any more issues… I'm sick and tired…." I did not realize until years later that Denise truly cared and did everything that she knew how to do in helping me overcome my pain. When people hurt they tend to have tunnel vision. That happened to me.

I dropped Denise off for work on the morning of August 6, 2002. After my failure in getting across to her that I was in severe pain and her continuing to tell me "It's not about you" I just mentally crashed. I called her mother and could barely speak the words, "I'm tired and can't do it anymore… I am in pain and don't want to live." I then assured her that I was going directly to Dr. McFarlane's office which was nearby.

Once I arrived at Dr. McFarlane's office I sat on the couch and then after talking I was so angry that I just laid down and faced the back of the couch. She knew exactly how to speak to her patients for she addressed me in a very soft and soothing manner. She stated that she knew that I was hurting and didn't want me to injure myself any further. She eventually became successful at getting me to sit upright on the couch. Then she proceeded to ask for my insurance card and contact number for Denise. Without force she gently asked me if I was willing to check into the University of North Carolina Medical Center for further evaluation and assistance. I told her that I didn't care to live because I was in so much pain and I hated my life. She continued her calm and soothing conversation. She even placed her hand on mine and convincingly stated that I would be okay. Once she persuaded me to voluntarily check into the hospital she began her quest in reaching the insurance company so we could get preapproved for my hospitalization. As I spoke on the phone I grew very agitated at the number of questions that the representative was asking. After a while I stated that I didn't want to answer any more questions and the lady continued anyway. I grew very upset and as tension grew I got up from the couch and dropped the phone and ran out into the lobby. We were on the mezzanine level and I headed for the rail and was about to jump. As I placed one leg on the rail I felt a nice smooth rub across my hand. Then I heard a calm voice say, "Jala, its Dr. McFarlane. I am here with you and you are okay. I want you to breathe slowly… It is going to be okay..." She convinced me to take my leg off the rail and back towards the wall. I wondered how Dr. McFarlane made it to the lobby so quickly. I barely remember me running to the rail. Dr. McFarlane gently rubbed my back and continued to express herself in a soft gentle manner. Then she told me that if I needed to sit in the lounge then it was alright. Instead of sitting on the furniture I decided to sit on the floor with my legs crossed in the Indian Style. She instructed me to continue to breathe slowly. I did so for a while until I actually felt myself calming down. My face was wet as tears ran down my face.

Once I was in a relaxed state, Dr. McFarlane invited me back in her office. She asked me if I was ready to continue the call to the insurance company because it was important business that needed to be handled prior to me going to the hospital. Prior to her redialing she spoke softly and made me aware of the expectations once I was to get back on the phone. Then she advised me to take ten deep and slow breaths. After she knew that I was ready for the phone call she redialed. This time I made it through the series of questions. I remember that I continued to cry and my head starting aching. After I finished speaking with the representative over the phone I laid back down on the couch. I was squeezing the heck out of the teddy bear that Dr. McFarlane gave me. During previous sessions she discovered that I liked stuffed animals. It reminded me of the teddy bears that Aunt Mae used to give me.

After the completion of speaking with the insurance company Dr. McFarlane called to have an ambulance come take me to the hospital. She set the expectations by telling me that an ambulance was going to pick me up. She further told me that there should be a driver and maybe one or two individuals in the back of the vehicle. After about 10 minutes or so the front desk called Dr. McFarlane and advised her that my ride was there. She told me that they were ready to take me to the hospital. As we walked towards the front entrance, she kept confirming that I was doing the right thing and that everything would turn out fine.

The drama intensified as I made it outside. The expectations that had been set were way off base. I didn't see an ambulance but I did see six police cars. Count them…one…two…three…there were six cops standing outside with guns and ready to take me to the hospital. I grew into an outrage. I started cursing and telling the officers that I wasn't going anywhere. My words were "It takes six of you motherfuckers to take me to the hospital...." I also told them that I wasn't going anywhere and "if I were white there would only be one or two of you." I continued to curse and Dr. McFarlane told me that I needed to calm down because I was causing a scene. I told her that the police were crazy and that I didn't care if they shot me because I wanted to die anyway. Finally she asked for the officer in charge to come speak with her. After a few words he approached me and began a nice and easy conversation. He stated, "Jala, we are only here to help you. We don't want to hurt you nor do we want you to hurt yourself. You are in enough pain." He continued then I said that I still didn't think it took six police officers to take me to the hospital. I agreed to go peacefully if there was one police man remaining and all other officers would leave. We negotiated and agreed that two police officers would take me in one police car. They then asked me to place my hands behind my back and told me that they were going to handcuff me for safety reasons. I followed instructions.

Once I squeezed into the back of the tight area in the rear of the police vehicle they shut the door. The two police officers started conversing with me in a very calm manner just as Dr. McFarlane had previously done. They spoke to me in a very humane manner. The officers asked me questions and wanted to know why I was hurting so bad. I explained that I had many issues and they responded that they were sorry that I was hurting. I also explained to them that I felt that I was a girl and didn't know how to deal with society. The officers had gained my trust by treating me in a gentle manner and after assuring me that they would not hurt me nor let anyone else hurt me. I began to calm down.

We were greeted at the hospital emergency unit by a few staff members. The two male employees appeared to be very nice and interested in helping me. However after I sat down with the receptionist I began to grow angry. She was rude and asked questions that raised my pressure. After she asked me a couple personal questions I told her that I didn't want to answer personal questions and told her that she had better hurry the hell up or I was through. She made another smart remark like, "You think that you are through... you are only beginning." I told that woman that if she made another smart ass remark that I would spit on her. She kept telling me that I was in handcuffs and I must have done something in order for that to happen. I told that bitch that if she kept fucking with me that I would kick her ass with or without the handcuffs. Both police officers stepped in and told me that I would remain handcuffed until I was secured in a room and once I had settled. The receptionist told the officers that she had completed her questions. They took me to a small room at the end of the hall. I remember asking if the room was a janitor's closet or something.

Once secured in the small room I was heavily guarded by both gentlemen. One policeman sat outside my room and the other sat in the room with me. After about ten or fifteen minutes one of the officers removed my handcuffs. A few minutes after I was told that Denise had come to see me. I told the officers to tell the hospital staff that I did not want to see her. She was turned away. I gave the staff member the keys to the car and told her that the car was at Dr.

McFarlane's office. One of the officers said that he would take Denise to the car. My two reasons for denying Denise a visit was that I was still angry at her for not hearing me out during the morning time and I also did not want her to see me in the condition that I was in.

After being medicated and sitting in the small room for many hours I was taken up to the floor. I was there on the Psych Ward and dared anyone to say anything to me. At first the nurse placed me in a room with an African-American male who was being discharged that day. Then after my nurse questioned me and found out that I was still suicidal I was moved to a room directly in front of the nurse's station. I attempted to close the door and was told that I had to keep the door open because I was on suicide watch. I commenced to cursing everyone out and kept asking them what the hell they were looking at. After a while my nurse entered my room and told me that I had to take a picture for my record. I stated that I didn't feel like taking a picture and to leave me alone. I don't remember how I was convinced to take the picture but I did. It was the worse mug shot that I ever took. Words would explain the picture as pure pain.

The staff attempted to get me to eat and I declared I was on a hunger strike. I knew that I was diabetic and didn't give a damn. I didn't really care if I lived or not. I went a week without food. I only drank a sip of water in cases where I had to take my medication. My arms itched from exposure to poison ivy behind my house. For every meal the staff continued to tell me that my tray was in the day room. I kept denying food and stayed in my room with my face to the wall. I became accustomed to that because I had done so for many weeks at home. Within a couple days I was moved to the end of the hall. One of the nurses tried to urge me to drink a cup of water. After refusing her offer she then asked me if I wanted some ice chips. I turned those down as well. Although I refused the ice chips she brought them to me anyway. I threw the pitcher with the ice at her and asked her what fucking part of "No" did she not understand? She immediately left my room without a word. I also picked up a box of tissue and threw it at the wall.

A few days went on and I continued my hunger strike. It was Friday and everyone was acting so chipper except for me. I continued to stay in my room so I only came into contact with the staff. The attending doctor and I had a disagreement earlier that week due to his dumb ass questions. He informed me that I was in "the gray area of being bi-polar." I told him that he was a crazy motherfucker and to get the hell out of my room. Well on this Friday he came into my room with a different approach. He acknowledged my pain and stated that he was sorry that he offended me earlier in the week but he was trying to get much needed information so that he could make a diagnosis. We began to talk and I told him of all my issues including the fact that I wanted to live my life as a female. He stated that the gender issue would be treated separately from my other issues. He thanked me for my time and appreciated me speaking with him. I began crying while speaking with the doctor. He told me that I was in good care and that he was sorry that I hurt. My cry was loud enough that it sounded like it was echoing throughout the hall. I felt like there was a ghost or monster inside of me crying out for help.

After the doctor had left the room I continued to cry and then my nurse came in the room. He stated that the staff was concerned that I was diabetic and wasn't eating. I told him that they couldn't make me eat and I wasn't going to eat until I felt like it. He advised me that my blood sugar had dropped and if it dropped below a certain level they would then be forced to feed me. I questioned him and stated that they couldn't force me to eat and if they were how would they accomplish their mission. He advised me that they would secure me to the bed with tethers and force a tube down my throat. I could remember the impact that I had when I saw my father strapped down at Henry Ford Hospital.

That following Tuesday afternoon Denise and Ace came for visiting hours. I refused to leave my room so the staff allowed them in my room. We were supposed to entertain our visitors in the dayroom. Once I saw Ace I gave him a huge hug. I told him that I was not feeling well and that I was in the hospital so I could be a better parent for him. He jokingly said "Yeah you need to stop banging your head on the wall." He remembered the time that I was so frustrated that I banged my head on my bedroom wall. Once Ace and Denise left I began to cry. I thought of the memory that I had of seeing my father tied to his hospital bed and said that there was no way in hell that I would allow Ace to see me in that manner. Around 9 o'clock that night I called the nurses' station and requested my nurse. I surrendered and told him that I couldn't allow my son to see me strapped down and therefore I would start eating. He told me to stay seated on my bed and that he would bring me some graham crackers and orange juice. My blood sugar probably dropped and therefore I was given orange juice; normally I would not be allowed to have orange juice. It was my favorite. I was very dizzy from lying in bed and not eating for the entire time that I had been in the hospital. So I began eating graham crackers and drinking juice.

As the days went by I continued to stay in bed and faced the wall. The nurses consistently encouraged me to come out of my room and join the various group activities. From what I was told the group activities ranged from such things as art class and group discussions. One instance occurred when a patient took a pair of scissors from the art class. This resulted in the staff conducting a strip search. The two nurses that were conducting the strip search entered my room and stated that they knew that I hadn't been out of my bed so they would just check my room and that there was no need for me to get undressed. I was only wearing my hospital gown anyways. Other patients wore their everyday clothing. I stayed in my bed for the majority of the time so there was no need to wear anything else but my gown. The nurses would get me up in the morning and ensure that I took a shower; which at that time was a major chore. The only times that I came out of my room was during meal times because I didn't feel like being bothered.

One evening, during dinner I decided that I would cooperate and come out of my room. I had developed an anxiety disorder and would shake real bad when around others. Dizziness resulted from my hunger strike and I walked very slowly in efforts not to fall. However I was getting stronger by the day. My dinner tray was placed on top of the refrigerator because I was told to come out my room whenever it sounded like the day room was quieting down. I needed help getting the tray off the top of the refrigerator. Most of the staff was busy so one of the nurses, whom it appeared was having a personal conversation on the telephone, asked me what I needed help with. Her tone was sort of harsh. I responded that I needed some help retrieving my tray because I did not want to drop it and make a mess. She snapped, "Whatever." Wow that set me off and I went into a rage. I pushed all of the papers and records that were on the top ledge of the nurses' station and started screaming and cursing. I called that nurse all kinds of names. She was called everything except for the name of God. The staff rushed to her assistance and directed me to my room. Denise and Ace had been waiting outside the locked unit for visitation. When they came to my room they both asked me what had just occurred because they heard a lot of noise and thought that they heard me screaming at someone. I explained the situation and told them that the nurse had made me angry. They visited for a while and left when visiting hours had ended. The Charge Nurse approached me after they left my room. I was staring at the wall while I was lying on my bed. She questioned me regarding my tantrum. I advised that the nurse was rude and I was only asking for some help. She instructed me that I shouldn't act in the manner in which I did and that I was required to sit in the Solitary Confinement room for two hours. I told her, "The hell with you and that I would stay there all night."

The room was made of Plexiglas walls so I could be closely monitored. I could see the nurses looking at me so I gave them my middle finger. I had been told to sit on the sofa that was in the corner of the room. In a defiant manner I sat on the floor. Within a couple hours a nurse came by and asked me if I was ready to behave and I told her to go screw herself. I then lay on the floor and remained there for the rest of the night. The Attending Doctor and some of the medical staff made their rounds the next morning and questioned me about the events that took place that previous evening. I explained my side and told them that since I was disciplined I felt that the nurse should have been as well and that an apology from her was in order. She refused to apologize and therefore I began my hunger strike again.

This hunger strike went on for a few days. In efforts to try to get me to eat the nurses kept reminding me of my son. They kept telling me to eat for him. I continued to refuse and stated that I would eat when I was damn ready. This behavior continued for a couple days until I received a phone call from the Director of the Cingular Wireless Call Center in Fayetteville. I was surprised by the call and felt like she was the last person that I wanted to speak with. I didn't say much, at first, but she voiced her support in telling me that everyone was concerned about me. I told her that one of my main factors for my depression included the stagnation of my career. I told her that I had goals and it seemed like she was making every attempt to bring my career to a standstill. She encouraged me to get better and that I had a promising career ahead. I told her that I wasn't eating and didn't feel well. I'm not exactly sure what she said but whatever it was I started eating again. I still demanded an apology from that nurse.

Speaking of telephone calls, I received one from my mother. We did not have a good relationship and therefore I wasn't in the mood to speak with her. Initially, out of respect, I let her lecture and question me. I did inform her that I had been suicidal and that the police brought me to the hospital. She stated that God would heal me and that I would one day have a testimony to share with others. She continued to lecture me on the reasons that I shouldn't want to hurt myself. After she asked me for my major concerns I told her that she was a major factor for the reason that I felt like I did. I told her that she wasn't there for my wedding or my college graduation and that was painful as hell. She became offended and made some comments that set me off. I told her that I didn't want to talk to her but she continued to speak her mind and I said, "The hell with you" and hung up the phone. Shortly after returning to my room I heard the phone ring. One of the nurses informed me that I had a call. I questioned who was on the phone and was told that it was my mother. I responded that I didn't feel like coming out of my room and talking on the phone in the hallway. I also told them to tell my mother that I didn't want to speak with her.

The strained relationship with my adopted mother coupled with the void of not having my biological mother in my life either left me feeling abandoned. As I lay in the hospital bed I would cry out, "I want my mother." Everyone could hear my uncontrollable cry and some staff members came to comfort me. When they asked me the reason I was crying I told them about me being adopted and how I always wanted the mother who gave birth to me. I also told them that I hated the fact that my adopted mother and I didn't get along very well. This was one of the major factors of my depression.

While sitting on my bed thoughts of hurting myself radiated through my head. We weren't allowed to use razors without supervision due to the fact that they could have been used as dangerous weapons. The rooms were securely guarded and there weren't anything in the room that I could use to hurt myself. So I thought, "What if I threw a chair at the window and broke the window and then jumped out of the window?" Just as my thoughts were going through my mind, a fine looking male nurse came into my room and asked me how I felt. I started crying and told him that I wasn't happy and that I didn't want to go on with pain. He stated that the reason that I was on the unit was so that I could get some help with the pain. He also asked me if I felt like hurting myself and I informed him of my recent thoughts. He advised me that he knew that I was suffering but that I would be alright. He left my room and within a few minutes the Charge Nurse came to my room and informed me that I was being moved back to the room in front of the nurses' station. She also mentioned that the door must remain open.

As the days passed the staff kept encouraging me to improve. It had been about ten days since I had been admitted to the hospital and I had been informed that the insurance company had begun to take issue with me being in the hospital for the length that I had been there. I was instructed that decisions were being made about placing me in a state institution. I was also told that the conditions weren't as nice as they were at UNC Chapel Hill. My response was that I could care less about where they sent me because I wasn't well. They informed me that they were trying to send me to Dorothy Dix, which wasn't too far from my house in Raleigh. That evening Denise and Ace visited me again. They both wanted me to come home and stated that they loved me. They encouraged me to follow the doctors' orders and get well. Once they left I gave deep thought about our conversation. I decided, "What the hell I can go back to my house and stay in my room." At least if I was back at my house I could lock my bedroom door and be left alone.

During that evening my nurse spoke with me and inquired about my well-being. I told her about my visit with Denise and Ace. It was time for me to go home. The next day, which was Friday, I was informed that I was going to be discharged. They contacted Denise and she stated that she would pick me up after she got off of work. She fulfilled her promise and escorted me down to the front entrance. I felt dizzy, but felt like I was ready to go home. We waited for the security to take us to her car. The security guard helped us get on the motorized vehicle and took us to the car.

The Aftermath of My Hospitalization

So I was released from UNC Chapel Hill Hospital and everything was supposed to be better. At least I thought that was the way it was supposed to be. It started out alright because when I got to my house I was greeted by Denise's mother and her boyfriend and they both hugged me and told me that they loved me. Denise's mother prepared a bowl of soup for me. I ate the soup and then headed to my room. I rested for the remainder of that evening.

On Saturday, Denise needed to go to Wal-Mart to purchase some dog food for Pooh Bear and I told her that I also wanted to try and go. She suggested that I stay at home because she thought that it may have been too soon to be in public. In trying to get better I wanted to force myself to be active and therefore I decided to go with her. At first I was okay but while I was standing in line my anxiety took a hold of me. I began shaking in a violent manner and then ran outside the front entrance. Once outside I fell to my knees and grabbed the yellow post in an effort to stop shaking. I began crying and then I noticed that Denise was standing over me and trying to help me overcome my anxiety. Once I came through she escorted me to our van and drove home.

Due to my anxiety I missed out on a very exciting concert. My house was located in what was known as the noise pollution zone. It was named such because we could hear, and some people would say be disturbed by, the noise from the concerts. Well we received some free tickets to the Luther Vandross concert. Boy did I enjoy his music, however due to my anxiety from being around people I had to miss the concert. Denise, her mother and boyfriend, and Ace all made the concert. I stayed in my bed and missed out. After they returned from the concert they told me how I missed it and how wonderful the concert was.

My sister, Blythe, would often call me and check on me. One day Denise and I drove down to Fayetteville so that we could pick Blythe up because we were going to cook out. My eating habits had gotten better and I moved on to solid foods. So I was ready for some barbeque. We spent the day listening to music and eating some good cooking which was prepared by Denise's mother's boyfriend. At the end of the day we took Blythe back to Fayetteville. I remember Denise and Blythe discussing my desire to live as a female. They both questioned the reason for me wanting to put myself through such misery. I told them both that my internal feelings were like a girl's and I had always told Denise, "I wasn't like other guys."

Trauma hit me on our way back to Raleigh. After we dropped Blythe off I almost killed a man. We were driving on Morganton Road and the night was pitch-black. This guy was dressed in dark colors and walked into the street. Before I noticed he was within a foot or so of the van. I almost ran smack dab into him and if not for the Grace of God I would have killed the man. I somehow swerved and missed him. Once I realized what had just happened I started an uncontrollable cry. I was so devastated that Denise became worried and made me pull to the side of the highway and she drove the rest of the way home. I kept screaming and crying that I almost killed someone. I cried the entire ride home. Once I got home I called Blythe and informed her about the incident. I was still crying and Blythe in a direct manner made me stop. I thought that her directness was very rude and mean. She kept telling me that she couldn't talk to me if I kept crying and my response was something like, "Don't you freakin' understand that I almost killed somebody?" Well she found a manner in which she calmed me prior to the end of our conversation.

On that Sunday I was in the bathroom and I was trying to shave. Then all of a sudden I became freaked out because I started hearing my razor tell me to, "Go ahead and cut yourself. Kill yourself. You don't want to live anyway." I was unaware, at the time, that the medication was the reason for this experience. I started freaking out and was wondering if I was crazy like Denise and her mother kept telling me.

As a result Denise called in on that following Monday and took me to my psychiatrist. While in my doctor's office my anxiety started working up again. Once my anxiety attack kicked into high gear I got up and ran outside my doctor's office and fell to my knees. Tears were rolling down my face. My doctor and Denise both came outside and made sure that I was alright. My doctor advised Denise that due to the experiences that I had over the past weekend that it might be a good idea to take me back to the hospital. I agreed and we went back to emergency.

Denise took me directly to the hospital and they escorted us back to the emergency room. They medicated me with a drug that put me in a daze. I do remember that we stayed in a room for a long time and I kept telling Denise that I was ready to go up to the unit and go to sleep. Finally, a nurse came and advised Denise that it was time for her to leave because I was about to be admitted and the unit was secured. She explained the visiting hours for the patients on the Psych Ward.

I had remembered my actions when I was on the unit a few days ago and I wanted to behave in a better manner. Blythe was a major factor in the decision to act like a responsible adult instead of the child that I acted like prior. She told me that although I was depressed I had no right to mistreat people. I promised her that I would do my best to control my temper but I also expected to be treated with respect. Therefore upon reaching the Psych Ward I greeted the staff in a proper manner. In fact the Social Worker whom I told off during the early days of my first visit spoke briefly with me and told me that she knew that I was in a lot of pain. I apologized for my behavior and she explained that she understood and that she knew that I meant no harm.

Once I was taken to the last room on that hallway I attempted to go to sleep. As I laid there I started hearing Gina say, "Dave put the bread away." This was freaking scary because she was in California and I was in bed in Chapel Hill. I tried to move past that but the demons in my head kept making me hear voices. I got up out of bed and ran down the hall asking a nurse to hold my hand. She instructed me that the staff wasn't allowed to touch the patients. I continued to cry and told her that I was scared. After attempting to make me relax she told me that the medicine was affecting me and that I had signs of schizophrenia. I had remembered that a few months ago when my psychiatrist asked me if I heard voices or saw aliens and I thought her ass was crazy. I thought that maybe I was the one who was crazy after the experiences that I had over the weekend and on this particular Monday. The nurse ordered me some sleeping pills and helped me stay calm and then helped me get back in bed and off to sleep I fell.

I stayed in the hospital for about three days this time while the medical team treated me for all the symptoms that I was experiencing. My anxiety was becoming worse and I often shook and cried. I became used to falling to the floor in order to stop from shaking. My doctor ordered me additional medication for both schizophrenia and anxiety. I was taking 13 pills per day, which included both my mental and physical illnesses. On that Wednesday I was released from the hospital and Denise once again took me home.

I told Denise that in order to keep my mind occupied I wanted to stay busy. So I tried to cut the front lawn and all of a sudden became very hot and started shaking uncontrollably. Ace and I often laugh at how his grandmother had to pour pitchers of cold water on me in order for me to cool off. Her boyfriend helped me make it upstairs to my bed.

I frequently conversed on the phone with both Gina and Blythe and they both assured me that I would get better every day. Gina and I had become very close over the years due to her being my brother's wife. Blythe told me that she would not allow me to have a pity party because it did not do anyone good. I mentioned to her that I also thought that she was depressed with all the issues that she faced. She agreed and said that one reason that she didn't visit me in the hospital was due to her depression.

I remember sitting in the rocking chair in my room with our dog Pooh Bear, a Heinz 57 that was mixed with lab and Rottweiler and many other combinations. I was talking to Derrick on the phone and began our conversation with questions about our childhood. I asked him if he remembered when I dressed up in our mother's clothes when I was younger. He told me that he did. I also asked other questions about our youth that would help me lead to my confession. I told Derrick that one of my major issues with depression was due to gender. I informed him that I always wanted to be a girl and I wasn't sure how people would accept me. Both Derrick and I had some trust issues from being placed up for adoption. I often felt abandoned and I hurt like hell when people rejected me. Derrick without hesitation gave me the overwhelming support that he had always given me.

A couple more months went by and it was time for me to return to work. Prior to that time a few events occurred that caused me more grief. Denise and I had previously purchased a Dodge Shadow and due to financial burdens we couldn't afford the car and it was repossessed. We made a lot of poor financial decisions in our younger day. Well the sheriff came to seize our house, van, and Mazda 626. Denise explained to the sheriff that I had just gotten out of the hospital due to being suicidal and that we needed to call and become updated on the situation. He agreed to give us a few days to straighten out the situation. I tried to call and speak with the debtor but felt my anxiety building so Denise took the phone and handled the remainder of the call. She resolved the issue and although we still owed on the car she somehow worked something out. Some kids were playing outside and started playing in my Mazda and somehow turned the lights on and left them on and caused my battery to go dead. These things added to my stress.

Upon returning to work I was greeted by my team and everyone expressed their concern and told me how upset they were that I didn't return their calls. I advised them that I was very ill and that I had become suicidal. Blythe continued to tell me not to spread my information because it wasn't anyone's business and that people might start looking at me as being crazy. It was bad enough that rumors spread quickly in the call center like they did between us so I needed to keep my information to myself. Blythe and I spoke about discussions that I needed to have with people about my gender. She wanted me to be careful, however it was something that I felt I needed to honestly tell people. I had struggled for years in keeping it to myself and I felt like a bubble that burst and wanted to tell everyone I knew. I remember telling my area manager and he appeared shocked because he had earlier counseled me because he believed the rumors and was thinking that I had an extra marital affair with Blythe. Once I told him that I was a transgender female he started telling me how he caught his brother in his garage kissing another boy when he was 11 years old. I advised him that I wasn't gay and that I was a female. He assured me that he would still treat me fairly, which he did. I advised him of my name, Jala Alyshia McKenzie also known as JAM. He laughed jokingly and said that the name was very fitting. (I will explain my legal name change in the next section.)

Like I mentioned earlier things were so stressful at the call center that I was informed that while I was on medical leave a decision was made by Cingular which allowed those who relocated the opportunity to return to the towns that they came from after the completion of one year. Schedules were about to change and I was being moved to Phase 3 and was getting an entirely different team. This team was very close and treated me very well. They accepted my gender and told me that if anyone had a problem then they were ignorant and that I should ignore them.

Denise and I were going through issues and I decided to leave her. We had a different approach towards Ace's education and we had difficulties because of that. She also had a problem with her husband living as a woman. I don't necessarily blame her for that because I would want my man to be all man. I was struggling with her mother and boyfriend living in my house due to my increased financial obligations. We had other strains on our relationship as well. Therefore in May of 2003, I made the decision to move to Fayetteville.

In setting up my utilities I had requested to place them in the name of Jala McKenzie and I had called Detroit to speak with my mother. I had forgotten that her Caller ID would read a name other that what she would have expected; it read "Jala A. McKenzie." Just about a year ago, the prior August, I had the hardest conversation with my mother in my attempt of letting her know about my gender issue. During that conversation, we discussed the fact that my outward appearance did not actually reflect who I was internally. The conversation began better than I imagined. After she asked me a few questions and I supplied her with direct answers she turned to religion. The turning point was when she asked me if I was attracted to guys. I advised her that I was a heterosexual female and that I was indeed attracted to "fine looking intelligent men." I also informed her that I frequented a club called the Spektrum because I was interested in the drag shows. I loved both the performances and the clothing that the performers wore. I advised my mother that my problem was that guys were always trying to holler at me and I didn't really want a man from the club. My mother transitioned the conversation into religion and doomed me directly to hell and told me that I was an abomination to hell. This was a major component of my depression. As I recall the conversation that took place during that particular telephone call, on that day in July, I struggled because my mother told me that she wanted nothing further to do with me and told me to get out of her life. This rejection was another major piece of my depression. I resisted the fact that she was trying to put me out of her life and continued to attempt to communicate with her.

So in my mother's attempt to kick me out of her life she gave me a valuable gift. In kicking me out of her life she gave me a contact number for the Children's Aid Society and told me that my biological family had tried to connect with me and that I should continue my life with them. This caused mixed emotions for me because I had drastically yearned for my biological mother but at the same time I truly appreciated being raised by the Burns' family. (I will discuss the details on meeting my biological family in Section 5). My experience with my biological mother was sort of different. The strain of depression was on her face because she had lost five of the six children that she gave birth. I could tell the stress and anger that she endured because almost every other word out of her mouth was a foul word. Something that I found disgusting was that my mother would spit the tobacco from her mouth into a jar. I thought spitting that stuff out was gross anyhow; but I just didn't think that it was becoming of a lady.

In August I relocated to Florida where my biological family lived. My sister, Patricia invited me into her home with the acceptance of her husband. I was excited to be reunited with my biological family but I still had major depression in my life. Denise had filed for a divorce and she also had nothing further to do with me except for the rearing of Ace. I found myself staying in the bed whenever I wasn't at work. As you know that is a sign of depression. I developed some anger because of my internal racial beliefs. During a normal Sunday routine of the family watching football my brother in law stated "Run nigga run" as he showed his excitement towards a player from the team which he rooted for was returning a kickoff for a long touchdown. I looked at my sister and asked, "What the hell was that all about?" She stated that her husband didn't mean anything by that, however I internalized it as this white man degrading my African-American race. The ironic thing about this statement was that several of my black friends would make the same type of comment and I wouldn't turn it into a major issue. Several weeks later I was asked to leave because I hadn't found an apartment and it didn't appear like I was making an effort to find my own place. I couldn't live with my mother because I knew that her depression would be too much for me due to my depression. Therefore I moved into a hotel for a few weeks. Then I moved back to Fayetteville.

Upon returning to Fayetteville, North Carolina I had discovered that the young lady that I allowed to live in my condominium had failed to pay rent and this resulted in my eviction. I ended up having to start over with my living conditions. Instead of having my lavish condo I had to settle on a small efficiency. I failed several times in my attempt to contact the girl who had taken over my condo so that I could get my furniture back. The girl continued to ignore my calls. Therefore I had to sleep on an air mattress and due to financial restraints it took me a while to get new furniture.

I became more depressed because I was trying to be cautious whenever I had visitation rights with Ace. So I would wear my female clothes whenever he was not around and then when he visited I would have to hide them and wear male clothes. Yuk this was a terrible feeling. I also became very lonely and hated spending holidays by myself. Blythe and I furthered our relationship and became close sisters.

My employment centered on working in the Lumberton location. Upon my return to North Carolina I was assigned to the straight line store that was located inside the Wal-Mart. The contract ended between Wal-Mart and Alltel so while we were waiting for our new store to be built I split my time between working on Fort Bragg and working in a R.V. that sat in the Shell Gas Station parking lot. Our new location opened on Fayetteville Road on the Black Friday of 2004. I had the honor of making the first sale in that store's history. I sold a vehicle charger. During that same time my regional manager and store manager consulted with the Human Resource Consultant and decided to allow me to transition on the job. I had to present my medical information to the entire sales staff. My R.S.M. definitely supported me but voiced his concern that someone from the Lumberton community might attempt to hurt me. In terms of my performance my sales soared. My store manager advised me that due to my customer care skills that my clientele base would be huge. In January, he had the pleasure to tell me that I ranked number three in the entire region for the prior month; which the Southeast Region had about 588 sales associates. I wasn't fazed and my manager continued to tell me that I really didn't understand the impact of that success. I continued to do my job to the best of my ability and my results elevated yet to another level. I ranked number one for both months of January 2005 and February 2005.

I relocated back to Charlotte in March of 2005 and transferred my work to the Alltel Sales Action Center. After a while, the career drive that I had lost as a result of my depression from the stagnation at Cingular, had become a difficult force to deal with. My issues of loneliness, my mother's rejection, financial concerns, career development, age, and other things started tugging and pulling me apart. These events led up to my third hospitalization, which took place at "Mecklenburg County Hospital."

Mecklenburg County Hospital
The Arrival of the Five Year Old Girl: Me

So as my mental issues mounted I became more depressed. My career was stagnant and I started thinking that my skill set and experience should allow me more of an opportunity than to be sitting on the phones as a sales and service representative. My brother was an executive for his company and I thought that I had that capability also. My gender conflict was also getting next to me because I was no longer facing customers because I was actually speaking to them via telephone. Customers kept addressing me as "Sir" due to the pitch of my voice and it irked me more than someone scratching their nails on a classroom chalkboard. I would often adjust my voice, which for me didn't take a lot of work because my voice was normally soft anyway. One day my manager was coaching me on a call that she had listened to and overheard me correct a customer who continued to call me "Sir." Her coaching was that a lot of females have deeper pitches and are mistakenly called "Sir" and that I should not even respond to customers who accidentally use the wrong personnel noun.

My depression deepened because of the lack of communications between my mother and me; no matter how much I called she did not want to speak to me. This was very hurtful. Another contributing factor was my age for I was approaching the devastating age of 40. Financial concerns were a final issue. No matter how much money I earned I continued to mismanage my money. Hey, what can I say? Girls love to shop and Alltel's Call Center was located in the middle of stores like Cato, Off Broadway Shoes, Wal-Mart and other desirable stores. Therefore this girl shopped.

The more depressed I became the more I started getting thoughts of hurting myself. My dear friend, Ericka, was also like a sister and I thought the world of her. She would notice that I slept everywhere I went so she recognized one of my traits of depression. I would share some of my issues with her and when she knew that I was slipping and starting to become a danger to myself she made her advice known. She suggested that I talk to someone as an attempt to deal with my pain. I also spoke daily with Blythe who had her own issues. One afternoon, while standing in my bedroom my thoughts of hurting myself started radiating internally. I shared this with Blythe and she suggested that I contact the Crisis Center. So I did as she suggested. I had been suicidal before and wasn't going back down that road again so I called the Crisis Center and stayed on the phone until I arrived at The Mecklenburg County Hospital.

My anger rose while being treated in the emergency room. The intake specialist kept asking me questions and it appeared that everyone was bothering me. I continually stated that I wanted to be left the hell alone but I needed help at the same time. One nurse took me in a room and started questioning me and asked me for my reason for being at the hospital. I went off and started yelling and asking him why did he think I was there. I had just told the medical staff that I was having thoughts of harming myself and that I was in a lot of pain due to issues that I was experiencing. He continued to question me and finally I blew my top. I started cursing him up and down and finally several staff members had to rescue him because they were alarmed by my screaming. I had caused quite a disturbance and there were other sick patients trying to be treated. One of the other nurses entered my triage room and persuaded me to take some medication that calmed me down.

Although I knew that I needed to be admitted I negotiated my admittance. Terms of our agreement were that the staff would have to refer to me as a female, respect and treat me as a female, place me on the women's side of the ward (The North Side), and help me get better. Wow. I was becoming skilled at using my negotiating skills for I remembered a few years back when I negotiated with the police when they took me to UNC Hospital in Chapel Hill. The nurses heavily medicated me so by the time they took me up on the unit I was in a daze.

I remember that my nurse asked me several questions and then took me to my room. Two nurses came in and stripped search me. They took all of my personal belongings, except for the clothing that I was wearing, and locked them in a locker. I then climbed in my bed and faced the wall and stayed there for several days. Our primary task while being on the unit was to get better. Therefore we were required to attend group activities, but I initially refused because I wanted to be left alone. After about five days I started attending some of the activities because my nurse was sympathetic and advised me to just try and attend but she made it clear that she wasn't going to force me. My nurse was very skilled and I looked forward to her shift. I attended a group activity where we listened to music and danced. Although my problem with my rhythm was still present, I enjoyed the activity regardless. I also attended a few other classes as well. The facilitators would often tell me that if I didn't think I could complete the session it was okay and that I could go back to my room. The patients were rewarded for completing their daily sessions by being allowed to go outside to the courtyard. There were many smokers and they were motivated by the opportunity of being able to smoke. I could care less because I didn't smoke and I normally stayed in my bed with my face towards the wall. There were several times when the floor was locked down, which meant that the privilege of going outside was revoked. I thought, "Hell we were locked down anyway because we were locked on the unit already."

I had several memories of different patients. The woman in the next room over was vomiting and really ill because she was addicted to drugs and was having withdrawal symptoms. She remained very sick for several hours and there was heavy traffic in trying to attend to her needs. There was another girl who had a disorder where she needed constant assistance. She continued to go back and forth to the nurses' station with different requests. I remember the nurses told her that if she was good she would be allowed to have treats. On her last day she was dressed in all red, including a red hooded jacket, and people from the facility that she was being transferred to came to pick her up. I thought of her as "Little Red Riding Hood." She asked, "Are you my owners?" In not picking on her I chuckled inside thinking, "Wow she was in a worse condition than I was." My memories also served me being asked to come play a game of Scrabble in the day room. I played my turn and placed a word on the board. One of the girls stated that I didn't know what the hell I was doing because the letters that I placed on the board wasn't a word. I grabbed the dictionary and proved that it was indeed a word and she grabbed the dictionary out of my hands and threw it on the floor. The unit was divided into the women and men sections which were separated by the nurses' station. Since my room was directly in front of the nurses' station I couldn't help but to take notice of the many different actions by the men. One guy came out of his room in his bare feet and was wrapped by a sheet and started telling the nurses that he was Jesus. There was another man that was acting like he was giving a Dr. Martin Luther King, Jr. speech. There was a third male patient that appeared to be walking while in a trance and kept trying to come over on the female side. There were many different characters that were locked in the Psych Ward.

Due to my mental state I found myself in several confrontations with the medical staff. I enjoyed the weekday staff more than the weekend staff. My thoughts were that since the weekday employees treated me as I requested that they were treating me with respect. The weekend employees, on the other hand continued to address me as "Sir" and "Mr. Burns." I freaking had enough and went off on them asking them, "What part of female don't you understand?" I continued to remind them that I was a girl. I raised the question for the reason I was on the female side of the unit. Several staff members stated that I was placed on the North Side so that I wouldn't get beat up or killed by the male patients. I told them that they all were full of it and if they wanted me to cooperate then they better start freaking respecting me and treating me as the woman that I was. My confrontations became so bad that the hospital security was called to calm me down. I questioned what they were going to do because if they planned on shooting me that was fine too because I was already in pain.

Several staff members had a very positive effect on me getting better and I am truly thankful to them. I reminisce on the time when a nurse asked me for my reason for feeling so bad. She also asked the important question, "What will make you feel better?" My initial response was that I didn't know but all I knew was that I wasn't happy. I began crying and turned to face the wall and she rubbed me on my back and comforted me by saying that I would be alright. She then left my room. Once I calmed down from crying I laid still and thought, "Could I ever be happy?" Then all of a sudden as I closed my eyes I thought of how much I loved Derrick and Gina and that I would be happy if I was a five year old girl that belonged to them. Derrick was my big brother and could never replace my father but Derrick was still awesome. When it came to Gina, I had the highest respect that I could have for a person. Oh how I loved her. So I began thinking that I would be happy being a 5-year-old little girl. This moment would impact my life for the next few years.

A social worker visited me and stated that she understood that I was hurting because of my non-existing relationship that I had with my mother. She told me that sometimes people have to look at a "Higher Force, someone bigger than life" and told me that she wasn't forcing religion on me but she knew that God was her "Higher Force." I turned to her and told her that I believed and loved God also. I also stated that my problem was because of my medical issues relating to my gender and my mother had doomed me to hell. I felt that I didn't deserve to go to hell because I was a good person and I believed in God. The social worker responded that just because my mother had an opinion it didn't mean that her opinion was the final word. I told her although that may be true it was still my mother and I was in an awful amount of pain. The social worker went on to tell me that she was also adopted and previously had a non-existing relationship with her father. She stated that it took much needed prayer and she developed a closer relationship to God. She stated that one day she and her father finally agreed to speak with each other. They had become like best friends. She told me in her sweetest, most loving and tenderly voice, "Sweetie, God loves you and your relationship with your mother may be fixed one day." She also told me that I had to learn how to "Let go.." This, my friend, was my most difficult challenge. I still struggle with letting go of hurtful things. There is a saying, "Let go and let God." This is a continued work in progress for me but I know that He is in control.

Other symptoms that I experienced including my depression were anxiety and schizophrenia. My anxiety was so bad that in order to control it I learned to fall to the floor. I often found myself shaking and crying so bad whenever I was around a group of people or whenever I had just had a tough conversation with someone. I remembered that I had several anxiety attacks while talking to Ace on the telephone. One of the nurses rudely told me that if I were going to have anxiety attacks while using the phone that my phone privileges would be taken from me. My thoughts were that instead of her helping me she was trying to make me worse.

Although I didn't really understand schizophrenia, I remembered my episodes during my hospitalization at UNC Chapel Hill. I knew that I wasn't crazy and the shit scared the hell out of me. One night I was trying to sleep and I began seeing monster-like aliens. I was so freaking scared that I got up out of my bed and ran down the hallway. I was crying and shaking and had told the nursing staff what I thought that I had just witnessed. They advised me to take a seat in the day room and gave me a cup of water and helped me calm down. I was informed that the medications that I was taking gave me the visions that I was having and patients normally would have such illusions. I tell you what, that was the scariest thing that I ever experienced. Those recent illusions reminded me of the illusions I had in 2002 when my razor was telling me to kill myself. Trust me; I'm not crazy, for it was truly the medication that I was taking.

After staying in the hospital for a little more than a week, the medical staff began questioning me about my condition. They informed me that my insurance company was starting to give them a hassle about my length of stay and that if I wasn't getting better I would have to be sent to a state institution. I remembered being told the exact same thing in 2002 and just like then I didn't really care. All I knew was that I wasn't happy. For the next couple days I was asked if I were suicidal and my comments were that I was in a lot of pain and that I brought myself to the hospital because I didn't want to become suicidal. Finally, my favorite nurse came and spoke with me and informed me that she felt that I could be discharged because they were planning on giving me a great plan of action and if things got worse that I was to call either the unit or the same Crisis Hotline number that I previously called. I told her that I was scared and I was still in a lot of pain.

Upon my discharge I felt a little distorted. When I first walked outside the hospital I felt like I was in a daze. The sunlight was very bright and I had trouble remembering where I had parked my car. I was unlike most patients that were discharged. I didn't have any family to pick me up from the hospital; for I was all alone. Once I found my car I drove home in a very gingerly manner. Upon my return home I found my cat was scratching from fleas. Prior to going to the hospital I would often let her go outside. I had been hospitalized for ten days and if it had not been for my apartment manager my cat would have starved. Instead of starvation, my cat had gotten a bad case of fleas. In fact the fleas were so bad that my apartment became infested and the maintenance crew had to treat my apartment. One of my neighbors took my cat to the shelter because I wasn't well enough to care for the animal.

After being at home for a few hours I had realized that I didn't have any money so I couldn't buy the medicine that I needed to treat my illness. Therefore I called the unit and was advised to go back to the hospital and meet with the social department in the basement of the hospital. After I drove there I discovered that there were many people waiting to be seen. I had difficulty being around a huge gathering of people and therefore I sat in a chair in the hall by two police officers. My patience began to grow very thin and I started to get a little worked up. While waiting to be seen I experienced two things that I will never forget and I'm hoping that they both were illusions. I thought that I saw a lady running through the door screaming that she just witnessed a man a few yards from the building who was attempting suicide. I heard her say that the man was holding a shotgun to his head and threatened to kill himself. For my sake of sanity, I will call the second experience an illusion. I also thought that I saw a patient being placed in a patty wagon that was about to take him away. The man was a heavy set white person dressed in black and white stripes. He was baldheaded and was chained to huge ball. Like I said in my efforts to deal with the incident I have always chalked it up as a side effect from the medication that I was taking. This was also some "not so funny" stuff.

After returning to my apartment I was greeted by my neighbors who said they hadn't seen me in more than a week and a half. I explained that I had been hospitalized due to my depression. One of my neighbors whom I didn't care for started telling people that I was a crazy bitch. I didn't like her because she was the type of person to start trouble with others. She also was a drug dealer and had a lot of traffic coming to her door. I went to see my property manager whom I really became comfortable with and wanted to let her know that I was home. The funny thing was that when I started to speak to her I couldn't remember her name. This was weird because I would normally go tell Debra hello on a daily basis. She laughed and stated that she knew that the medicine was playing tricks on me.

As for my living conditions, my apartment was a wreck. I hadn't felt like cleaning or cooking. I had pizza boxes stacked almost to the ceiling and I hadn't really cared for pizza since my early college days. I didn't want to sleep in my bedroom so I basically stayed on my couch for several months. I would sleep there every night and my clothes were in my other bedroom so I would get dressed in there. For some unknown reason I continued to avoid the bedroom where I first started getting thoughts of hurting myself.

My treatment continued as I became a patient of the Partial Hospitalization Program at a facility in Concord, North Carolina. The treatment included education on pain management, anger management, coping skills, and other items. I completed the Partial Hospitalization and began some improvement; enough so that I could return to work.

I decided to call my manager and let her know that I was released from the hospital and that I was going to be off work for a few more days. My manager showed me some compassion and stated that she looked forward to my return. I also called Blythe because I hadn't spoken with her much while I was in the hospital and I missed her very much. She informed me that she was planning a trip to come see me within the next couple of days.

The Aftermath of Mecklenburg County Hospital

I am a firm believer that God places people in the lives of others for special purposes. There were several people who tried to help me fight my battle. Gina, my sister-in-law, was more than my brother's wife. She was my inspiration and guide. After telling her that I felt like a five year old and that I wanted to be a child she said that older adults didn't want to treat 40-year-old adults like children. She recognized my pain and stated that I had been through enough pain in my life but I could overcome my obstacles. Although she was extremely close to my mother she would take battle with her because she didn't think that my mother should ostracize me. Gina recommended that I read a book that her cousin, June Cross, wrote entitled "Secret Daughter: A Mixed-Race Daughter and the Mother Who Gave Her Away." This was also an autobiography that could help others such as me. Gina's cousin and I had commonalities such as we both were biracial, struggled with our relationship with our mothers, and had hurdles to overcome. I read and thoroughly enjoyed the book but due to my level of depression I didn't fully benefit from the reading. I realized that June had many struggles due to her relationship with her mother and the fact that she was biracial during the 1950s caused even more stress on her life. Without me telling her entire story I will say that June overcame her hurdles and is quite successful in her career.

Of course there was my big brother, and by now you know, how much I adore this fine young man. Derrick would encourage me to fight my battle and not let things control me. He would instruct me to focus on the "Things that I could control" and not to focus on things that I had no control over. Derrick instructed me to read several books. One of the books spoke about the thoughts that a person radiates out would reflect back to that person resulting either in negative or positive results depending on the thought process. I viewed Derrick as a very intelligent, caring, and kind person; but he had zero tolerance for nonsense.

Blythe would call me on a daily basis and tell me to "Get up out of bed." Due to my depression I would often be found in bed during my off days. I would rather sleep my pain away instead of actively fighting my depression. Blythe was having her own difficulties and would tell me that she couldn't afford me taking her into a deeper depression. She loved me and made me part of her family but could not tolerate me having a pity party. I often felt that she didn't understand my situation and that she was cruel and mean towards me. I felt that she didn't show me the same appreciation that I showed her. However, she was fulfilling my void by allowing me to be part of her family. My sister, Blythe, was a very direct but loving person. She helped me more than one could appreciate.

Denise and I continued to talk but the majority of our conversation was related to Ace. I wanted a deep friendship with her because I always felt that she was a nice person. People have flaws and no one is perfect. In my eyes she handles work and educational issues different than I did. My concern was the manner in which Ace would be impacted. Denise struggled with us becoming close friends because of the so called struggles that I put her through. She described me as being controlling and emotionally abusive towards her. I could understand the manner in which she felt on both topics. For example, my demand of her to treat me as a female while having intimacy would have abused many people emotionally. I don't think that I could have dealt with my husband wanting to be treated the same as I. Furthermore, from what I observed many of my family members had issues trying to control others. The result of my mother's childhood was that she became very controlling. The impact that she had on Derrick and I caused us to have issues with controlling others. I actually became aware of my issues and often caught myself in the act and had to learn how to temper my control. Denise was very helpful towards my battle of depression. During my discussion with her regarding me wanting to be a five-year-old child she would tell me to "Woman up." In other words I should stop wallowing in pain and fight my battle. She also would state that people would not tolerate a grown ass woman acting like a child. Although the severing of our relationship was a major factor in my depression she found ways of helping me cope. She was a blessing for me although we both recognized that two women weren't going to make it in our relationship. I am sure that I caused her pain although it wasn't intentional.

Jamie, my new sister, was also a co-worker of mine at Alltel. In an effort to help me with my mental state our manager positioned Jamie and I directly across from each other. Jamie would often have the biggest smile that one could have and was very pleasing in her attempt to get along with others. She would often mock my telephone calls with others by repeating my conversation with my customers. Jamie would hear me say, "This is Jala," then I would slowly spell my name for customers, "J-a-l-a McKenzie." My sister would slowly shake her head while she would be mocking me. One day I was sort of bored and while on one of my calls I started cutting my hair. Jamie looked up at me and placed her customer on hold; then she told me to place my customer on hold; then she scolded me as if she were in fact scolding the five year old little girl that I was. It was funny. My hair had all kind of unevenness all over my head. Jamie was my dear compassionate big sister and we grew very close. I also looked at Jamie's sister as my big sister. She would often tell me that if I was a good little girl she would read stories to me and she would make good on her promises.

Another person that I grew close to and viewed as a sister was Ericka. I met her while living at Steeplechase Apartments. Although she knew that I was depressed she didn't allow me to just sit and drop further into my depression. Ericka always wanted to cook out at the apartment swimming pool or just hang out and talk girl talk. She was new to dealing with transgender people but she took a liking to me because I was a genuine person. I took a liking to her because she was one of good nature and always seemed to help others. This sister could get down with the best of them when it came down to being the "real deal." After discussing my issues she would often say, "So what are you going to do about it.... Jala you can't just complain about your problems, you must do something about them."

I had interactions with many others but these people mentioned above had a profound impact on me as I fought my battle of depression during the next few years. During this time I continued my work at Alltel and also increased my interaction with people more than I had in the past. I began to realize that my relationships were a blessing from God because the average person would not have tolerated the drama that I brought. I am honored to have had these individuals in my life.

Upon returning to work at the Alltel Sales Action Center I was greeted by my team which consisted of several new employees. I was still in a lot of pain and continued to act out while at work. My manager had moved my seat a row away from my team and my feelings became hurt because of that action. I also was given my Employee Annual Review and I contested my results. I was one of the best sales reps in the department but my behavior had impacted my results. Therefore due to my evaluation I sank lower into my depression and really started tripping. For example, whenever our team was supposed to be in a huddle I would stand away from the group and gaze into space and ignore the business at hand. I also would tell my manager that "I wanted to be her little helper and that if I was a good little girl I would like to be assigned the job to help her." She kind of smiled and said that she wanted me to concentrate on my job. Another incident occurred where I made suggestions to my manager so that our team's performance would improve. She rejected my suggestions and I stomped my feet as I walked back to my desk. Another occasion occurred when flashlights were passed to the floor for some type of celebration and I sent the team an email suggesting that we shine the flashlights in our manager's face while she was attempting to conduct a huddle. While I was off work I found this doll that I took to work with me. When you pulled the doll's string the doll would say, "Give me a big hug." So while in the huddle I pulled the doll's string. The result from both the flashlight and the doll incidents was that I received my first write-up ever. In my write-up I was instructed that I was required to take an Alltel online course on "Being professional in the work environment."

Moreover, I continued to struggle with my pain but attempted to fight through it in order to get better. My therapy included both group and individual treatments. I attended an evening session which educated me on skills for handling my emotions. I also attended individual counseling, which allowed me to address my pain. I was instructed to complete a daily journal for writing problems down. This seemed therapeutic for some people but it didn't help me much. Actually I detested my journal so much I grew more and more angry. One day my therapist suggested that I write my problems on small sheets of paper and place them in a box. I was also instructed to drive to the top of Cherokee Mountain and throw them off the mountain. So I followed the instructions and I felt somewhat better.

As my employment continued at the call center I made several attempts to overcome my depression. I continued to face adversity while working at the call center. Several encounters took place that continued to turn me into a ball of turmoil. My 40th Birthday was November 11, 2005. We had previously donated money collected from our team so that we could celebrate the birthdays of our team members by giving them a birthday card and cake. The team failed to collect money for my birthday and therefore I felt isolated. Being in the state of mind that I was in, I decided to "show them" and I took a payday advance for $300 and made my "famous spaghetti," purchased my own birthday card, bought me a nice outfit to wear to my birthday party, and purchased a "Little Princess" birthday cake. When I arrived to work on that following Monday everyone was surprised about the party that we were about to have. It was rumored that I made the meanest spaghetti with shrimp, crab meat, cocktail sausage, Italian sausage, meatballs, and the works. The cake was designed for the 5-year-old girl that I'd turned into. I instructed my manager to have the team sign my card and present it to me. Wow. I must have been out of my mind in my attempt to educate my team on how to properly celebrate everyone's birthday.

My so called childhood, outside of work continued. I also shared a Princess Cake with Ericka and the rest of my neighbors. Some of them laughed at me out of ignorance. My true friends wanted me to be happy and they enjoyed singing Happy Birthday to me. I also participated in other childish actions in order to fight the pain that I was suffering. Blythe would often laugh with me because I would drive around town with Cuddles fastened to my front seat. Cuddles was a lavender teddy bear that I had won at Carowinds Amusement Park in Charlotte. Just like a little angel, I would snuggle up with Cuddles whenever I went to sleep. I was all alone and didn't have anyone else to sleep with; so why not Cuddles. Blythe, Jamie and I also exchanged Christmas gifts during the Christmas of 2005. While I gave them gifts for adults, I was happy to get Bratz Dolls and accessories. I enjoyed being the little girl that I was (at that time). Coping like this helped me deal with my depression. This was reminiscent of my thoughts that I had while I laid up in the hospital bed in Mecklenburg County Hospital during October 2005. These childish activities made me happy; at least for the moment.

While on the job, I was tired of just being a sales representative for I knew that I had much more talent and experience to just settle on an entry level job. Therefore, I had made up my mind that I would battle the issue regarding career stagnation. I knew that in order for me to progress my career I would have to transfer back to the retail channel. I continued to achieve monthly awards for my sales results. In December 2005, I was the top rated performer in overall sales. There were more than 130 other representatives in the sales center and I was ranked number one overall. Several months I received honors for being in the top three in various categories such as overall sales, feature sales, accessory sales, net activations, and a host of other areas. During the beginning of 2006, a change in teams occurred and this was a major step for me. My new team was built of a complete roster of all-stars. I indeed increased my focus because as a team player I wanted our team to finish as the top team on a monthly basis. We went so far as to order "Dream Team" shirts. Our manager was awesome because he was a very experienced sales person. His prior experience included insurance sales and he taught the proper manner in which to do Consultative Sales. He also taught us how to ask open ended questions and how to bundle items in our closing offer. Our team was the bomb.

Although I was ecstatic to be on my new sales team, I encountered an experience that was very hurtful. Our Charlotte Sales Call Center was challenging the Youngstown Sales Center in a week long All-Star Challenge and I was left off the All-Star Team. While I was one of the best sales people in the call center I was left off the All-Star team because I was viewed as being a negative person (wow talking about humility). I was very upset about this and I just had to deal with it. I spoke my opinion to my manager and his assessment was that I deserved to be on the team because I was truly an all-star but we both realized that my attitude made a negative impact on my image. I had adverse feelings towards the manager heading the All-Star team because I felt that she was the deciding factor on which representatives were on the team. Several members of the call center stated that our team lacked my presence. Early in the competition she sought my advice in addressing the sales of features. Although I remained pissed off at her I agreed that I would offer my advice due to my being a team player. The team appreciated my input. Even though our team made a comeback and the competition was close we lost. My thoughts were that everyone learned a valuable lesson. I realized that my negative behavior, although it was a result of my pain, had a major impression of my overall performance. Hopefully if another opportunity arose I had wished that the decision makers would seek to find the reason that an individual was acting different from others.

As my days continued at the Sales Action Center I continued to reach milestones for sales. I reached out to a couple of Human Resource Consultants and was advised that they would attempt to return me to the retail channel. I continued to produce outstanding sales results and received many sales awards. A sales recruiter set an appointment up with a store manager and me. That store manager spread his enthusiasm regarding my presentation throughout the retail channel. My forty-first birthday was much different than my fortieth because I was celebrating three events simultaneously. While I was on a sales call with one of my customers I looked up and I saw a group of six managers carrying a bunch of balloons. One read "Happy Birthday," another announced "Congratulations," a third one stated "Happy Anniversary," and the others were very colorful. I celebrated the following dates: November 10th was my third anniversary for working at Alltel; November 11th was my forty-first birthday; and the following Monday, November 13th was the date that I was to report to the brand new Alltel Store at Rivergate Shopping Center. What would you expect? Jala had her doll at her desk and politely pulled the string and the doll said, "Give me a big hug." This 6-year-old girl was really happy.

The time spent at the Rivergate Store was of quality because not only did I set my mark with my sales results; my career advancement also was on the upward spiral. I normally led the store's scorecard and I was usually in the top five in the market (about 100 or more employees). I immediately took the leadership role in our store because I was the most experienced and I was the only one familiar with both software systems. After a few months my manager supported my role into the "Manager Development" program. As a member of this program I was responsible for mentoring other sales associates and I had to attend monthly meetings. The district's top management team, up to and including the market's vice president, was excited about my entire presentation.

On September 11, 2007, I was promoted to market assistant store manager and assisted in managing 6 different stores. Immediately after I was advised that I had been promoted my mother had called and informed me that my uncle had passed. I had advised my brother that I wasn't sure if I was going to attend the funeral because I did not want any drama during the grieving time. My brother called our cousins and informed them of my transition. During the family dinner I sat directly across from my mother and she pretended that she didn't have a clue of who I was.

Upon returning to work my initial task as A.S.M. was to fill the manager's void at the Gastonia, North Carolina store. Once a store manager was hired I then resumed tasks that my regional store manager assigned. My R.S.M. stated that I was his eyes and ears for the things that were going on in his stores. The various store managers afforded me the opportunity to manage the stores whenever I was at their locations. During my time in this role I participated in two exciting proceedings. I was assigned the task of assisting in a software systems convergence in Hickory, North Carolina. I was one of the few that were familiar with both the Cellware and the Unity Point of Sales operating systems. My dedication resulted in my gaining much respect from the store manager, her R.S.M. and other market leaders. I also spent my 42nd Birthday in Little Rock, Arkansas while I was participating in The Alltel Coaches Camp. This camp was an intense training that taught the leadership "How to take care of Alltel's most precious assets." The various vice presidents would greet our class and tell us that if we were not able to take care of the employees with the utmost care then we might as well not become members of management. While in Little Rock, I was invited to a telephone interview for a store manager position in Mathews, North Carolina. I must point out, that during my stay in

Arkansas, I took the opportunity to visit The Clinton Library. This tour was a real tear jerker for me.

Once I arrived back in Charlotte, Jamie threw me a 7-year-old Birthday party. My theme was the Bratz Dolls. My Auntie Jen made me a Bratz Doll cake. Jamie and a representative from my Shelby Store bought me all kinds of Bratz Doll gifts. Blythe also presented me with special gifts. Once this party was over 2 of my employees from the Shelby Store took me to Chuck E Cheese in Gastonia, North Carolina. This was definitely making up for time lost as a child when I would have rather lived my life as a little girl. This made me happy.

My stint as A.S.M. only lasted for two months prior to getting promoted to store manager at the Summit Square Store in Winston Salem. In the capacity of store manager I had the pleasure to help my representatives develop their careers. The most important goal that I wanted to accomplish was to make my team know that I would make them my precious assets and that they were in good care with me as their leader. I would often cook out for my team and give them weekly incentives to produce at a very high quality. My store received the top quality award for "Feature and Accessory Sales" for the month of December 2008 in the region. There were 26 locations in our region. I had the pleasure to extend my friendship, which I acquaint as an extended family to my entire store. I am still very close to Samuel Perez and Nadine McCraw. I am also very good friends with the fly –girl named Ashley Wright. She reminded me of a mix between Beyonce' and Monica. My entire store would voice, all in unison, "Jala definitely took good care of us." I did let my store know that I was the little 8-year-old girl that wanted to have fun. Whenever someone asked a question my answer would often be, "Errr I don't know." I had my team rolling. On the contrary, I was a very effective leader that showed a deep compassion for my team and had the desire to make our store one of the top quality stores in our market.

I also represented our store very well at the staff meetings and other events. One of my peers would often tell me, "Jala, your Summit Square Store is putting up numbers that the district hadn't seen in years." The entire staff respected me for items that our store brought to the table. I enjoyed many relationships with all of our managers and am still friends with two of the former Alltel managers.

So it appeared that everything was sailing smoothly. I was advised by the Charlotte Sales Recruiter that if I did a good job that it would not be long before I would be promoted to R.S.M. I had planned on serving as store manager for a couple years before I addressed my desire to advance to regional manager. Once I proved myself as regional manager my plan was to press forward to the regional vice president position and then close my career out with whatever advancement the company saw fit. All of a sudden my ship came to a halt. The announcement came during the 2nd Quarter of 2008; Verizon purchased the majority of Alltel. Therefore my career had come to another stand still and I again plummeted into a deeper depression.

My support cast held me firm for a moment; only to see me crash again. Derrick and Gina would give me support but I also could feel them growing weary of my suffering. Blythe continued to have her problems and she couldn't continue to carry my burden. I would often contact Ericka and Jamie by telephone but I had moved an hour and a half away. I sorely felt like I was missing something special.

Forsyth Medical Center
I Want to Be a Baby

Babies need love and since I had dropped into a deeper depression I was that baby and therefore I needed love. I failed a final attempt to make peace with my adopted mother in 2007. For the fourth time she refused to accept me as her child. I had finally given up and since that time I lived my life without a mother. I again had been abandoned and was hurt by the rejection. Another uncertainty for my career had raised its ugly head up and the pain was oozing from me like a soldier shot at war. Health concerns were definitely present due to not properly caring for my diabetes. My blood pressure was normally slightly elevated and I had other medical conditions. My financial situation had gotten better but wasn't where it should have been at that point in my life. I couldn't afford my gender reassignment surgery and sorely wanted my completion. I felt all alone and wanted to be loved.

Once the news of the Alltel acquisition took place I did everything that I could do to hold on. Verizon built a huge store directly across the street from our Alltel store and I saw it as an intimidation tactic. I attempted to assure my team that they would be okay. I, however, did not feel that I would be protected. Several of my representatives would tell me that I would survive, even if it was as a sales representative. They did not understand the fight that I made in order to advance my career. After eleven years of hard work in my wireless field I should have at least been at a regional manager level. I felt as a failure because I always internalized the success of my brother. I always felt that success, at least in my mother's eyes, was to be placed on a pedestal and to be in power over others. Much of my anxiety was because she had raised Derrick and me to succeed and now I have fallen and was unsure in which manner to advance. My relationship with my boss was once unshaken but now it had crumbled to pieces. I shared the information about my transition because I trusted him and soon found out that was a huge mistake. Our relationship eroded and I felt undue pressure that I wasn't meeting his expectations. Verizon had closed my store in April 2009 and my employees performed until the very end. I was told that I would co-manage the Bridford Park location in Greensboro and that my hours of work would be extended. Since I was salary my pay would not increase. After much endured stress I lost my battle and collapsed further into depression. I was having pains in my side and decided to go to urgent care. The doctor asked me a lot of stress related questions and one of the questions I should have answered differently. In focusing on my relationship with my regional store manager I became even more depressed. My depression landed me in the Emergency Ward at Forsyth Hospital. After an overnight evaluation I was instructed that I was being placed on medical leave immediately and was to begin The Partial Hospitalization at Forsyth Behavioral Center.

I was accustomed to taking Cuddles with me everywhere I went except for work. So Cuddles accompanied me to my therapy. This time I didn't want to be 5, 6 or even 7 years of age; I actually wanted to be an infant. I began wearing adult diapers and invested in several pink bottles and pacifiers. I informed the medical staff that I wanted to be treated like a baby because a baby was loved. I was tired of living the adult life and told everyone that I didn't want the responsibility of being an adult. In fact I didn't want any responsibility; I was tired. The group sessions became a bit too much for me and I felt myself slip even deeper into depression. I began to get the feelings of not wanting to go on. Even with Blythe's continued pushing of me to get out of bed so that I could attend my sessions I just couldn't go on. It was a struggle just to take a shower and do other daily activities. The charge nurse consulted with the doctor and recommended that I admit myself to the Psych Ward at Forsyth Hospital.

Upon my entry to Forsyth Hospital I was dressed in a diaper and was carrying Cuddles for she had every right to travel with me everywhere that I went. When I finally was taken up to the locked unit on the Psych Ward I told the nursing staff that if they wanted me to cooperate they needed to treat me like an infant. I told them that I wanted diapers, bottles and pacifiers. I was told that since I was a baby and in my room by myself they feared that I might choke and they refused to fill my request. Wait, do you mean to tell me that I failed at something that I had proven to be successful at twice before? My negotiation skills must have been on the decline because I couldn't get my way. While in the interview room my nurse allowed me to keep my diapers and I stay dressed in my Onesie. I even had my one piece pajama set with the feet. The nurse promised me that if I cooperated, that she would feed me ice cream prior to her leaving at the end of her shift. I was a good "Little Jala" because I looked forward to my treat. The staff would come in my room to check on me and would tell me that I was "as cute as a button." I continued to be on my best behavior and the nurse kept her word. She sat me up and fed me rainbow sherbet ice cream. She tricked me though. She mixed my medicine in with the sherbet. During each spoonful she spoke to me as though I was a little baby. Oh how I felt loved; but I was mistaken because she avoided me during the rest of my stay.

I did my normal routine which was to lie in the bed with my face toward the wall. This was different because this time Blythe came to visit me. She scolded me for telling a nurse off when the nurse addressed me as a "He." She also got on me for spitting out the medication that the nurse was attempting to give me. Blythe told me that if I was going to act like a child then she would direct me as a child. She recognized the pain I was in but told me to take that damn diaper off and that I looked stupid as hell. She told me that I definitely wasn't acting like the diva that I had become. Once she left I took the diaper off and put my adult clothing on. I also started participating more in group sessions.

I was instructed to do the best that I could in group session and I had permission to go back to my room in case my anxiety increased. I gave a complete effort in trying to retain the materials taught in group. The doctors ordered me some real strong medication that both controlled my mood and which heavily sedated me. My stay in the hospital was much shorter than my stays in the University of North Carolina Medical Center and The Mecklenburg County Hospital. I was released from the hospital within a few days and directed back to Partial Hospitalization.

Blythe picked me up from the hospital and took me to her house in Charlotte. I remember that I was so sleepy that I crawled into bed. I told Blythe to order a dinner for her and her husband as a treat for taking care of me. Once I was in the bed for a while, with my favorite Dora the Explorer program on the television, Blythe came up to check on me and she leaned over and kissed me on my forehead and tucked me in like she normally did for her 4-year-old son. I was half way passed out and couldn't tell her how special that made me feel. Her husband agreed to let me stay at their house for a while because the Forsyth's Nursing Staff had informed Blythe that I was hurt due to the lack of love that I felt and that I was very lonely.

One condition for my release from the hospital included my continuation of the Partial Hospitalization program. While in Partial Hospitalization I had to pledge, "I contract not to hurt myself or anyone else." I also agreed that if my feelings increased and I felt a desire to become dangerous that I would contact the crisis center or go back to the emergency room. We were required to wear name badges that identified both our names and group that we were assigned to. The two groups were Mental Behavior and Substance Abuse and of course my assignment was Mental Behavior. Therapy consisted of education on topics such as anger management, coping mechanisms, overcoming anxiety, and several others. We were treated in both individual and group therapy sessions.

One evening after hospitalization I travelled to Jamie's house in Charlotte. My son, Ace, had feelings for this girl who, lived in New Jersey and he made a trip to visit her. He had joined Job Corps in order to finish his high school education. Well once Ace was ready to leave and return to Job Corps he realized that he lost his bus ticket. He called both Denise and I and neither of us had any money. Thus I became in an uproar because for that one night my son was homeless. I feared that someone would hurt him. I couldn't sleep and stayed awake crying while sitting on Jamie's couch.

Once I arrived for Partial Hospitalization the next morning, I was weary from worrying about Ace. I started crying really bad and my anxiety had risen very high so the charge nurse took me to the Relaxation Room and allowed me to lie on the couch until I recovered from my trauma. I was found once again crying as though there was a ghost inside of me. The nurse gave me a teddy bear because I had left Cuddles in the car and she gently rubbed my back until I fell asleep. When I woke from my nap I got up and rejoined the therapy session that was in progress. The medications kept me in a daze and were supposed to temper my mood. I continued Partial Hospitalization for a little more than a week and then I was discharged from the program.

I spent much time at Blythe's house because she was attempting to help me overcome my depression. She would often comment on my mood, which became hard to handle. Instead of being in a continuous uproar I became very quiet and distanced myself from others. She struggled at my site. I would often be seen looking straight down at the floor or cement when sitting outside. I had zero energy and the "Old Jala" had disappeared. Oh how Blythe would say that she wanted her "Jala" back. I would continue to ask Blythe to read me stories and at first she resisted. Finally she stated that if I tried to become more active she would then treat me to a story. There were several times that she would read to both her 4-year-old son and me.

My twelve weeks of FMLA had come close to expiring and it was time for me to return to work. Upon my arrival I was told that my job was eliminated and that I would be laid off. While transitioning out of the company I was employed at two different locations. During the last 30 days of employment the managers getting laid off had the option of staying at home and receiving pay. I chose to continue to work for several reasons. My first reason was that it wasn't in my nature to stay at home and not work. I only stayed at home when I needed to recover from my illnesses. Secondly, I wanted to keep my job because I feared the fact that I wasn't hirable because of my gender issue. My thoughts were that society lacked open-minded people that would give me a chance of employment no matter what credentials I had. I also wanted Verizon to know that I wanted to maintain my employment with them. Finally, I believed in earning my pay and didn't want to stay home and get paid for not working. Three days prior to getting laid off my old district manager called me and offered me a job. She stated that she was impressed with my desire to work and knew that I was struggling with the fact of my possible layoff. She also informed me that she did not have a management position available but she would be more than willing to promote me within a six month to year time table once I successfully demonstrated my sales skills.

The medication had severe effects on me and almost caused me to lose my job due to performance. I would interact with my customers almost in a zombie-like manner. My energy level was very low and I was moving around the store in a very slow manner. As a result I would not meet my monthly goals for sales. Several customers made comments in reference to something being terribly wrong with me because I didn't have any enthusiasm. Mark Anthony, one of my former employees from Alltel, would tell me that he wanted his "Old Jala" back and that I needed to come off of the medicine that I was taking. I eventually went back out of work in an effort to get my medicine readjusted. I went back into the Partial Hospitalization at Forsyth's Behavioral Health.

While in the Partial Hospitalization program my worries about keeping my job continued to grow. However, I became active in group discussions and for the first time started listening to what the therapists had to offer. I learned various healthy coping mechanisms for my anxiety and depression, methods of anger management, methods in dealing with my hardest issue of "Letting go" and other topics as well. My medication was adjusted and I began to get more energy so that I could function and return to how I was prior to taking the medications. I stayed in the Partial Hospitalization for about one week prior to returning to work.

It Took Tragedy to Turn Things Around

Upon my return, my sales results drastically improved and I became more involved in assisting our store in its overall improvement. My results would place me as not only one of the best sales representatives in our location but my success rate helped me become one of the top performers in the Triad District. There were several months where I led the district in various sales categories. I also began helping our management staff with whatever tasks they requested. For example, I helped coach other associates in areas that I was performing well. I also assisted in leading various segments of our Friday morning store meetings.

Although my performance had gotten on track my anger had gotten the best of me and my overall performance was deemed negative. My once promising career had become stagnant again as a result of the Verizon buyout of Alltel. While my goals had been for me to become a regional manager for Alltel within the next year or two I had settled for a sales representative position. I did not have a desire to manage for Verizon and became very frustrated. Thus I started saying many negative things about Verizon. It was not the fact that I hated Verizon. It was the stagnation of my career which exasperated me.

Tragedy struck in December 2010; starting with the death of my God Sister, Kimberly "Perfect 10" Donaldson. While in the hospital she departed this life on December 3rd. Kimberly was characterized as a very beautiful brown skin diva that was a very professional woman. Kim was very smart and had also spent her time as an educator for the Detroit School System. Of her many accomplishments she had achieved one goal that I wished that I could reach; she crossed line as a Delta. Kimberly successfully completed her M.B.A. and was a devoted businesswoman.

Derrick, who was very close to Kimberly, had just left Detroit because of taking care of our mother who was also on her deathbed. Therefore in representing our family it was a must that I supported my God Family. Just as God moved when my father passed, He moved again. My mother and I hadn't spoken in four years and I had been advised a few weeks prior that she requested to see me. However, each time I called her home I was advised that she wasn't ready to speak to me. After spending time with my godmother, Mrs. Donaldson, and after being urged by my mother's caregiver I decided to take Kimberly's program by the house. As the caregiver answered the door I advised her that I had only wanted to drop the program off and that I was getting on the road to head back to Winston-Salem. The caregiver told me that I needed to come in and see my mother and at first I refused. My thoughts were that I didn't want to make my mother uncomfortable because I felt that she was already not well. I finally decided to give in and go check on my mother. As my nerves mounted I sat in the living room as my mother was prepared to see me. While I was escorted into her room I felt nerves stir throughout my body. I witnessed my mother's poor health as her skin barely clung to her body. My hair was braided in long micro braids and I thought that I was very pretty. As my mother struggled to speak she asked me if I were "Dave" or "Jala." In knowing that she disapproved of my transition and in acknowledging that she was in pain I gave her the answer that she wanted to hear; I softly replied "Dave." As my mother tried to speak she began to cry. I attempted to ease her pain by telling her that I thought that she was a good mother. I didn't quite understand her crying. I wasn't sure if she was crying because of her sorrow for kicking me out of her life or due to the pain which my gender crisis caused her. The rest was a big blur. As I left the room I fell into the caregiver's arms and began my cry for I had witnessed my mother's end on that December 12th day.

As I drove back to Winston-Salem I called my Cousin Barbara in Chicago and discussed the events which had just occurred. She and I agreed that Kimberly's death had been for a reason because it had given me one last chance to make peace with my mom. I also spoke to Mrs. Donaldson and was advised that her opinion was that Kim's death had served a purpose.

When I returned to work at Verizon my mood had worsened. I was struggling with my son, whom on that December 3rd day had totaled the car that I had just given him. I also took Kim's death and my mother's condition to heart. I was often reminded that others witnessed a lot of anger in me. On December 18th I became upset because a sales representative closed a sale that I had worked for very feverishly the night prior. I got into a huge disagreement with my manager due to the loss of my sale.

Exactly one week to the day of last seeing my mother I was hit with another tragedy. As I sat in the Verizon employee parking lot I received a text from my friend and former employee, Nadine, asking if I was working that day. Just as I was in the process of replying my brother had sent a text saying, "She just died." Our mother departed this life on December 19, 2010. As I reported to work I couldn't speak due to my emotions. As tears rolled down my face I showed the duty manager my phone. I then began to cry and thought that I would try to take my mind off of the situation by trying to work. As I attempted to open my cash drawer I decided the best thing to do was to leave. I called Blythe and headed to Charlotte where she and her husband attempted to comfort me.

After giving Derrick some time to grieve I attempted to get myself together and stayed at Blythe's house for a couple days. On Tuesday I went and picked up my son and headed to Detroit. Once I arrived at the house in Detroit I felt awkwardness because of all the pictures that were hung throughout the house mine was not found. That disturbed me badly. After making calls and trying to help Derrick I suggested that we try to have a Christmas dinner. Our cousins Irene and Nicole and a friend of ours attended the dinner. This was the first Christmas day that I did not spend alone in seven years. As family arrived from Atlanta and Chicago I started to witness one of my major issues of my depression. I had sorely missed being with family. My family said the same thing that my godmother had said a few weeks earlier. They all stated that even though my mother specified that she didn't want anything to do with me they had not kicked me out of their lives.

During my final view of my mother, during her services, I placed a note under her arm that read, "Mother I forgive you, please forgive me." This was another attempt of letting go of the pain that I suffered due to our relationship. As several speakers gave remarks they kept speaking to Derrick and I felt ignored for they hadn't even recognized me. Several people informed me later that they didn't have a clue that I was even there. My appearance had certainly changed from the last time that they saw me, which was ten years ago.

The night prior I had pondered a decision to accompany my brother and give remarks at our mother's funeral. Initially, I resisted because I felt that she would not want me to speak at her funeral. First of all she made a statement many years ago at Derrick's wedding that hurt me for a long time. She told me to try to sound intelligent when I gave a toast at his wedding. Again that impacted me because of me not being my brother's equal. The second reason that I had not wanted to give remarks was that this would have been the first time that the members of the church, which I grew up in, would have seen my transition. I was deeply thinking of my mother and did not want to show any signs of disrespect to my mother and therefore I struggled in giving my remarks. After careful thought I reconsidered because I didn't want my brother to make the journey alone in giving his remarks. My goal was to give him the same level of support that he had always given me. Thus I joined him as we gave remarks on the passing of our mother. I stated that this service was a celebration and that my mother was going to enjoy her Home Going. I further explained to the congregation that our mother instilled two values in me that carried a lot of value. She instilled both principles of Christianity and education in both Derrick and me. As Derrick addressed the church he mentioned that I was a "tough act to follow." After he had wrapped up his remarks both Derrick and I embraced.

After the funeral my brother was attempting to put my mother's things to order. As I went into her bedroom in my effort to help my brother I spotted my mother's will, which was lying on the bed and I became very disturbed. She directly detailed in her will that Derrick was left with her financial estate and due to me being transgender and courting men that I was to be left with nothing. I read other hurtful things and ended up just leaving the room and going to bed. No one truly understood the pain I felt. Again it was the same pain that I struggled with throughout my life with rejection and abandonment. Derrick and I engaged in an argument the next morning because he felt that it wasn't fair for me to sleep while other members of the family tried to organize our mother's belongings. For the first time that I could remember I snapped on him due to both the anger and the pain that I had suffered. We later made up. After the argument, Derrick commented that as he went through my childhood pictures he did not remember seeing any picture of me where I was smiling. The majority of pictures showed a frown on my face.

My manager had called me and advised me that it was time for me to return to work. Upon my return, in which I wasn't ready, I struggled to work on the sales floor and face my customers. My manager, Fantastic Feletia, called me in her office and told me that she wanted me to focus on doing what I did best, which was help people. She wanted me to focus on helping our customers and in performing my sales job. It was a very difficult day as I had to leave the floor several times as my face swelled with tears.

As the days got easier I made plans to go to San Mateo, California to spend my brother's birthday with him because I knew that it would be tough due to him spending it without my mother. He turned 47 on April 6, 2011. My second motivation for visiting my brother and his family was so that I could watch Maya play softball. She was heavily recruited out of high school as one of the nation's best catchers. I had never observed her playing softball before. She had experience playing on the travelling softball team prior to college and had several years of experience. During the first weekend we watched Stanford play a series at home against Arizona. We celebrated Derrick's Birthday on April 6th by taking him out to dinner to a "5 Star" Caribbean Restaurant. That following weekend we headed to Los Angeles to witness the Stanford-UCLA series. While on my vacation I suffered 2nd degree burns on my foot while trying to make breakfast for Derrick and Gina. My vacation was further enjoyed because of the wonderful time that I spent with my nephew, Jamil.

When I returned to Winston-Salem my doctor took me out of work for a couple weeks so that my foot could heal properly. While out of work I attended an engagement dinner for my cousin in Douglasville, Georgia. The atmosphere of sitting in a room with 16 family members was a chill filled experience. After our full spread of dinner and deserts, the family sat around and shared comments about each other. The lack of being around family had been a major element of my depression. My family showed me the love that I had lacked during the past few years.

On my drive to Douglasville I called my sister, Patricia, who I previously lived with in Florida and mentioned that I had only spoken to Karen via telephone but never had the opportunity to meet her in person. While in Douglasville, my cousin who I refer to as "Playboy" loaded up his van with his daughter, her fiancé, her friend, and myself and we headed to Woodstock to see my biological sister, Karen, for the very first time. The experience included a van of five African-Americans pulling into a driveway of a short Caucasian woman. I made jokes that the neighbors were going to think that trouble was brewing. We spent a couple hours together as the guys went downstairs to play pool and us ladies stayed seated in the living room chatting. This evening in May was a very heart-warming experience.

After I returned to work and shared the pleasantries with my co-workers, some employees mentioned "So you found your real family?" My response was that I grew up with my real family and that Derrick and Gina and their children were my real family. They were the ones that I had belonged to during at least 40 years of my life. I am very appreciative of the fact that I had the pleasure of meeting my biological sister. (I will further elaborate about my experience with finding my biological family in the Adoption Section of this book.) I continued to work at Verizon and had started feeling much better because of being reunited with my family. Throughout my early life I had also been taught about the importance of being "with family" by several members of our family; especially my father and my uncle.

Karen had also planned a wedding that was scheduled on July 27th in Gatlinburg, Tennessee. It was a honor for me to be invited to the wedding. It was a beautiful site. We hung out and participated in various activities. The guys wanted to partake in go cart racing and we ladies joined in the fun. We also had a wonderful dinner at Bennett's Barbeque in Pigeon Forge. The wedding took place at Cupid's Chapel of Love. Karen was so excited about getting married that she discovered that she left her wedding dress at the cabin so the wedding had to be rescheduled for later in the day.

Our other sister, Patricia, and I spoke on the telephone the night before the wedding and she shared her disappointment for not being at the wedding and she asked that I try to record the wedding. I advised her that pictures were not allowed in the chapel and I devised a scheme that would allow her to enjoy Karen's wedding. I decided to begin a phone call with Patricia while outside the chapel and as I entered the chapel I laid my cell phone on the pew and continued the call so that Patricia could witness the ceremony. Afterwards I took a picture that said "Turn off all cell phones." I figured if a rule was made to be broken I would be the one to break it.

The wedding was beautiful. Both Karen and the man that she was marrying looked so gorgeous that I called them Ken and Barbie. The Maid of Honor was stunning as well. She was a good fit for her role, however my thoughts were that since I was the sister I should have been the Maid of Honor. How dare I have that thought because I had just met Karen two months prior?

After returning to Verizon I worked for a month prior to injuring my right knee. I had previously injured my knee playing football and jumping off a wall while training at the Marines Officer's Candidate School. This time my knee slipped out of joint and I was in severe pain. I continued working on my bad knee until orders for a M.R.I were issued by my primary care physician. I received my results on August 18th and was placed back on medical leave. While on medical leave I went back to Georgia so that I could attend my cousin's wedding. Upon meeting up with my family I was overjoyed with what being with a family was really like. The wedding was held at the Westin Hotel at Atlanta's Airport. The scene was wonderful and so was my cousin.

Once I returned from Georgia, I met with my orthopedic surgeon and began my physical therapy. The goal was for me to get my leg strong enough to have the surgery. Due to FMLA Job Protection Laws I returned to work on October 7th. Since I was hobbled the management team decided to relocate my work station to the front of the store. Upon my request my station had previously been at the rear of the store. I preferred the location because it wasn't as noisy as the location in the front of the store. However due to medical necessity I was grateful that I was moved. My results continued to be among the best in the District. Yet on December 5th I reported to work and was feeling ill. After I attempted to open my cash drawer I informed my manager that I was sick and had to leave for the day. Blythe called to check on me after several hours of me napping and advised me to come to Charlotte in the event that I had to go to the hospital. After suffering from pain throughout the night and after the continual urging by Blythe I went to the emergency room at Carolina Medical Center–University. After several tests and a cat scan I was informed by the emergency doctors that they were concerned about my gall bladder. It had been severely infected for a very long time and emergency surgery was scheduled. My diabetes was severely out of control; my glucose reading was 527 upon being treated in triage. My surgeon spoke with me about both conditions and advised me that if I hadn't come to the hospital when I did I would have died within two weeks. She also told me that if I don't get my diabetes under control I would also die an early death. People had mentioned that to me before but I was so depressed that I didn't really care. This time it was different hearing it from my surgeon. The fact that my doctor stared me directly in the eye and told me that I was going to die caught my attention. Her advice was that I stop letting things stress me because stress also impacted my diabetes. At that moment I decided to remove myself from anything that caused me undue tension. I soon found myself walking away from unhealthy situations and thinking that, "It's not worth my health." Wow, what a dramatic change in my mental health for I had struggled for many years in my efforts at "Letting go."

After being released from the hospital Blythe took me to her house so that I could recover enough so that my cousins whom I refer to as Socrates' and Playboy came to pick me up and take me back to Georgia. I named my one cousin Socrates' because he always analyzed statements of others and he attempted to present his conversation in a logical manner. I would state that I appreciated exercising my mental state in such a manner. The one item that I practiced was his message regarding being patient. I actually used the tactic of being patient during my sales process and my results soared upon my return to Verizon. While earning my bachelor's degree in history I became very fond of my studies of Greek history and Socrates'. His famous quote touched me deeply and I began sharing this with my direct reports both at Cingular Wireless and Alltel. Socrates' said, "Only a fool knows everything." My cousin appeared to also have issues with my gender because he would often use the inappropriate personal noun when addressing me. He would often refer to me in the masculine; which I detested.

I became endeared to my other cousin as well. I called him Playboy because of the way that he handled himself with the ladies. In my opinion he was by no means a womanizer but he would often speak about his attractiveness to certain women. He would also treat me as the true lady that I was. I would often find my cousin opening doors for me and being very sensitive to my needs. Playboy was a true gentleman and my thoughts were that any woman would be pleased by the manner in which he carried himself. He was very organized and stated that he treated his life as a business. I found the information very useful because many of my mental issues were caused because my life appeared in chaos. Therefore I tried to adopt some of my cousin's techniques. For example, my cousin always wrote his thoughts down on paper. I decided to begin taking notes of certain things on my Galaxy Tablet.

I enjoyed my Christmas Holiday with my family. This was the second Christmas in a row that I spent with my family. Previously I had spent many holidays sitting on the couch fighting my tears as I felt lonely. Due to my surgery I was blessed with the opportunity to spend this Christmas with family. Due to the betterment of my financial affairs I had begun to be able to afford gifts for my family. I am a person that loves to give to others and I love doing for other people. This was the second year in a row that I was able to purchase quality gifts for Derrick, Gina, Maya, Jamil, and Ace. I tell you that this was very therapeutic for me and allowed me to reflect on my childhood when Aunt Mae would bring Derrick and me large trash bags of toys. My internal reflections allow me to feel overjoyed when I can spend money on other people and therefore I had much gratification during the Christmas of 2011.

Upon returning to work in late December I began to practice the things that my cousins taught me. My sales results were taken to a higher level as my sales for accessories and Home Phone Connects had become the best in the district for two months in a row. However on March 16, 2012, I again fell ill. My knee finally gave out and I suffered excruciating pain. I ended up having my surgery in Charlotte on April 18th. Playboy and Socrates' again headed to Charlotte to take me back to Georgia. A major event occurred a week prior to my surgery that would change my total way of thinking and also became a huge step in my overcoming depression. My cousin Irene, from Detroit, had called me while I was at Blythe's house and informed me that she wanted me to read a book by Pastor Joel Osteen. His book, "Everyday a Friday: How to be Happier 7 Days a Week" was a very inspirational book that changed my views on a lot of things. Pastor Osteen told several stories in his description of how people interact in life. One of the stories that he shared involved four men and two sacks. Three men were carrying two sacks while walking. The fourth man asked each man about the contents in the sacks. The first man said that he was carrying all of his bad thoughts and negative feelings in the front sack and was supposed to be carrying good things in the sack on his back. The man stated that he was overburdened by the bad experiences and was being weighed down and couldn't move forward. The second man was the opposite of the first for he was carrying all his good thoughts in the front and bad thoughts on his back. He stated that he was being dragged down by the sack carrying the bad thoughts and couldn't go any further either. The third man stated that he was carrying all the good things in the sack that was on his front. He stated that he had a hole in the sack that was on his back and all the bad things were let loose from that sack and he thought that he could fly. After giving heavy meditation to this reading I focused on the art of "letting go."

Without telling Mr. Osteen's entire book, I found something else very crucial in my life; he mentioned the act of forgiveness. Joel stated that how can we expect God to forgive us if we can't forgive people that have wronged us. I also gave heavy thought to this and reflected on all the poor experiences that I had with my mother and realized that in order for me to get well I had no choice but to forgive my mother. As I stated on my mother's death bed, she was truly a good woman. She and I just had difficulties for whatever reason. My brother had found tapes of my mother recording her thoughts about the anxiety that she had due to some decisions that I made. Just like several of my patterns were developed as a child my mother's issues were also developed while she was young. My maternal grandmother was deceased and she was raised by her sister. Mr. Osteen also made mention of not criticizing others. While growing up, I found my mother being very critical of many things that I did. Without me thinking that she was only trying to help me, I started to resist her instructions because of the manner in which she presented her ideas to me. After doing my reading on this topic I can honestly say that I had forgiven my mother 100% and now am at peace.

My dear friend, Sam, who considers me as part of his family soon learned that I appreciated Pastor Osteen's reading and suggested that I also read Pastor Joel Prince's "Destined to Reign." This reading further impacted my well-being because of my gender conflict. There are some Christians that are so religious that they only understand the laws and lose focus on Grace. My mother was one of those people for she condemned me to hell due to my gender issue. I was troubled for many years because I did not want to go to hell and I transitioned due to medical reasons. Many religions excluded the gay, lesbian and transgendered communities from their churches. Therefore I had stopped going to church because I felt that I could praise God in the privacy of my home. I also felt that I would not go anywhere that I wasn't welcomed. Furthermore I felt that I wasn't doing anything wrong and that if I would have been partaking in wrong doing then the church should have been willing to welcome me with open arms in their efforts to save me from my sins. This issue had become detrimental to my health because I wanted to be active in the church and had allowed others to discourage me. Well Pastor Prince pointed out the principle of Grace. It states that believers in the Grace of Jesus are already saved. Jesus died on the cross so that all of our sins could be forgiven and that if my gender transition was a sin (and it has not been proven to me as of this writing) God has already forgiven me. After reading and understanding this I thought really hard about Grace and I developed the understanding that God forgives people for sins regardless of the debt; as long as we believe in His Grace. This reading helped me further overcome my depression.

Throughout my depression I participated in both healthy and unhealthy coping mechanisms. People become depressed because of a whole lot of reasons and they cope with depression in various manners. While in Douglasville, Playboy had indulged in one of his drinking binges. This was a coping mechanism for him. This binge started on May 20th for he had started drinking that night. He woke up on that Monday and advised me that he couldn't take me to therapy. He slept until about 8 or 9 that night. The same thing happened the next morning and continued until that next Sunday. As Playboy was trying to recover from this experience he began having hallucinations. On that next Tuesday he began hearing things around 10 a.m. He thought that I was speaking to him. Then he started hearing "drilling" noises. He also started seeing things that weren't present for he thought two people had entered his home. He then started searching his house while carrying his pistol. Although he doesn't remember he carelessly pointed the gun at me while attempting to dislodge the bullets from the gun. This activity carried on throughout the day. I reflected back on when I was in my last foster home and I became very frightened. Playboy was standing on the lower tier of his house and started arguing with a man he thought he saw. I contacted Socrates' and Playboy's daughter. I also stayed covered up under my sheets in an effort to stay out of the way on this terrifying event. Around 8 o'clock I made an attempt to divert Playboy's attention by watching his favorite team play basketball on television. While watching his Oklahoma City Thunder lose the game he advised me that he had called the police earlier that day. I told him that I didn't hear the police. After the game concluded I attempted to go to sleep and was awakened to what I thought were footsteps running up the stairs. After waking up I heard Playboy on the telephone with a female police dispatcher. The police were dispatched out to Playboy's house for a 2nd time. After an officer approached me with questions I advised them that they could get their answers from Socrates'. A few hours after that I was picked up and taken to Grayson to become a house guest of Socrates'. I had trouble sleeping that night and stayed awake crying. The next morning I had found out that Playboy had called the police for a third time. This time he opened the door to let the police in and the police report reflected that as he opened the door he was carrying two knives and a gun. He was blessed that he hadn't gotten killed by the police. He was taken to the hospital to have his medical condition checked out. Please believe me when I say that this was a horrific experience. Again people employ coping mechanisms in order to avoid pain. Some mechanisms are healthy and some are unhealthy.

Throughout the ten plus years of my depression I experienced many things. Through all of my activities I have overcome a lot of my issues. Although I sorely miss my father, I am dealing with his death better as the days go by. Due to my performance on my job my financial status had gotten better.

I continue to live my life as intended and I have become an effective member of society. My faith has grown and therefore I have learned to "Let go and let God." I have truly forgiven my mother for the transgressions that she made against me. I have become acquainted with my family and the closeness is beginning to resurface. I am continuing to work on my physical well-being. Overall, I am headed in the right direction and truly feel that I have overcome my clinical depression.

Bringing It All Together
Overcoming Depression

The question of whether depression is innate or developed is a common discussion. I believe that it is both. My experiences show that my biological mother was institutionalized during her pregnancy with me. The non-identifying information that I received described Carla as being clinically depressed. Early patterns that were contributing factors to my depression included abandonment, rejection, anger, and trust. I felt abandoned because of my being placed in the adoption system. Therefore the rejection of being without my biological mother had psychological effects on me. I suffered with the issue of "rejection" for many years. One example included being denied a promotion to management four times prior to finally being promoted. Another example of rejection involved being left off the Alltel Sales Action Center's All-Star team. I had many other rejections throughout life. In fact I continued to internalize my gender issue and did not tell others due to the fear of being ostracized. In my opinion the "rejection" issue caused concerns with trust because I felt that I couldn't trust people because they would end up hurting me.

My interactions during my times of depression impacted my relationship with others. For example, Denise suffered a lot of stress in trying to explain to our child the reason that I was acting a certain way. Due to the anger management issue that I had I often screamed and cursed at people. This interaction would often sever relationships. One time my son tried to duplicate an embarrassing event that I had. Once I was released from UNC I shaved my eyebrows and as a result I had a gaping hole in them. He then proceeded to shave his eyebrows as well and also had a similar result. My son often acts out in frustration and screams and curses at people like I did. I believe that my relationship could have been closer with Derrick but I think that my depression had an influence on our bond. We are still close but I think that we would have been much tighter if not for my behavior during my depressed days. Gina and I are very close but I often feel that we would have had a tighter bond also. Blythe often tells me that I am overbearing on her because of me always being dejected. She also has issues in her life and has become hardened towards my situations. Due to my anxiety I have had many problems trying to socialize with others.

There are many reasons that people become depressed. I had many reasons for my depression, however I realized that as time went by my issues had less impact. The death of several loved ones contributed to my depression. I felt abandoned whenever I lost a close relative. For example, it took many years for me to overcome the loss of my father. Once he passed away I felt like I was left on a deserted island. My brother is an awesome individual and through hard work became very successful. I felt that I was also capable of becoming successful but I always compared myself to Derrick and always seemed to come up short. Therefore I sunk into a deep depression due to the lack of progress in my career. It had become so bad at one point that I lost my drive to succeed. I truly believe that I inherited clinical depression from my biological mother. Joel Osteen speaks about "The generational curse." He says that we have choices and can break the curse of our predecessors. My actions caused strains on relationships and I often found myself alone. My mother put me out of her life; my ex-spouse divorced me; and there is much distance between my son and I. A most important feature of my depression was the inability to "let go." During my stay in Mecklenburg County Hospital I was often told that I had to "let go" of the pain that I had because of my sour relationship with my mother. In addition to having strains on several of my relationships I also had anxiety when trying to socialize with others. I did learn, however, that I had to overcome this anxiety while at work in order to be a successful sales person. Perhaps this was another reason why I acted out at work. Although my financial stability was a great factor in causing me much pain, it got better over time. To this day I still struggle with making sound financial decisions. My physical health has been poor and therefore it affects me mentally. Obviously, my conflict with my gender was a major issue because I didn't really know how to express my transition to others for the fear of being harmed. Being the religious person that I was raised to be, I struggled when Christians became critical of me and separated themselves from me because of my gender. I also didn't want to go to hell for transitioning.

Pastor Joseph Prince wrote a book entitled "Destined to Reign." The book is as powerful as the name itself. Prince states that many Christians hold people accountable for the laws that were written in the Old Testament and ignore the fact that the New Testament speaks of the Grace that we received as a gift when Jesus died for our sins. Prince stated that when Jesus arose and prior to sitting down at the right hand of the table He stated, "I am finished." This, according to Pastor Prince, meant that Jesus was saying that He completed the task laid before him by our Almighty Father. In saying this He meant that He was crucified in order for Believers to have eternal life. Joseph points out that the laws in the Old Testament are important because we should understand how awesome this gift is. Grace saves us from repercussions that we would face if we didn't believe in the Grace of God.

I was also enlightened during a visit by my mother's pastor during my grieving process. The pastor from Metropolitan Baptist Church visited Derrick and me in order to help us during our hour of need. He conducted the conversation in a very compassionate way. The question of the manner in which he was going to address me during his remarks became part of the conversation. My response was that it was about my mother's Home Going and not about my feelings. I told him that I felt that the older people of the church would probably take issue with my gender. I further informed him that I was struggling with the fact that my mother deemed me to hell because of my transition to female. He stated that he wasn't saying that I was living in sin, however if I were and I believed in Grace then I would be saved. He further stated that all my sins would be thrown into the Sea of Forgetfulness. The pastor backed his statements up with scripture. It took me a few months to process what I was told and this conversation was very helpful with me overcoming this obstacle. I truly love God and look forward to spending my eternal days "Walking around Heaven."

Although I should have been encouraged that factors of my depression were getting better I couldn't see it due to staying focused on my negative thoughts. I was hospitalized in 2002 because I had become suicidal. Some of my issues were becoming resolved over time but I didn't realize it. Once I started getting thoughts of hurting myself in 2005, I decided to seek immediate help. While hospitalized this time I decided that in order to become happy I wanted to become a 5-year-old little girl. I struggled with "Letting go." However my issues were not as bad as they were in 2002. In 2009 I admitted myself into the hospital for a final time while wearing baby clothing. I was seeking love and I was lonely but my issues weren't as bad as they were in 2005.

There are both unhealthy and healthy coping mechanisms when dealing with depression. Early in my depression I drank and smoked every day. Alcohol is an agent that leads to depression and is unhealthy. I also locked myself in my bedroom in order to avoid others; therefore I became isolated. While hospitalized I did not want to participate in group activities because I was too focused on my pain. During this time I made myself worse by focusing on my problems instead of doing something about my issues. Pretending to be a child and a baby were also unhealthy mechanisms.

Healthy mechanisms included caring for my pets. Pooh Bear was the family dog that we had while we lived in Raleigh and Scarface was the dog that I had during my stay in Winston-Salem. It is said that caring for pets helps people fight the issue of loneliness. In my late stages of depression I was willing to read healthy topics on religion which helped me understand Grace and also realize that others had things worse than I did. My reading and the fact that I had extra time due to being on medical leave with my knee afforded me the opportunity to write my book. This writing was very therapeutic. Ironically I failed at my attempt at journal writing during the 2005 phase of my depression. Although I struggled during the early portion of this section on depression I made it through and completed the writing. Another thing that Joel Osteen stated in his books was that everyone should make a habit of having a good laugh at least once a day. Many people agree that laughter often reduces stress. I have found that the more I laugh the less I feel depressed. Overall, I have begun to practice healthy activities in order to climb my mountain of overcoming my depression.

Overall, depression is a serious illness and some people may not completely understand the sickness. Depressed people still have to interact with others while fighting their battle and the interactions could cause further pain. In sharing my experiences I hope that my readers could understand what depressed people suffer through. Even though I had many hospitalizations, and became harmful to myself, I overcame my agony. You too, my friend, shall overcome yours. Loved ones of those suffering, I beg you to understand and help others climb the hurdles that they face. In the end I am still standing.

For those who have inquiring minds relating to gender transition I have decided to have a special treat in my next section. I will speak about my experiences and back those up with medical information that pertains to me and then I will provide a few interviews that will give a full perspective of gender transition. One of the interviews is with a post-operative and the others are with pre-operative females. I have also included an interview from a medical professional. My goal is to share the various views and experiences in an effort to educate my readers towards gender transition. Please enjoy.

David shortly after being adopted in 1972

Derrick and David at the World Trade Center

Derrick and David in the early 1980's

David looking depressed

Overcoming depression with the help of my family

Gina and Jamil in April of 2011
At Stanford University

Jala and Derrick at their
mother's funeral on
December 28, 2010
Detroit, Michigan

Gina Gregory-Burns and
Jala McKenzie-Burns at
their mother's funeral
December 28, 2010
Detroit, Michigan

Derrick and Gina
November 2010
San Mateo, CA

Jala and Derrick
April 2011
Napa Valley

Gina, Jala, Maya, and Derrick
November 2010
San Mateo, CA

Gina, Jala, Maya, and Derrick
April 2011
Stanford softball
Maya played softball for Stanford

Jamie and Jala
October 2006
Charlotte, NC

Maya Sylvia Burns
Stanford University
Graduation
June 17, 2012

Jamil Gregory Burns
2010 High School
Graduation

Cousin Irene Fountain-Burns, Jala,
Cousin Nicole Burns, and Derrick
Mother's Funeral
December 28, 2010
Detroit, Michigan

SECTION 4

GENDER TRANSITION

The Transgender Community
Another Component of Society

Society is composed of a whole lot of different elements. Of those elements are a bunch of different types of people. Yet they are still people. Some individuals have black hair, some have brown hair, and others may have grey or white hair. Their eyes are also different. Please don't forget that the skin tone is different as well. People come in all sizes, shapes, and forms. Friends, I introduce to you the Transgender Community.

In order to help you understand a transgender individual let me share the Wikipedia, The Free Encyclopedia's definition with you, "Transgender is a general term applied to a variety of individuals, behaviors, and groups involving tendencies to vary from culturally conventional gender roles....it is the state of one's 'gender identity' (self–identification as woman, man, neither or both) not matching one's 'assigned sex' (identification by others as male, female, or intersex based on physical/genetic sex)." In other words a transgender person's mindset is different from the body which one had at birth. Wikipedia goes on to say, "Transgender does not imply any specific form of sexual orientation." Transgender people can be heterosexual, homosexual, or bisexual. A heterosexual person is one that is attracted to the opposite "sex" or "gender." A homosexual person is one that is attracted to the same "sex" or "gender." A "homosexual" person is also referred to as a "gay" person. Not all transgender people are identified as being "gay." C.J. writes in the "Scarleteen Sex Ed for the Real World" that there is "The typical gender system is known as the 'gender binary'." Many scholars feel that there are more gender identities than just the normal male and female types. While reading a message on the grooby.com website I was taught another reference for those in gender transition. There is also the affirmed female and affirmed male.

Transgender people go through various psychological and medical tests in order to determine if a person has a "Gender Identity Disorder." People suffering from this disorder are said to also have a gender dysphoria. This means that the person is not happy with the gender that one was born with. Many transgender people become depressed because they don't know the exact manner to handle their disorder. However gender dysphoria is not seen by all medical professionals as being a mental illness. Personality tests, blood tests, MRIs of the human brain and other exams are performed when diagnosing a transgender person. Once a person is deemed transgender by their doctor they can begin hormone treatment. Low amounts of testosterone can lead to a condition called "hypogonadism." Some doctors prescribe an estrogen enhancer and a testosterone blocker for transgender females. Doctors also prescribe testosterone enhancers for transgender males.

In order to have gender reassignment surgery a transgender female must live in that fulltime role for a minimum of one year. As a result many of the transgender community have difficulties in both their work and home lives. There are some very supportive people but there are also people who don't accept transgender people. I think that the reason is because of the lack of education about people in their transition.

The following section will reveal my real life experiences so that an accurate depiction of a transgender woman can be made. In bringing a complete picture I will discuss various topics such as medical, social, and mental aspects. Finally, in my efforts to demonstrate that even transgender people are different, within our own classification, I will reveal the complete picture by sharing several interviews with you.

My goal in writing this section is to educate society on gender transition. The readers will be able to look inside the minds of transgender people so that they can get a complete understanding. My friends, you will be able to understand the battles that we, as transgender people, struggle with on a daily basis. Please enjoy the reading that I present to you. Overall, my goal is to educate society about my people, the Transgender Community.

My Gender Transition

There are two schools of thought regarding sexual orientation and gender identity. Some scholars believe that both are innate behaviors and that people are born with these characteristics. Others believe that patterns are developed through experiences and make a person's composition. I firmly believe that both sexual orientation and gender identity are innate and that patterns are developed over a period of time. I believe that my physical development started prior to birth and that I learned gender patterns throughout my life. When I was about the age of 3 or 4 my foster father would call me a sissy. I was beat up throughout elementary and middle school and called names like "Shirley Temple" and "Debbie." After getting beat up I would often cry. Although I am not in total agreement, crying is often associated with things that girls do. I used to call my best friend by the name "Daddy." It is not a normal behavior for boys to refer to other boys in that manner. While in boot camp my strength didn't match that of other recruits and my drill instructor asked me if I had a penis or a vagina. By being the clown that I was I answered a vagina. I enjoyed an order that one of the visiting brothers made me do while pledging. He made me envision wearing a red fitted dress and red pumps and he ordered me to talk to my line brothers in my most sexy and feminine voice. Most males wouldn't have enjoyed that task; but I found it as a turn on. I started wearing makeup and female clothes during my middle school years. I remember the days when there were half days at school and I would be at home alone and I would dress up. I would wear my mother's clothes and would use oranges to create my breasts. Whenever I heard a car drive into the drive way I would rush to take the clothes off and I would then rush down the stairs so that I could remove the makeup. I would continue dressing up while in college, but I was in the privacy of my own apartment. Therefore I say that I was born with a less physique than other guys my age and I formed my gender identity at an early age. I also found out that my pituitary gland was smaller than the normal size of a male's pituitary gland.

During my stay in the University of North Carolina Medical Center, in 2002, I stayed in my bed thinking about my gender crisis. The medical staff recognized my depression and other mental illnesses and they told me that my gender crisis was a totally separate issue. In the Fall of 2002, I began hanging out with Blythe and furthered my transition. One memory serves me while we were visiting Virginia. This was my first time leaving my own domain dressed as a woman. Apparently I wasn't too passable at the time because a girl in her early 20s made a rude comment saying, "Elvis had left the building" as she was making fun of me. As I practiced my education of applying makeup I called Belk's in Raleigh and scheduled a makeover. Wow. This was an awesome experience for the sales lady treated me just like any other girl and she taught me the art of applying makeup. I also started going to the salon to get my eyebrows waxed. In the spring of 2003, I moved to Fayetteville and started hanging out at the Spektrum because I enjoyed the drag shows. Although my pattern of having a lack of rhythm continued throughout my life I once imagined participating in a drag show. I figured that I wasn't skilled enough to perform at the club so I performed for several friends at my apartment. I remember Blythe and her husband laughing at me. Blythe accompanied me to the Spektrum several times so that I could become comfortable hanging out. She and I would also practice walking in heels and switching our behinds in ways that men would appreciate.

I often became lonely because I lived by myself and I wanted to feel loved because I didn't have any immediate family in the area. So I began to crave attention and started enjoying when men started flirting with me. I remember leaving the club and guys would holler at me and attempt to get a piece of tail. One time a guy was calling me over to his truck and like the inexperienced tramp that I was I went over to him. He got out of his truck and the next thing I knew he had my red dress raised and had me leaning over his truck as he was doing things to me that shouldn't had been done in public. Another time a guy grabbed my arm and placed his other arm around my waist and tried to escort me to my car. The next thing that I knew the boy's tongue was half way down my throat as he was French kissing me. One night a sports agent and I sat in the VIP Lounge and he kept massaging my legs and breasts. I enjoyed the attention because I felt the love that the man was showing me. However at the end of the night instead of just exchanging numbers he asked me if he could take me to Waffle House. I didn't think anything of it and agreed to go with him. After having an early morning breakfast the man wanted me to drive him to the park so we could make out. I told him that I wasn't comfortable with that because I had just met him. He informed me that I was acting like he was some type of murderer. Although I was scared I told him that wasn't my thought at all. He then proceeded to pull his pants down and asked me to kiss his private and for some reason in my nervousness I did as he requested. I then asked him for his address and took him to his house.

In August of 2003, I relocated to Venice, Florida to live with my sister. I didn't hang out at clubs that often but I did dress as a female and often went out shopping. Just like at Belk's I scheduled a makeover at Dillard's. This sales lady did an awesome job but she also attempted to sell me everything in the store. I remember while living in a hotel I decided to go to the Comedy Zone to see BET's very own Monique. The usher asked me if I mind sitting at the corner of the bar, which was located at the front near the stage. She warned me that the performers normally pick on people that sat in the front. I agreed anyway. During Monique's performance she made several jokes about me. Her final joke was in reference to giving a man oral sex. She looked at me and said, "I'm talking to you too Bitch." The audience roared in laughter.

After returning to Fayetteville I resumed hanging out at the club and focused on meeting men. While working at Alltel, in Lumberton, I met a police officer who told me that he was attracted to me. He complemented me on both the look of my body and the view of my rear end. The officer ended up visiting me at my small apartment. A couple days later a woman came into the store and mentioned that she needed to order a phone for her husband. As I pulled up her account I took notice that the police officer's name was listed on her account. She pointed out that the name on the account was her husband's. I excused myself and went to the rear of the store and let out a loud laugh. I found it hilarious how some married men tried to cheat on their wives. I wasn't having any of that and I refused from then on to take any of his calls. He came by my apartment one day and I refused to answer the door. The situation fizzled out.

While working in Lumberton my manager would ask me to help fill in at the Fayetteville Wal-Mart Kiosk I met a very friendly Christian lady, named Gina, who I befriended. She was beautiful looking, with her long hair, and had a beautiful personality. She invited me over to her house several times. She celebrated my 39th Birthday with me as well. In becoming close to Gina I shared information with her about my gender transition. I also informed her of the difficulty between my mother and me due to her religious beliefs. Gina advised me that God loves all His children and that she didn't think that I was doomed to hell because of my Gender Identity Disorder. She would comfort me and also included me as one of her female friends. Gina soon left Alltel and as I relocated I lost touch with her.

While hanging out at the club I met several transgender girls, who were often referred to as "t-girls," and they were prostitutes. I would hang out in the parking lot with my friends although they were soliciting for money. They would tell me that I didn't need to get caught up with their activities and that whenever traffic began to pick up I would be instructed to go inside the club. Many military men from Fort Bragg would frequent the spot. I recollect a man that was in the army drove up in a truck and asked me if I was one of the "chicks with dicks." I advised him that I was in my transition and continued my way into the club. It appeared that most of the men waited outside the club in their efforts to pick up women. I soon realized that a lot of married men were attracted to transgender girls.

I became friends with many of the girls and was invited to one of their houses where they were giving each other breast implants. This was an underground activity and was very risky. This activity aroused my interest so I decided to call Raleigh Endocrine Association because I also wanted my breast to be enhanced. An appointment was scheduled and I took my next step in my transition. The doctor ordered several tests prior to ordering my hormone therapy. My hormone test resulted as me being "abnormal for a male and normal for a female." This meant that my testosterone level was low for a man and my estrogen level was normal for a woman. The normal testosterone level of 300 ng/dL is considered low for a man. My level was 124 ng/dL. My doctor also ordered an MRI in order to view my pituitary gland and the result came back that my gland was small like most women. The purpose of this gland is to send signals to other glands and organs and to direct them to produce hormones. My doctor prescribed Estradiol and Spironolactone so that my hormones could properly develop for the woman of my nature. After a few months of taking this treatment my breasts began to develop. I was told that my breasts would probably develop to a size "C." I also had the results from two different Minnesota Multiphasic Personality Inventory exams. Both times the tests results were identical. The exams were set up of more than 550 questions and some of the questions were rephrased to ask the same question in an effort to make sure that the examiner was telling the truth. My results read, "She answered the questions honestly and was consistent with her responses." The system had read my correct gender and stated that my answers showed that I was a depressed girl who was also immature.

I continued my therapy with Kimball Jane Sargent, at Diverse Solutions, and learned many interesting activities that different communities perform in order to help families adjust to dealing with the transgender family member. My therapist told me that when a person transitions to a different gender it is as though the person of the gender of birth had passed away. Members of this particular community gathered their family as though they were having a funeral for the old person and the person would come out dressed in the appearance of the person's former gender. The family would tell stories of how much fun they had with the person of the former gender. Then the person would come out dressed in the gender of the new person. The family would burn the clothing of the old gender and welcome the new person into the family. They would discuss items of what they looked forward to from the new person.

I was also educated on the method in which children overseas are treated in regards to choosing a gender. There are those that allow children to wait until a certain age to decide their gender. During this time, patterns develop and the child starts acting in either a masculine or feminine manner. At this point the family sits down with the child and helps that child choose the desired gender. I thought that this was amazing because this would seem to create happier people in society.

I first started bringing more attention to my appearance when I lived in Fayetteville. I would find myself standing in the mirror for hours each day. I would try to fix my hair to various styles. Many times my hair was in so much of a fuss that I would get aggravated. Therefore one day I decided to go to one of the salons in Fayetteville and get my hair treated. My hair was formerly worn in naturally tight curls. Well I went to the local stylist and was informed that my hair was a fine mix between Caucasian and African-American so the stylist gave me a reverse perm which loosened my curls into a more feminine style and I began wearing long loose curls. The stylist also tinted my hair of a medium auburn color. After looking in the mirror I was amazed at how beautiful I looked.

Now that I had my hair in the manner in which I preferred, I now wanted to start focusing on my makeup. I also stood in front of the mirror for long periods of the day in my attempt to master the technique of applying makeup. I would often go to places like Belk's in order to get a makeover and learn tips in applying my makeup and I became a huge fan of the Clinique products. I used the three step process for cleansing my face. I also became familiar with the various makeup products and began building my makeup collection. I would often become frustrated with making my eyes up for this was the hardest part of my routine. To this day I find myself practicing the makeup application process in front of my bathroom mirror.

I began making frequent trips to the nail salon so that I could get my eyebrows and nails done and I would always request to get my eyebrows waxed in a thin high arch. The art of eyebrow waxing was to shape them to fit the woman's face. I just thought that a high thin arch was sexier. At first, I wanted to get my nails done with acrylic nails and then changed to the gel nail style. I often enjoyed the pedicure process for the beautification process of my feet but I struggled with the removal of the dead skin from the bottom of my feet. Whenever the technician would scrape the dead skin from my feet I would normally break out in laughter. My feet are very ticklish. I would often enjoy placing my feet in the wax because it was so relaxing. The technician would often paint a design on my big toe and my finger.

In terms of hair removal, I received the Cool Glide Laser treatment. The process would make my face very soft looking and worked wonderful results. The process normally took about 30 minutes or so. At first it was very painful and I would often feel like my face was being stapled. The person treating me would place goggles over my eyes so that the elements would not blind me. She would then use a cold applicant to chill my face. Then she would use the laser to zap my hair from my face. I was happy once the process was complete but I felt much pain during the procedure.

Now that I was working on my body, it was my time to shop. Let me tell you, this was my hobby. While I lived in Fayetteville, I loved shopping at Ashley Stewart's and Cato's. The clothes were very attractive and the staff was friendly. They would treat me like every other female customer and I received courteous service and was allowed to use the female fitting room. My boot collection grew due to the love that I had for boots. I found, for a period of time, that I was not buying a lot of pants. I was a girl that enjoyed wearing dresses and stockings because I felt that my look was more feminine.

Sunday nights were my relaxation nights. My tub would be lined with candles and I often soaked in bubble bath while listening to my music. I would shave my arms, legs and behind. A girl shouldn't be hairy and I made sure that I wasn't. I found myself soaking in the tub for long periods of time because I found a way to wind down and get focused on the week ahead. This was my special treat.

My voice was the next item that I would concentrate on. It wasn't the normal deep masculine voice but some people would sometimes refer to me as a male. So I often found myself practicing the pitch of my voice. I was often thrilled to frequent the drive through at fast food restaurants and I found myself wanting to hear the fast food worker answer my order so that I could see whether I passed their exam. If I heard a "Thank you ma'am" I knew that I was successful in my quest. Initially there was some disappointment because I would get addressed as a male but after a while I met much success.

I was determined to be what the transgender community called "passable." I read a lot of materials listed on the internet or in books and I could relate to the frustration that some faced in getting addressed in the wrong gender. It hurt my feelings whenever someone addressed me in the gender other than what I was.

I continued working in Lumberton for a few more months after being allowed to transition on the job. In March of 2005 I transferred back to Charlotte and began working in the Sales Action Center. I struggled with customers not addressing me in the correct gender. There was an incident where an employee from a different department questioned my gender and then starting laughing at me. I reported the issue to my supervisor and the issue was addressed.

Upon my relocation to Charlotte I attempted to transfer to another endocrinologist, but the doctor in Charlotte ended up not treating me. This was a crucial point for me because my breast had started to develop quite nicely and my face was becoming softer and my body was taking on a more feminine appearance. This transition was basically due to my hormone therapy. Due to not being treated by the endocrinologist in Charlotte I had stopped taking my pills and as a result my breasts appeared to shrink and then my mental health started to suffer.

Two events occurred that further enhanced my transition. Due to my age my doctor scheduled me for a mammogram. I was told that since I was approaching the age of 40 that from that point on I had to schedule an annual mammogram. Although I felt clamped down like a cow and twisted like a pretzel my results came back normal. The second occurrence involved the process of changing my name. Both management and the Human Resource Consultant were very supportive of my name change. On January 31, 2006, I appeared in front of the Magistrate for the Charlotte Courts. I previously processed the paper work in order to have a court date scheduled. Jamie accompanied me to court and we met my attorney, Cory Williams, whom I now consider my friend. He was a well-dressed African-American male that was well spoken and was very educated. As my attorney addressed the magistrate he spoke very convincingly and his tasks appeared very simple. The magistrate looked at me and stated that according to my appearance and dress that the decision in this case would be very easy. She looked down at the paperwork and signed it immediately without having to give it a second thought.

In the course of choosing my name several developments took place. One evening after work Blythe and I went to a Mongolian Barbeque restaurant in Fayetteville. While sitting at the bar we watched the news program on television. There was an anchor named Jala and I thought the name was very pretty. Blythe definitely favored it over the previous name that I had wanted. Blythe thought that the name Daneshia was too ghetto so she surveyed many people to see if they agreed. Once those people gave their opinions I decided against the name Daneshia. As a manager at Cingular I had a young lady on my team whose middle name was Alyshia. I told her how much I admired that name and I adopted the name as my middle name as well. For many years I had thought about having a strong last name. Corretta Scott was a strong black woman and therefore I gave much thought to the last name Scott. Jamie's last name was also Scott. Blythe on the other hand liked the name McKenzie as a middle name but I preferred Alyshia over McKenzie; therefore I choose the name Jala Alyshia. I thought that the name McKenzie fit me perfect for a strong black woman; thus the name Jala Alyshia McKenzie. My son had pleaded for me to keep my last name the same (Burns) and I told him that I really wanted my last name to be McKenzie. As I gave it further thought and as I sat down at the courthouse to file the paperwork I chose the name Jala Alyshia McKenzie-Burns. I was happy with the name because I thought that it was pretty and very fitting for me. I am also glad that I kept the last name Burns because it allowed my son to continue a bond with me and it was my adopted last name. This date of January 31, 2006 was a special date for two reasons. I could celebrate my name change and my sister, Patricia's birthday.

While in Charlotte I developed close friendships with several people who accepted me for who I was. Since all of my family members lived out of state and I was experiencing a lot of loneliness I adopted these people as family members. I had my own family right there in Charlotte. Jamie would visit and allowed me to visit her frequently. When I first met her she did a lot of partying. We would hangout on Friday and Saturday nights for mid-night bowling. Several friends would gather up and drive to the bowling alley in Matthews. The scene would be that of a party life atmosphere and the overhead lights would be turned down and music would be playing on the overhead speakers and we could watch the music videos on large screen televisions. In 2005, we celebrated Jamie's Birthday and there were several other parties going on at the same time. I noticed that a few people were receiving bowling pins as a birthday present, but I didn't see Jamie receive one so I scouted around to find a way to get her one. My thought was that "If other people were given signed bowling pins then I'd better make sure that my sister had one." So after walking around the bowling alley for about twenty minutes I spoke to the manager and purchased one for $20. I tried to get her boyfriend to distract her while everyone else was signing her pin. She was really happy when we presented her the birthday present. Jamie smiled at me and said, "You go Little Jala." After that we partied until about 3 a.m.

One day Jamie came by my apartment to check on me because I was going through my depression. She was accustomed to seeing me dress in a very sophisticated manner while at work. While taking her throughout my apartment I showed her my walk-in closet. The spacious closet was lined with my boots. She was amazed and said, "Girl you got some boots going on up in here." Understand that I had a thing for boots. I loved wearing my 2-inch boots because they made my legs look thinner and I could really work myself as I swayed around switching my tail in the sexiest way. I loved suede material boots, knee high boots, short and sexy boots, and just about any other type of boot. My closet was also filled with various dresses and skirts. Jamie would tell me that I had it going on. She and I became very close friends and adopted each other as sisters. Although she was my junior by 20 years I would call her and her younger sister my big sisters. They would treat me as their little sister.

Whenever I visited Jamie she would always do my hair and my makeup and I would enjoy the fact that she would make me as pretty as could be. She used to sell Mary Kay products and would always find a way to give me some products. She would often give me her clothes that she no longer wanted. This was my girl and we loved each other as sisters normally do.

My other girl, Ericka, was a party girl also. I met her when she was in her late twenties. This girl knew how to party and believed that life was too short to sit around in misery. She would often tell our neighbors in Steeplechase that we were going to have a cookout at the pool. We lived in the horseshoe and everyone was very tight. We all would cook a dish and bring it to the poolside; while the guys would grill out. We would drink beer and just chill. After chilling at the pool we would bring our chairs outside and sit in the horseshoe and enjoy each other's company. There were some neighbors that had a problem with that and would call the police. We confronted the police one night and stated that we were just relaxing with each other and weren't too loud so we weren't sure for the reason that they were called. We did actually get pretty loud during the 4th of July in 2005. All of the families got together in the horseshoe and lit fireworks. We didn't need to go to the annual fireworks show because we were having our own show. One of the guys kept teasing us ladies by rolling the fireworks at us because he was just having fun. There was no harm intended. He threw one at me and in my attempt to avoid it I fell to the ground and everyone laughed. We indeed had a wonderful time that holiday night. I would often flirt with my neighbor because I thought he was cute and he would normally flirt back with me. I remember telling him that I would ride him like a cowgirl and the whole group busted out with laughter. They were all cool and my neighbor knew that I was just flirting. Besides he had a girlfriend that lived with him and I knew her from working with her previously at BellSouth Mobility.

Ericka actually called all her girlfriends one Saturday afternoon to gather at her apartment and we were scheduled to have fun. It was a girl's day and about six or seven of us gathered around and had girl talk and then we started talking about sex and other girlie things. The next thing I knew Ericka had brought a dildo out from her room and we started talking about doing oral sex. All the girls urged me to show them how to make a guy happy by doing things by mouth. She placed a condom on the object and handed it to me. I was thinking, "Why me?" Of course it was me because of my gender transition and I was a little different from the other girls.

Ericka would often try to bring me out of my shell and although she was well aware of my mental state she would try her best to make me snap out of my depression. She would tell me that other girls would say things just to see if I would respond. For example, Ericka would often tell us how much she wanted to have children. The other women would comment about having kids and at first I would just sit there and listen. Ericka would often say, "Girl you need to join in on the conversation because the other women were looking for your response." My thought was that I was transgender and couldn't have kids in the manner that I desired so it wasn't a need to comment. Ericka would tell me to comment anyway; besides we were all gathered to have girl talk.

In helping me further transition into the woman that I am today, Ericka would tell me that there was no need to tell people that I was a transgender female. I made a habit of telling people that because I believed in being upfront and honest with people. She would tell me that I was just a female like all the other girls and that it was like I was discrediting myself when I mentioned transgender. The neighbors were aware of my transition and I didn't need to broadcast it to the world. Soon thereafter I stopped mentioning the word "transgender" and just introduced myself as Jala.

Blythe relocated to Charlotte a year after I did. So I had my sister back. I would spend a lot of time with Blythe and her family. She would try and toughen me up by not allowing me to sit around and pout and we would do girlie things like practice walking in the sexiest manner so that whenever we were around men we could win them over with our sexy attitudes. One evening Blythe was spending the evening at my apartment and she decided to flat iron my hair and all of a sudden there was a knock on my door and I went to answer it. To my surprise it was my first friend that I met when I first moved to Charlotte in 1998. He previously had only known me in my masculine appearance. I was further surprised because he didn't recognize me. After opening my door he stated, "Ma'am, I used to live at this apartment and I was wondering if I might use the mailbox key so I could get my mail." I gave him the key and when he returned from retrieving his mail I called his name and he was surprised that I knew him. After being flooded with several questions I advised him that he was my first friend that I ever met in Charlotte and that I worked with him at BellSouth Mobility. I made him aware of my former name and that I worked with him and then we both embraced with the nicest hug. He was not disappointed about my transition and admitted that he didn't recognize me because instead of my hair being in tight curls it was long and pretty. He expressed that I looked sexy and pretty at the same time. This really put me at ease and he and I became close friends and I would often give him a ride to work. He was my main man and I thought that he was a really nice gentleman.

Gina and I would often speak on the telephone. She was a very warm person who nurtured me and made me feel that I belonged. If she and I had lived close by I may have been able to fight through my depression much quicker. From my impression my sister understood Gender Identity Disorder because she was a doctor and was educated. Whether she completely understood or not I'm not sure but in her very loving manner she made me feel comfortable. I was missing my mother and Gina appeared as a mother figure to me. The manner in which she carried herself reminded me of Aunt Mae. When I told her that I was a five-year-old she told me that adults don't want to treat other adults like children and she would tell me to act like the grown woman that I was.

Of course Derrick was very supportive in my transition. I travelled to California twice within a five month period starting in November 2010. I went out to California in November to celebrate my birthday and in April to celebrate his birthday. I was thrilled to be introduced by him as his sister. Derrick would often spoil me by taking me out to eat or taking me sightseeing. In November we visited Botanical Gardens at Berkley, Alcatraz, Oakland, and many other attractions. We also had the privilege of enjoying the Reuben Stoddard concert. In April I had a chance to do something that I hadn't previously been able to do; I witnessed my niece, Maya play softball. She was highly recruited as a catcher out of high school. She was a very popular player due to her experience of playing for a local team. We also celebrated Derrick's 47th Birthday by taking him out to a Caribbean restaurant. Jamil and I had an opportunity to chill out a few days. Both Maya and Jamil respectfully enjoyed their Aunt Jala. I thoroughly adored hanging out with the "West Coast Burns."

It appeared that the further I advanced through me transition the more education on Gender Identity Disorder became available. For example, I was watching the "60 Minutes" documentary on television one day during the year of 2007 and the program was discussing the topic. The commentator was discussing two 6-year-old twin boys as related to their gender. The first boy was deemed a "normal" child because he wanted to play with cars, trucks and other traditional toys that boys played with. His twin brother was more interested in playing with dolls and things that enticed little girls. As patterns developed the second twin appeared to be happy wanting to be a little girl. The commentator interviewed both the parents and each child and learned that the family was willing to accept each one. The later youngster stated that he felt as though he was a girl and therefore wanted to be a female. As I reflected on this I had memories that were prior to my adoption when I played with my girl cousins and was more interested in things that they played with instead of the traditional things that boys amused themselves with. I also reflected 30 years earlier when I was watching several talk shows that had transgender guests discuss the topic. During this time period these affirmed females appeared strange and would often be ridiculed because of their gender. One day in 1984 I called the phone number for one of the programs and told them that I also wanted to be a female but was scared to say anything. The lady I spoke with mentioned that I needed prayer and that I should talk to someone about my issue. Therefore I could appreciate the fact that people in today's culture are beginning to open their minds so that they can understand what it is like to be different in terms of gender.

While in Charlotte I continued to concentrate on my appearance for my look was everything to me. I would learn to color my hair at home and I would also flat iron it as well. I was often very nervous whenever anyone wanted to take scissors to my hair. I hadn't really had a haircut since my interview with Alltel when I first moved to Florida in 2003. In fact that wasn't really considered a cut. It was only a trim. My hair, when flat ironed, would hang below my shoulder. I also enjoyed getting my hair braided with micro braids. I felt the longer my hair the more girlie I looked.

I also continued to go to the nail salon so that I could get my nails and eyebrows cared for. Actually I found a salon directly across the street from the call center. The staff was very friendly and treated me very well and I would always enjoy relaxing with the other ladies. The more time that I spent in the salon the more comfortable I became with the process.

I would often take part in my favorite activity of shopping. Once I relocated to Charlotte, I found myself enjoying my time at Dot's, Ross Dress for Less, and Victoria's Secret. I stockpiled my closet full of dresses, blouses, skirts and sexy panties and bras. I enjoyed looking very nice whenever I went to work. I didn't go out to the club as much as I did in the past but I believed in looking the part whenever I was on the job.

Although I didn't hang out in Charlotte as much as I did prior to moving there, I did go out a couple times. During the spring of 2007 I went to the Scorpio Club due to my wanting to watch the "Drag" Show. While at the club I met this superfine looking stud of a man and we drew to each other. He started visiting my apartment on Sunday and we would also hang out at the midnight bowling at the bowling alley in Matthews. I would invite this young man to my apartment every Sunday and I would create the atmosphere that most men enjoyed. I would cook a special dinner for him, give him the remote control to both my television and my heart, and we would cuddle up and spend the evening together. This was a really enjoyable time. I often speculated that I had an intuition that he might be married. After calling his cell phone one afternoon and getting his voice mail I received a return call. To my surprise there was a female voice on the other end and she asked me for what reason I called her cell. I stated that it was by accident. However, I mentioned it to him and was told that the person was his sister. I questioned his response and asked him if he was married. Our dates became more infrequent.

In terms of my job, I continued to work in the Sales Action Center until November 10, 2006; which at that time I transferred back to the Retail Channel. I was the most experienced and tenured sales representative at our Rivergate location. The store had only been open for three months prior to my transfer. My transition was very smooth and no one really questioned my gender. I worked in a sales and service position until September 11, 2007; where at that time I was promoted to retail assistant manager. On December 7, 2007, I relocated to Winston Salem as a result of being promoted to retail store manager. Throughout this time I had decided to drop the word "transgender" because as my girl Ericka had stated a few years prior, either I was a woman or I wasn't. I had physically and mentally become the true meaning of a female.

I managed the Summit Square Store until April 2009 at which time my store was closed due to the Verizon acquisition. After working at a couple stores in Greensboro I was offered a sales position at the University Parkway Store in Winston-Salem. While at that location I meet several friends and developed some relationships. Nadine became a very close friend of mine and we also treated each other as family. We would often find ourselves in front of her barbeque grill cooking chicken wings. She had become one of a few people in the Winston Salem area that I had informed about my gender transition. Nadine was very accepting and advised me to continue to live as myself regardless of how others might feel. My reason for telling Nadine was that much anxiety had built up to the possibly of losing my job and the scare of not being able to gain employment due to my gender transition. She was both very comforting and encouraging in regards to my gender and being able to find employment. Throughout the years, Nadine and I have established a very close relationship.

Yaria was another person that I became very close to. Now this was my girl because of the bond that we created due to deaths that occurred in our families. While on medical leave for depression in 2009, I met Yaria. At this time she was working at the CVS Pharmacy that I would get my medication filled at. Yaria and my bond became closer in 2010 because we both had relatives that passed. Her grandmother died in November and my mother deceased in December. Yaria's grandmother raised her and from what I could tell she did a wonderful job for she was quite a wonderful person. Her personality was as bright and as her sunny face. While on medical leave for my knee she separated from Verizon. After her separation I mentioned to her about the topics in this book. She stated that due to our closeness several co-workers had asked her about my transition. Her response was "Jala is my girl and if you had any questions you need to direct them towards her." Yaria was also aware of the challenges that I encountered with my mother. She gave me a different perspective of my mother's relationship. She told me that although I was adopted as a young boy and in my mother's eyes was seen as a son, our relationship was actually that of a mother and daughter. Her perspective was that although this wasn't true for all mother-daughter relationships it was true that a lot of daughters were are not close to mothers. In fact many daughters and mothers would have estranged relationships. I took it a step further by saying that a lot of girls become "Daddy's little girl." I was very close to my father and the only regret that I had was not telling him the entire story about me. The relationship between Yaria and I is one that I most definitely cherish.

I also established a good bond between Valerie and myself. I came to know her because we both were former Alltel managers. Due to her professionalism and the manner in which she carried herself I became very impressed with her. I also recently told her about my gender and she informed me that it didn't matter because if people truly cared about me my transition wouldn't make a difference. She definitely accepted me for the woman that I am today.

An important relationship that I must mention is that between my God Family and me. On December 3, 2010 my God Sister, Kimberly, died at age of 46 and I was really saddened by the news. I called my godmother, Mrs. Donaldson, that evening so that I could express condolences and get information regarding the events. She had told me that she heard that I currently lived my life as a woman and that she wanted to express that their family hadn't kicked me out of their life. It was my mother who accomplished that. Upon arriving to Detroit and going to their house I met my God Family in the appearance of Jala for the very first time. They embraced me and Karen, the God Sister whom I had gotten really close to told me that I was pretty, but she still saw a little of "Dave" in me. My entire God Family had always been special to me. Mrs. Donaldson, Kenneth, Kathryn, Karen, and Kimberly have always been great and very influential in my life.

Karen and I had long talks about my relationship with my mother and also about my gender transition. She accepted me but still didn't have a complete understanding, which I thought was normal. After telling her that I was looking to start dating again and that I wanted a heterosexual male, she stated that it may be difficult because many gay guys would be attracted to me because my body had male components. Although I have several gay friends, I am a heterosexual woman and am looking for a heterosexual mate. I further explained the situation and she stated that she understood. I have stayed in contact with my God Family ever since the death of Kimberly. Her death also served as an event that brought me back together with the Donaldson Family.

Throughout my professional career and daily encounters I met several persons of transition and developed friendships. In order to provide a complete story of the transgender world I have provided several interviews in the next few chapters of this section. My goal in interviewing my friends is so the readers could fully appreciate the experiences that we encounter as transgender people. It was my hope to educate my audience because although society is beginning to accept us not everyone understands. Kimball Jane Sargent provides her psychological expertise on the topic.

Transgender Interview
Kimball

In 2004 I began seeing Kimball Jane Sargent (Diverse Solutions; Raleigh, NC) for my Gender Identity Disorder. She has helped me with issues of depression and gender. Kimball has helped me become more confident in the person that I am. One project that she encouraged involved creating a collage for a 5 year plan for where we wanted to be at that time. I have been to a few of Kimball's Holiday functions and have truly appreciated them. She is a true professional that has helped me through my process of transition.

Jala: What are your current qualifications with treating the transgender community? What is your title? How long have you contributed to your profession?

Kimball: I am an individual and family psychotherapist, board certified by the American Nurses Credentialing Center. I received my undergraduate degree from the University of North Carolina at Greensboro in nursing. I then received my masters in public mental health nursing from the University of North Carolina at Chapel Hill. I am also a full member of the World Professional Association of Transgender Health Care and have presented several times at their conferences since 2005. I have worked with the Transgender community since 1997. My studies of transgender care have lead me to Europe four times. I have scrubbed in on gender reassignment surgeries with both a transman and a transwomen. I love working with persons from the transgender community.

Jala: What is the most critical issue that you discovered when treating transgender persons?

Kimball: What I really treat when I work with transgender people is shame and fear.

They have an immense amount of shame and guilt because they are hiding their true identities. They are continuously shape shifting to fit into the people's lives around them and to try and not be discovered. Transgender people continuously live with the fear that those closest to them may abandon them if they learn who they really are. This creates a very lonely life.

Maslow said that we are all working towards self-actualization. All healthy people have a desire to live with integrity. Transgender people know that they are out of integrity and they begin the process of transition and often seek the help of a therapist so that they can overcome their fear and shame. When they come out to the world and start living their true lives, they break free from the shame and fear.

Jala: What is your definition of transgender?

Kimball: Gender is really a web. We all have male and female personality traits, but we have a core identity that for most of us is congruent with our genitals. For transgender people their genitals are not congruent with their core identity. Not all persons who are transgender will make a complete transition. For some, dressing in the clothing that is congruent with their other identity periodically meets their need. Most people who are transgender, however; feel that they need to make a complete medical transition with hormones and surgery to live a congruent life. The individual is the expert on his or her life and they must decide what they need in order to live a complete life. The transgender person's definition of being transgender is what is most important.

Jala: In protecting patient confidentiality please describe your most memorable experience relating to your patients.

Kimball: I had a client from another country that was referred to me by a local physician. This person was living full time in her new gender but did not believe that she would ever have the money to have surgery so she carried a lot of shame related to the incongruence of her body. At our first meeting she told me that she only had small mirrors in her home because she couldn't accept the lower half of her body. This young woman cried when she learned that the surgery could be affordable for her. She didn't have a computer and had no access to the internet, which is where most transgender persons learn about the process of transition. She took on a second job, sold her truck and bought something cheaper and saved as much money as she could for a year. At the end of the year she had the money she needed to have her gender affirming surgery. When she came back to see me after the surgery, she thanked me for giving her a new life. She told me she now had a full length mirror and pride in her body. It is gratifying to help someone feel whole.

Jala: Please describe the process a person of transition must experience in order to complete the person's transition including GRS.

Kimball: Gender transition is individual for each person. The World Professional Association for Transgender Health Care provides the Standards of Care which are a guide for persons who would like to transition. However, transition is unique for each individual. Being transgender is a self-diagnosed issue. Counselors and therapists who are educated in gender transition can be very helpful in guiding people through the process. Helping them find affirming and educated medical providers to help with the medical transition is important. There are individuals who transition without the help of a counselor, but just as going through divorce or other major transitions, using a therapist can make the process much less painful.

If the person sees a therapist, they will help them find their medical team. The person works through whatever issues they feel they need to, comes out to family and friends, comes out to work and begins to live full time in their true gender. After living in their new gender for a year, they need two letters from qualified mental health providers and then they can have their gender affirming surgery.

Jala: I mentioned that different cultures adopt various traditions in helping family members adapt to one's transition. Please share a couple of these traditions with our readers.

Kimball: In the United States we don't have a lot of rituals, but rituals can be very helpful to people when they are going through life transition. One that I recommend to my transgender clients is having a party just before they go full time. Their family and friends come together and they have a bonfire and the clothing of the old gender is burned. The transgender person and their family and friends take turns talking about things that they love about the old life and what they will miss about it. The transgender person then goes in and comes out dressed in the clothing for the new life. The person shares their feeling about their new life and their family shares their hopes for the future. This ritual provides a way for everyone to openly grieve their losses and move on to the new life for the transgender person.

Jala: What activities do you sponsor for the transgender community?

Kimball: I provide support groups for transmen and for transwomen on a monthly basis. I also sponsor a community holiday party once a year for transgender persons and their family to give a safe space for anyone, no matter their stage of transition to come and socialize and feel supported.

Jala: I struggled with my mother's opinion of me going to hell because of my gender transition. Please explain your opinion of religion as it impacts transgender people.

Kimball: Faith is a very important part of many people's lives. I find it incredibly sad when people feel separated from God because they are transgender. I talk with my clients about the God of their understanding, which validates whatever faith belief they have. I tell them that God created them. God knows their heart and he loves them. It is my hope that for those transgender persons whose faith is important to them, that during their transition, they can resolve the wounds that their faith communities may have inflicted on them through the years. I often refer my clients to faith leaders who are supportive of the transgender community so that they can work through these issues if they need more than what I can provide in our counseling sessions.

Jala: What advice would you give transgender people that deal with depression? What would you tell those who kept their gender identity to themselves and were afraid to share with their family and friends?

Kimball: Depression is a common problem for people who are transgender. If the transgender person is struggling with depression, then they definitely need to work with a qualified mental health professional during their transition. They may or may not need medication. Depression often improves as transgender individuals work through their personal issues during transition.

Jala: What advice would you give to family members and close friends of transgender people?

Kimball: It can be very difficult for the family and friends of transgender people to accept their transition. We all make home movies in our lives and we have dreams about the people in our lives and what our relationships will look like in the future. When a person transitions, those around them loose their dreams. They must grieve.

Many years ago I read a letter that a trans women had written about her transition. She said that her family was very supportive when she told them but that she became very sad when she learned that her father cried the night of her surgery because he had lost his son. At the time she was telling this story she said she understood her parents now. She said that when she lived as a male she would go home and lie on the couch and her mom would cook for her and when she got ready to leave her Dad would walk out to the car, pop the hood and they would talk about the engine. She said that now when she goes home her and her mom go shopping and cook together. Whenever she got ready to leave her dad would go out and tell her not to stop at any dirty gas stations to use the rest room, not to stop at any rest areas after dark, and not to let her car drop below half full on the interstate.

She said that trans people need to be patient with their families. You do have to let them grieve and then celebrate the new life.

Jala: Is there a difference between gay, lesbian and transgender? Please explain.

Kimball: Gay and Lesbian are descriptions of sexual orientation. Transgender is a word that describes a person's gender identity. These are two totally independent issues. People who are transgender can be heterosexual, bi sexual, gay or lesbian.

Jala: I mentioned my hormonal tests, psychological exams, pituitary gland results from my MRI and other medical information. In your professional opinion, how does all this tie together in terms to my gender transition?

Kimball: There is testing that can be done, however being transgender is primarily a self-diagnosed condition. People often would like to have a litmus test that would say for sure that they are transgender. I am glad that we don't have a test like this. Even with conditions like arthritis where there are blood tests that are supposed to be definitive, medical professionals know that there are individuals who have all the symptoms, but do not test conclusively. It would be awful for someone's experience to be negated because the blood test or the scan did not conclusively diagnose them as transgender. If a person has questions as to whether they are transgender they should work with a therapist. They will find the answer within themselves.

Jala: Is the topic of transgender innate, learned, or both?

Kimball: In my opinion this is a medical condition and is innate.

Jala: I state in my book that I am afraid that I may not get hired by other companies because of my gender transition. Am I valid in my reasoning? How can I overcome this obstacle?

Kimball: On April 21st, 2012, the Equal Employment Opportunity Commission (EEOC) ruled that transgender and gender non-conforming individuals have protection against harassment or discrimination at work. EEOC announced that Title VII, the Federal Sex Discrimination Law protects employees who are discriminated against because they are transgender. This ruling should help Jala when she is seeking employment and when she obtains her new job.

The other thing that I tell transgender persons is to work on their self-esteem and continuously tell themselves that they are capable and competent and will obtain a great job. Because what people put out into the universe comes back to them.

Jala: My goal is to educate people about transgender people regarding transition. What might you say to both the transgender community and those that are not transgender that would educate society as a whole?

Kimball: Probably the best education for people is to have the opportunity to meet, talk, and have a relationship with someone who is transgender. All of the "ism's" are born of ignorance and fear. When people learn that transgender individuals are just the same as the rest of us, then their fears and negative beliefs end.

Jala: What advice would you give transgender people that want to date? How might they initiate the dating process? Are there venues outside of clubs and chat rooms that the trans community might utilize in order to meet people that may become interested in them?

Kimball: Dating for transgender individuals is the same as for the rest of the population. Finding the right partner is a numbers game. The more people you meet and date the better your chances of finding a life partner. The other piece is that you must believe that you are lovable and that you will find someone to have as a partner.

I encourage people to get out of their homes and engage in activities that they enjoy. It could be going to church, working with political groups, hiking…etc.

If a person has not completed their medical transition, I encourage them to let a potential partner know that they are transgender before their first date. The reason for this is to prevent the potential mate from feeling they have been deceived and putting the person into a potentially dangerous position. Once a person has completed medical transition, there is no need to tell everyone that they are transgender before beginning to date. Let the person get to know you and if you think you want the relationship to go further than just friendship, then share with them.

Jala: What advice would you give that would impact society as a whole in relating to this topic?

Kimball: I see the changes that are occurring between the transgender community and the general society as a civil rights movement. There have been so many positive changes since 1997 when I started working with the community. Things are not where they need to be but things are changing. They will continue to change if transgender people continue to choose to live their lives with respect and if they continue to speak out when injustices occur. People who are transgender have the same desires as all of us, they just have a challenge that most people don't' know.

Jala: In your opinion please describe the impact of pituitary glands in developing one's gender? What impact does X and Y chromosomes play on transgender people?

Kimball: This is probably a more complex question than can be covered here. We know that a persons' chromosomes do not necessarily determine their gender. People with androgen insensitivity syndrome have XY chromosomes but are female bodied and most of the time self identify as female. There are a number of intersex conditions in which the chromosomes do not accurately define the gender of the individual. Therefore the chromosomal make up doesn't really mean much to a transgender person.

Jala: What advice would you give parents that recognize patterns in their children that are opposite of the norm of their gender at birth?

Kimball: Children should be allowed to participate in whatever healthy activities and sports that they choose regardless of the perceived gender of the activity. Allowing children to experiment with different activities helps them learn what activities they enjoy. The activities that a child chooses will not change the child's gender or sexual orientation. If a girl decides that she wants to learn carpentry, it doesn't mean that she will grow up to be a transman or a lesbian. It simply means that this is an activity that she enjoys. Allowing a boy to take part in dance doesn't mean that he will be gay or a transwoman.

If a child tells their parent that their gender and their body don't match, then they need to take that child to a gender specialist. Every child that self identifies as transgender will not grow up to be transgender; however, they need a safe space to explore their feelings. They need support and a space to experiment and figure out what feels most comfortable for them with their gender. Their parents also need education to learn how to best support their children.

Jala: What is your final thought that you would leave with the readers on this subject? What are your strongest message that you would want readers, both trans and non-trans people, to understand? Is there anything that you would add to the interview?

Kimball: The only real problem that transgender people have is those who are not transgender. Trans people know who they are and usually how they would like to live, but they have to live with the fear of losing the people they love, being ridiculed for the change in their lives and struggling with their transition which is usually not paid for by insurance in the United States.

When we plant flower gardens, we include as many different flowers as possible. If we would look at our world and our friends this way it would be so much better. Transgender people just need to be accepted for who they are and allowed the same opportunities that everyone else has.

Transgender Interview
Rachel

Rachel is a young lady that Blythe and I met while visiting a pet supply store. We thought that it was wonderful that Rachel was a strong enough person that she was able to live life according to her gender. She was very professional and carried herself in a very caring manner. Rachel and I shared our commonality of our gender transition. It is a real treat when you meet someone else that is transitioning because people struggle with their internal conflict. Please enjoy her interview because she has a lot of information that would help you understand her struggle. Rachel is a very exciting pre-operative transgender female.

Jala: Please describe your overall experience as a transgendered female.

Rachel: With the decisions that I made I gained more experience. As I became older I became more comfortable and the further the journey the happier I became.

Jala: At what age did you discover that you had a gender conflict? Were you accepting of your conflict or did you try to fight against it?

Rachel: Around the 4th grade… I started looking at boys… I liked boys…and I internalized it.

Jala: Did you have a problem disclosing your identity to others? Please discuss further.

Rachel: I got picked on as a child. I was treated like a girl. I had long hair and I put my hair high on my head in a ponytail to differ from how the boys wore ponytails. I walked and talked like a girl. I also used my hands a lot.

Jala: Were your family members accepting or did you encounter challenges from them?

Rachel: My mother's side had ten brothers and sisters. Three of the girls married preachers and they were very religious. My brother came out when he was 16 years of age and they treated him like shit. Once I made my decision I didn't go around my mother's whole side of the family.

Jala: Are you planning on having gender reassignment surgery? What steps are you taking in your preparation? What obstacles are you facing? Have you chosen a doctor yet? If so where is the location?

Rachel: I would like to. My main problem is financially. I started my transition around the age of 16 with my hair removal. I've done all my psychiatric stuff. Several doctors are willing to sign off on my surgery. I haven't chosen a doctor yet because I want to get my money ready first.

Jala: Do you think that laws will past so the insurance will cover the surgery?

Rachel: I don't think that it will happen in my lifetime but it should.

Jala: Are you having any hesitancy in terms of having your surgery? If so what are your concerns?

Rachel: My concerns are for after having surgery. I wonder how intimacy would change. I also heard that problems with incontinence, holding urine.

Jala: What would you say to those that challenge your transition?

Rachel: Depends on if it was someone I already knew then I would try to explain and educate them. I would try to answer their questions. If it were someone that I didn't know or didn't care about I wouldn't give a shit. Everyone has their own opinion and I can't change opinions to those that I am not close to.

Jala: How do you feel when others use the improper personal noun when describing you?

Rachel: I find it very rude. It is as they are trying to be mean and cruel. It makes me angry.

Jala: What is your most challenging experience when it comes to your gender identity?

Rachel: My hair, it gets on my nerves. I'm obsessed about it. It drives me crazy because I can never get it just right.

Jala: What is your best memory relating to your gender identity?

Rachel: I first started going to the Phoenix Rising in Asheville. It was a Transgender group. It felt natural being around other transgender girls. Everyone supported each other and it was a great thing.

Jala: What would you say to others who struggle with their gender identity?

Rachel: I definitely say find a support group to go to. Be prepared to lose your family in the process. Start new and fresh… work on your hair removal and go from there. Also save money.

Jala: Describe your experience when you first started dating as a transgender female.

Rachel: Well I would go out to gay bars at first because I was doing drag shows prior to my transition. Therefore I found people who liked that. In looking for dates I used a couple websites. I use outpersonal.com and tsdating.com. I believe that when dating transgender girls should be honest and straightforward. Be upfront.

Jala: I'm scared of the pain that anal sex would have during intimacy so I become intimate in other ways. What is your take on intimacy?

Rachel: Get a dildo so that you can get used to sex. It gets the pain out of the way and it works because you can control it.

Jala: In your opinion what is the difference between gay, lesbian, and transgender?

Rachel: In my opinion gay men like gay men; lesbian women like lesbian women. Transgender is not the same area because it's not a sexual thing. It's how transgender people see themselves and how the world sees them.

Jala: Did you face any challenges in the work environment once your employer became aware of your gender?

Rachel: Yes, when I started living as a transgender female I worked in a plywood factory and got harassed everyday by co-workers. There were "redneck" men that harassed me. Managers would tell me that I had to change the way I dressed and acted. I told them that I would go see an attorney. The plant manager told them to leave me alone. I also worked for Bi-Lo for six years. The customers complained about me using the restroom. Every year I had to meet with Human Resources at corporate. I saw this as harassment.

Jala: Did you ever get your name changed?

Rachel: Yes, I had my name legally changed in 2000. It was a very liberating experience.

Jala: What do you feel about same sex marriage?

Rachel: I think that they should definitely be able to get married. The church and state should remain separated. This is a legal issue. Anyone that cared about another person so much and wanted to get married should be allowed.

Jala: Do you have a role model? If so explain the reason for picking the person as your role model?

Rachel: I don't really have a personal role model but I do have certain popular people that I look up to. I look up to Maya Angelou and Oprah. I have collectibles by Marilyn Monroe. The common theme is that each one of these ladies have been through some type of torment in their lives and became stronger through it. This makes me think about life in a more positive way.

Jala: Are you a religious person? If so how do you address those that ostracize you because of your gender?

Rachel: I'm looking for religion. Most religious people don't care about my views. I don't mind it if they aren't paying my bills; then they don't matter.

Jala: If you could leave an impression on those who question your gender what would the impression be?

Rachel: Just that, I guess the impression would be that I stand up for what I believe; I follow through on what I believe; and I am myself no matter what.

Jala: What are your final thoughts on transgender ideas that you feel will help society as a whole?

Rachel: I think that more education is needed on this topic because people see other people as being different and they shouldn't treat the people any different than they want to be treated. The adults should teach their children that people are different. I am talking about family education.

Jala: Do you have any other information to add about the topic?

Rachel: In Houston, Texas there is a transgender organization that helps transgender people with their financial concerns related to transition. They also give moral support. There should be centers that help with transitions in more of a financial way.

Transgender Interview
Cindy

Cindy is a very interesting young lady. She is a post-operative transgender female; she had her surgery when she was 40 years old. She also married a charming gentleman. I had the pleasure of meeting this inspiring person while working at Verizon. She was a customer that had taken notice of me several times while visiting our store. Cindy informed me that although she could tell that I was in transition she didn't think that many other people knew. She told me that I was very passable but she had been around the transgender community for years. She stated that she wanted to help me with my transition process. Please enjoy reading Cindy's interview. My goal was to share the thoughts of a female who was experienced in the process of the gender reassignment surgery.

Jala: Please describe your overall experience as a transgendered female.

Cindy: That question is on so many levels. All of my paperwork is squared away indicating and legalizing me as a female. Once the paperwork was complete I fulfilled my lifetime dream and became married. I married Charles. It was my dream come true. I am now a "Happy girl."

Jala: At what age did you discover that you had a gender conflict? Were you accepting of your conflict or did you try to fight against it?

Cindy: Probably about 10 years old. I never told anybody prior to surgery. I had surgery when I was 40 years old. Prior to surgery and telling people I would just dress up in the bedroom. Two, three years prior to surgery I dressed fulltime.

Jala: Did you have a problem disclosing your identity to others? Please discuss further.

Cindy: No by the time I told anyone I was too old to care what others thought of me. I was about fifty years old before telling people. I went to my mom's funeral in a dress. I shocked a lot of people because they were not aware of my transition.

Jala: Were your family members accepting or did you encounter challenges from them?

Cindy: I have one brother that hasn't spoken to me since the surgery. I also have three brothers who have accepted me.

Jala: Tell me about your experience with you gender reassignment surgery.

Cindy: Leading up to surgery it was life as usual for me. I let people know that I was having the surgery and most people accepted it. Charles and I headed out to Colorado with smiles on our face. A week later I felt like I had been through a hamburger grinder. I looked like I had just gotten out of the hospital from being in a rough car wreck. In terms of the actual surgery I had to prepare by shaving my private. I had to make sure that I was in decent shape because my doctor doesn't like doing surgery for anyone over 200 pounds. I was about 170 pounds. I reported for surgery around 6 am and I came through around 5 p.m. I had the lower surgery and breast augmentation. I was in quite a bit of pain and my body doesn't react to pain pills. My recovery took a few weeks and I had to use dilation.

Jala: Do you have any regrets in terms of having your surgery?

Cindy: There are times but most times I like it. My regret is that I have a deep voice. Sometimes I wish that I hadn't had the surgery but that's few and far between.

Jala: What would you say to those that challenge your transition?

Cindy: I ignore them. They don't deserve my response. I keep going and other people's negative attitudes don't concern me.

Jala: How do you feel when others use the improper personal noun when describing you?

Cindy: It bugged me for a year or two. It doesn't now. I just sort of got used to it.

Jala: What is your most challenging experience when it comes to your gender identity?

Cindy: My most challenging experience was getting my driver's license changed. The employee at the Department of Motor Vehicle office didn't like it. Other than that I have no other problems.

Jala: What is your best memory relating to your gender identity?

Cindy: Getting married.

Jala: What would you say to others who struggle with their gender identity?

Cindy: Be sure of what you are doing before you do it because after you have done it, it's done.

Jala: In your opinion what is the difference between gay, lesbian, and transgender?

Cindy: Transgender is the sex; lesbian and gay are the states of the mind. I'm not saying that gay is by choice but transgender goes to the heart of the soul.

Jala: Did you face any challenges in the work environment once your employer became aware of your gender?

Cindy: No, I have always been my own boss. I had a dump truck company at the time.

Jala: What do you feel about same sex marriage?

Cindy: I don't see anything wrong with it.

Jala: Do you have a role model? If so explain the reason for picking the person as your role model?

Cindy: No, I don't have a role model.

Jala: Are you a religious person? If so how do you address those that ostracize you because of your gender?

Cindy: No, I'm not a religious person. My parents were deceased before my transition.

Jala: If you could leave an impression on those who question your gender what would the impression be?

Cindy: I would give them four knuckles right across the nose. No seriously, if people don't warm up to me I just walk away.

Jala: What are your final thoughts on transgender ideas that you feel will help society as a whole?

Cindy: I would tell other transgender people to be themselves instead of hiding. I would tell non-transgender people that everybody is different and every situation is different.

Jala: Do you have any other information to add about the topic?

Cindy: No, you just about covered every topic.

Transgender Interview
Sila Michaela

My friend, Sila, is a successful screen writer and is a very special person whom I had the pleasure of meeting through The Diverse Solutions organization in Raleigh. I thoroughly enjoyed our interview; this was my first Skype session ever. Sila is a very feminine lady who is also very intelligent. She is one who has faced much criticism from others during her initial transition in the 1990s. Due to society's pressure she returned to living her life as a male; which was very frustrating for her. Therefore she is now living her life as the woman that she is. I very much enjoyed our session and appreciated her mannerisms. Due to previously changing her name and then reverting back to her old name she is now currently working to get her name changed again. However North Carolina Law states that a person can only change their name one time. She is diligently working to fight to change this law with help from various LGBT organizations.

Jala: Please describe your overall experience as a transgendered female.

Sila: It's very positive. It didn't start out like that though. I had issues with people in Wal-Mart. Most people are accepting. My family is starting to come around. My dad refrains from using male pronouns. I rate my experience a 7 ½. My son is interesting and awesome as well. We are seen as a mother and son relationship.

Jala: At what age did you discover that you had a gender conflict? Were you accepting of your conflict or did you try to fight against it?

Sila: At first I fought it and my mom said that I couldn't wear my sister's stockings and other clothing. I started at about 6 ½ or 7. My mom found my sister's clothes in my drawer and she was concerned about family issues. My mother placed our family on a pedestal. Symptoms for dyslexia are the same as gender issue problems because I was born in a male's body but I was a girl.

Jala: Did you have a problem disclosing your identity to others? Please discuss further.

Sila: There are two examples and I couldn't have gotten it done without Kimball's help. She urged me to write letters. I dreaded telling my cast members in the film that I wrote. Anywhere from 70-75% of the cast accepted me. Some continued to call me a "he." I had difficulty telling my family. My mother didn't accept me but my father tried. It was also a challenge letting people know at my work. My immediate supervisors were all right with me but it was their bosses which forced me to resign. I was also afraid of my landlord. I thought that I was going to get kicked out. My son's teachers are fantastic. The Vision Impaired Teacher cried and inspired me.

Jala: Were your family members accepting or did you encounter challenges from them?

Sila: My first transition was from 1995 to 1999. I went back to living as a guy due to the pressure. My hardest thing was telling my ex-spouse. My dad was accepting but he used the wrong pronoun. My mom wasn't accepting during my first transition. I think that she knew all along but didn't want to accept it. I handled it better the second time. I had letters to explain. This time period is better than how it was in the 1990s.

Jala: Tell me about your plans for gender reassignment surgery.

Sila: I plan on having it as soon as I get the money. I'm going to either Pittsburgh or Brazil. I'm sure in the next couple years that I will be having surgery. A friend works at Food Lion and I was told that their insurance will pay for the GRS and the after care.

Jala: Do you think that laws will past so the insurance companies will eventually cover the surgery?

Sila: Not in another 10 years…I could be wrong…knock on wood… when Obama gets re-elected he will approve "Same Sex Marriage" and pass other measures. Then Hillary will get in and will support it. I believe that Hillary will finish what Obama started and will be good for the transgender community.

Jala: What would you say to those that challenge your transition?

Sila: Get out the way or I'm going to knock you out…I hate it for you but I am going to keep being me.

Jala: How do you feel when others use the improper personal noun when describing you?

Sila: I feel like they are blind because they don't see. They are stubborn and they don't want to change. It was like in Wal-Mart when they referred to me as he. It was embarrassing. The customer service rep and the customer service manager frowned upon me. They kept calling me a "He" but when I mentioned a person in my film they started perking up and then stated that they don't tolerate discrimination. I decided to call corporate and asked them how I know that I won't be harassed by Wal-Mart in the future. They told me that I can be sure that I will not be harassed by that Wal-Mart again.

Jala: What is your most challenging experience when it comes to your gender identity?

Sila: My hair is a big issue. The hair that I wore in 2009 was a wig. I began using Rogaine because it has a better percentage of working. A lady told me that Rogaine is good. I buy my hormones online.

Jala: What is your best memory relating to your gender identity?

Sila: There are so many. I enjoyed when my son's other mom read me an email that she told him to listen to Michaela. She was mentioning me as a she.

Jala: What would you say to others who struggle with their gender identity?

Sila: As Winston Churchill says, "Don't ever give up." I say don't ever go backwards; I did and shouldn't had. You can't cure this with a pill. I definitely say don't put yourself at the end of a gun.

Jala: Describe your experience when you first started dating as a transgender female.

Sila: Oh God. I hadn't had that experience yet. There was a guy and we went to Austin, Texas where there were a lot of trans people… probably the only Texas City that accepts transgender people.

Jala: Anal intercourse during intimacy could be painful so I become intimate in other ways. What is your take on intimacy?

Sila: I've never had it so I don't know. I have had to authenticate it. I have had toys.

Jala: In your opinion what is the difference between gay, lesbian, and transgender?

Sila: I think that if I am with a male and I am as a female then I am a heterosexual. If I was attracted to other females then I would be a lesbian.
Jala: Did you face any challenges in the work environment once your employer became aware of your gender?

Sila: There were some issues. I went to the Department of Public Instruction and on the first time I used the female restroom. The next time I went there a sign was posted that read, "For Real Women Only." I'm sure that they knew about me in the office and this was just awful. My immediate supervisors were great. Some people from the Office of Migrant Education came and were talking to me and all of a sudden the department heads were scrambling to break up the meeting.

Jala: What do you feel about same sex marriage?

Sila: I'm all for it and it's the greatest thing in the world. I think that if two people of the same sex or gender who love each other should be able to get married.

Jala: Do you have a role model? If so explain the reason for picking the person as your role model?

Sila: Oh goodness…well… that's a very good question. I would probably say I don't have any transgender role models; but probably Bruce Springsteen and Reggie Robins. Whenever I feel down I will put on Bruce Springsteen's music. The words of his music always spoke to me and were encouraging and related to me. I love the words to one of his songs, "I was working on a dream." That relates to me because I am working on my dream. I like Reggie Robins because he is a self-help guru.

Jala: Are you a religious person? If so how do you address those that ostracize you because of your gender?

Sila: Well, I kind of go up and down. I grew up Catholic. It hurts when I hear the Pope express his opinions; he just doesn't get it. I go to church that is more accepting of me; but I have become an atheist because I didn't feel that God was there for me.

Jala: If you could leave an impression on those who question your gender what would the impression be?

Sila: I would say the impression is that I am a lady and I allow people to be who they are. You can feel the way you do about me; but you got to love me because I love you. You should look at me at a diligent woman like my mom. Everyone deserves equal protection under the law. I am a southern cat.
Jala: What are your final thoughts on transgender ideas that you feel will help society as a whole?

Sila: We are doctors; lawyers; mothers and dads; and we are parents. We have hearts and we bleed red blood just like everyone else. We believe in the Golden Rule and we aren't very much different from other people. I am trying to catch up with myself for who I am. We aren't perverts or commit pedophile crimes; we aren't child molesters. We are not criminals.

Jala: Do you have any other information to add about the topic?

Sila: Well there are some laws like gender marker laws that are so difficult to change. In Greece it's easy to get markers changed if people wear women's clothes. The American Medical Association says that it's a Medical Condition. They recommend that the insurance companies pay for the surgery because it's necessary and it's not domestic.

Jala Answers Her Own Survey

The purpose in answering the survey listed below is so that the readers can get a full specific on the issues that I faced. In the earlier reading I shared my transition experience and my hope is that after you have read the survey below you could understand my thought process. As the earlier reading indicates I have not had the gender reassignment surgery but do plan on my completion once I become healthier.

Please describe your overall experience as a transgendered female.

Jala: My overall experience has been heart-filling. My focus has been on overcoming my depression due to my internal conflict with my gender transition. I have tried to educate many people about the topic because a lot of people don't really understand what it means to transition to a gender different than what one was physically born with. There are many obstacles.

At what age did you discover that you had a gender conflict? Were you accepting of your conflict or did you try to fight against it?

Jala: I actually discovered that I had a gender issue during my middle school years. I was about 10 or 11 years of age. I tried to fight it by participating in sports; joining the Marine Corps; pledging a fraternity; and getting married.

Did you have a problem disclosing your identity to others? Please discuss further.

Jala: Yes I had a problem disclosing my identity to others for fear of losing relationships with friends and family members. I had been in many fights due to being biracial and I was afraid that I would get beat up if I disclosed my information to the wrong person.

Were your family members accepting or did you encounter challenges from them?

Jala: My brother has always supported me with the occurrences of life in general. My sister-in -law, Gina, also is very supportive and we are very close.

My logic is that she is very understanding because of her medical profession. My mother on the other hand, struggled with my transition and therefore kicked me out of her life. My son also struggles with my transition and is not as close to me as I would like.

Tell me about your plans for gender reassignment surgery.

Jala: I have to get well physically first. Then I plan on contacting a surgeon in Canada. I originally contacted his office a few years ago. I will continue my psychological counseling and will continue my hormone therapy.

Do you think that laws will past so the insurance will cover the surgery?

Jala: Yes, I think that laws will eventually pass where insurance coverage will include gender reassignment surgery. In my opinion it was amazing for our President to support same sex marriages. I think that was a monumental step towards GRS.

What would you say to those that challenge your transition?

Jala: I say that critics of transgender individuals should educate themselves. Transgender people are different but are still people. We carry many mental burdens due to trying to be acceptable by society. It was so bad that I once was suicidal.

How do you feel when others use the improper personal noun when describing you?

Jala: It hurts really badly. I equate the improper use of personal nouns as someone continually punching me in the stomach. The sound of it is worse than the scrape against a chalkboard.

What is your most challenging experience when it comes to your gender identity?

Jala: Two things come to mind. The first thing is educating society towards things that transgender people experience. The second thing is getting my driver's license marker switched to female.

What is your best memory relating to your gender identity?

Jala: My very first makeover at the Belk's store in Raleigh. I actually called the store ahead of time and told the salesperson that I was a transgender female. She was very comforting and accepted me for the person that I was. She treated me so gentle and didn't mind me being a transgender female. She treated me like a girl should be treated and I looked so pretty when she was done.

What would you say to others who struggle with their gender identity?

Jala: Be true to thy own self. Major depression is not worth fighting your internal conflict. There are many understanding people in society who genuinely care and support transgender people.

Describe your experience when you first started dating as a transgender female.

Jala: I started hanging out at the Spektrum in Fayetteville because I wanted to watch the drag shows. The guys would holler at me as I left the club. I craved the attention and loved it. I dated a few military men, police officers, and a sports agent. I humbly say that as I look back on these experiences I could have carried myself in a better manner.

Anal intercourse during intimacy could be painful so I become intimate in other ways. What is your take on intimacy?

Jala: Yes, I don't like pain. Therefore I found other ways to please the various men that I dated. In pleasing them I got my satisfaction.

In your opinion what is the difference between gay, lesbian, and transgender?

Jala: Gays and lesbians are in relationships between two men or women. Transgender is where a person transitions into the proper gender. I view transgender people in the same manner that I see hermaphrodites; but instead of having two different sex organs a transgender person's mind is different from the body.

Did you face any challenges in the work environment once your employer became aware of your gender?

Jala: Upon addressing the Alltel staff in Lumberton I was supported by management, human resources, and the sales staff. My only challenge was when I worked in the Sales Action Center. Due to my voice some of my customers would refer to me in a masculine manner.

What do you feel about same sex marriage?

Jala: I believe that if two people love each other enough to want to get married then it should be allowed. Marriage should be a bond between two people who love each other.

Do you think that laws will ever pass so that the insurance companies will cover gender reassignment surgery?

Jala: Yes, I do. It was a big step for the President to endorse same sex marriage and I think that will lead to changes in insurance where GRS will be covered.

Do you have a role model? If so explain the reason for picking the person as your role model?

Jala: My brother, Derrick, is my role model for life because of his many successes. I read and become inspired about transgender people that face challenges. For example I have been inspired by the following people: The high school Homecoming Queen in Florida, Miss Singapore and her mission to become Miss Universe, and the girl who revealed her gender after coming back from war.

Are you a religious person? If so how do you address those that ostracize you because of your gender?

Jala: Yes, I am a very religious person. I love God. One hurdle during my depression included the so called Christians who rejected me. The pastor of my mother's church shared with me that if I was committing a sin, which he wasn't sure, my sin would be thrown in the Sea of Forgetfulness. Although I don't feel that my gender is a sin because of medical reasons if I was committing a sin then I surely believe in Grace. Jesus paid the ultimate price so that our sins would be forgiven.

If you could leave an impression on those who question your gender what would the impression be?

Jala: My impression would be for those individuals to become educated so that they can open their minds to the transgender community. Transgender people are human too.

What are your final thoughts on transgender ideas that you feel will help society as a whole?

Jala: Just educate yourselves to the challenges that transgender people face. Help them instead of placing pain on them and become more acceptable of them. People are different from one another.

Do you have any other information to add about the topic?

Jala: The information not contained in this survey should be covered in my book. I hope that this survey and the previous interviews will shed light on my readers.

Bringing It All Together
Gender Transition

Gender transition is a difficult topic to understand. As society advances more people are becoming more accepting of the transgender community; however people will become more educated towards the topic as further information is provided. People are more sophisticated regarding transgender people than they were 20 or 30 years ago. Without having a full understanding some people still refer to people that are born a different gender than at birth as "freaks." I am here to tell you that Gender Identity Disorder does not make an individual a "freak."

My opinion is that in order for society to accept the transgender community people have to be able to understand them. Further information has to be provided so that people can become more educated on the topic. Although it is true that there are some people that are closed minded, I do not believe that everyone is unwilling to open their minds to the issue. Many people have crossed my path and have shown that they support me although they don't really understand me. My goal with interacting with people is to invite them to ask me questions so that I can inform them about me and therefore they will become more familiar with me. I tolerate people who want to find more out about my gender transition more than I tolerate people that take ignorant actions towards me and disrespect me. Education is a key to helping society accept people that are different.

Several people come to mind as I take notice of the advancement that society has come in reference to accepting people that are transitioning in gender. While exploring my Android phone I decided to download an application that discussed transgender news. I read several interesting topics that I will share in my book. I was elated when I read about the high school girl that was transitioning and had gained enough support from her friends so that she became the Homecoming Queen. The blogs about this occurrence was mixed. There was much support for this student; however I still read comments from people that lacked education on this topic. It moved me so much that I decided to post my comments in support of this young lady. Another article that I read involved a young lady who got beat up because she was using the female's facilities in a restaurant. I felt that this was a very ignorant thing due to the harm that this transitioned woman received because of her being transgender. Another example of my reading included an article on "Chaz." The article discussed his transition to male. I found this unique because from a woman's view I was more aware of transgender women than I was of men that transitioned. Although I supported "Chaz" I also had to become further educated so that I could understand what the thoughts that men who transitioned dealt with. I was enlightened to discover that the topic was bigger than me and that I wasn't the only one dealing with a gender identity issue. I reflected a few years previous on reading a book about a person that was transitioning to male.

Not only are there many articles relating to transgender people, there are also several current events that have been aired on the television. One situation that I became overjoyed with involved The Miss Universe Pageant. A young lady, Miss Singapore, had successfully completed gender reassignment surgery and won her battle of being allowed the opportunity to compete in the Miss Universe Pageant. There was also a recent news segment about a person who was in the military and served in Iraq. She made her gender known once she returned from overseas. These events encouraged me because I could definitely see that society was becoming more educated and accepting of transgender people.

In my quest to get my readers to understand the information regarding the transgender community I focus on the medical factors that a person has experienced. Medical factors would include both the physical and the psychological. As I mentioned earlier in this section people are different in a variety of ways. In order to make this world a better place I challenge you to become more understanding of the difficulties that we as transgender people encounter. An example of some of my fears included me not being able to gain employment due to me being a transgender female. Although I have a college education, many experiences, and a pattern of success I still feel that due to the unwillingness to accept transgender people there are many employers who are unwilling to hire me. I remind you that my medical history provides both mental and physical testimony of me being of the female persuasion.

Transgender people go through many obstacles as a result of being different. Although society has gotten better there are still people that ridicule us. In completing our transition we face challenges of being accepted by our families and the communities in which we live. In order to be considered for reassignment surgery we are required to live as our desired gender. In living as our preferred gender we often question whether we are going to be passable and accepted by others or if we are going to face harassment by people that don't truly understand us. We also live with the fear of facing obstacles in completing our surgery. For example, some of us are afraid that we will never be able to save enough money to cover our surgery. In order to be able to have the surgery due to medical risks many transgender people have to overcome health concerns. Some people in their transition lose the support of family and friends due to their desire to have the surgery. There are many people that are critical of the transgender community and say "God created people as male or female." While I believe this there are many people born with a different gender than what their physical appearance reflects. There are different people born with both sex organs. God has created us all as unique individuals and I believe that each person, however their differences, are made to complete our society. As I heard one of my friends say, "Each person is like a puzzle piece and when properly fit into the puzzle of society we all benefit."

Overall, it was my goal in writing this section to further educate society on the transgender society. In my mission I wanted to share my transition with you so that you could understand what I went through during my transition. I also wanted to share interviews of other transgender females. This purpose was to grant my readers the understanding of what other transgender people faced. In interviewing the medical professional such as Kimball Jane Sargent I had hoped to have the medical condition further explained so that the readers would become more educated.

In leaving you with this discussion I ask that my audience become more willing to learn about gender transition and that you continue to become open minded because people are different. I hope that this section was informative and allowed my readers the willingness to discover more about gender transition. I hope that the next time that a person encounters a person of transition that the person does not rush to judge the transgender individual but I hope that the person opens both the person's heart and mind towards the gender identity. As we focus towards the final topic of this book, on my adoption and finding my biological family, I hope that you continue to enjoy my story.

Jala McKenzie
October 2003
Fayetteville, NC

Jala McKenzie
October 2003
Fayetteville, NC

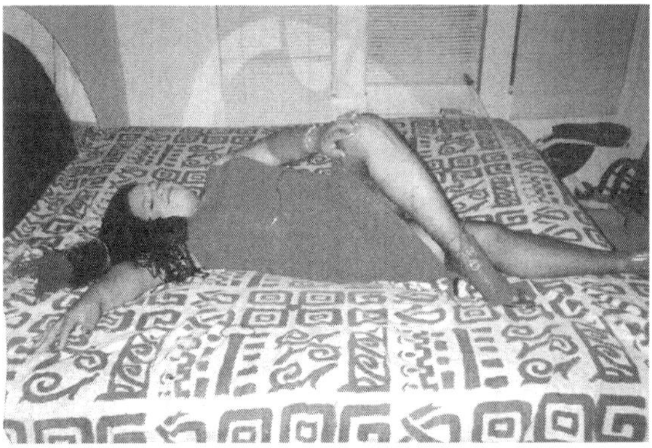

Jala McKenzie
October 2003
Fayetteville, NC

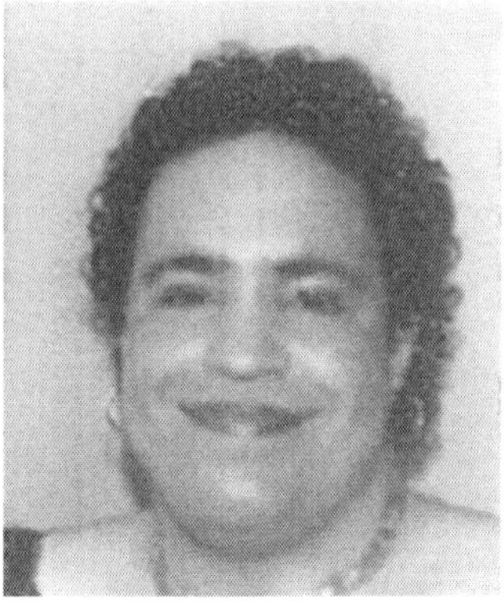

Jala McKenzie
February 3, 2004
Venice, FL

Jala Wine Tasting
April 2011
Napa Valley

Jala McKenzie
July 2012
Charlotte, NC

Jala McKenzie
July 2012
Charlotte, NC

Jala McKenzie
July 2012
Charlotte, NC

SECTION 5

ADOPTION and FINDING MY BIOLOGICAL FAMILY

Howard and Willa Burns

Announce the Adoption

cf their Son

DAVE BERNARD

Born: Nov. 11, 1965 *Arrived: Mar. 24, 1972*

History of Adoption

In trying to understand adoption I traced the history back to Roman times when abandoned children were picked up as slaves. These children were raised in a situation that closely resembled guardianship. Adoption is the parenting of young children where their rights and responsibilities are shifted from one set of parents to the new set of parents. The process of adoption has many influences on everyone involved.

There are many reasons that a child may be placed up for adoption. One result of a survey conducted by the U.S. Department of Health and Human Services showed that between 70 and 90 percent adopted children because they elected to give a child a well needed home. The variance in this survey was due to the multiple types of adoption. Children are placed for adoption for several reasons which could be deemed voluntary or involuntary. Some children are born in under developed countries and therefore become adopted by parents that wish to give them a better environment. Some women want to adopt due to infertility. Relatives may adopt children whenever their relatives are at risk of losing a child. Women that have been raped could give a child up for adoption because of the mental strain that the woman suffers from the crime. It was very possible that racial concerns were a reason that I was given up for adoption in 1965. My siblings were forcefully taken by the State of Georgia and were then placed for adoption.

Studies show that adults adopt children for various reasons. Adults may just have a genuine love for kids and therefore invite them into their families. There are times when a family has multiple children of the same gender and want to have both male and female children. Some families that only have one child may consider adoption instead of giving birth to additional children. People that are not in relationships may decide to adopt children. Some people are too involved with their careers and don't want the experience of pregnancy. Some families decide to adopt older children because they do not want to deal with the steps needed to care for infants. As I grew older I found out that I was adopted by the Burns' family because they wanted my brother to have another child to grow with.

Although many people adopt children with good reason, there are impacts on the child being adopted, the biological family, and the adopted family. Often times people value adoption as parents contributing to society; which is definitely true. People, however, don't see the impact that an adoption may cause as the overall picture develops. Often times adoption produces wonderful results for the adopted child. While other times the adoption becomes a strain for those involved.

Adopted children are negatively impacted in several manners. For example, I have struggled with issues of abandonment, trust, rejection, and anger. While growing up many other children would tell me that I was adopted because my mother didn't want me. Therefore I felt different from the other kids because I felt rejected. Many adults tried to redirect my thinking by telling me that I should feel special because a family decided to adopt me. Throughout my life, I have had issues of trust. Through my experiences of my adoption and in going to different foster families I developed trust issues. These issues often surfaced during my career. I would often think that my career was stagnant because my boss didn't like me and therefore I couldn't trust my superiors in terms of my career development. I have had difficulty handling rejection. Although it appeared that my father's favorite answer to me was "no," his instruction did me well as he was very influential in my end result. There are others that have answered me in the negative and I often engaged in debates. During my time at BellSouth Mobility I interviewed multiple times in order to be promoted to manager. The rejections that I received hurt very bad and I think I was impacted more than normal due to rejection issues that were deeply rooted in me due to me being left for adoption. In the end, I became a better sales person, in my current profession, due to my capabilities to overcome obstacles and the challenges that I face when my customers answer me in the negative. As a result of abandonment, trust, and rejection issues I have amassed much anger and experienced more than ten years of depression. As a result, I have strained many relationships because of actions taken in anger. Derrick has often told me, "You are in control of things…things should not control you and make you mad." He is absolutely correct and therefore I focus on the things that I can control.

Not only does the adopted child develop unhealthy issues there is also an impression left on the biological family. Although my biological mother gave birth to me while in a mental institution, it is my humble opinion that she had every right to be depressed afterwards due to giving five of her children up for adoption. Four of my siblings were involuntarily taken from my mother. Emotions including anger, humility, pain, distrust, and others accumulated due to her loss of five of her kids. Society may not understand the difficulty that a mother faces when she has to give up her children. My mother not only gave up one child, she gave up five and from what I was told she would have lost her sixth child if she hadn't moved from Georgia when she did. Imagine the mental strain that developed over her lifetime from losing the children that she gave birth to. My sister, Patricia, became very angry because as she grew older she found out that the adoptions could have been avoided and was hurt because she was left wondering about her siblings. Other family members were also affected by the loss of the children given up for adoption.

The adopted family also develops certain experiences through the development of relationships with the adopted child. Although I didn't feel very close to Derrick, as a child, as we grew older we have become very close. The normal sibling rivalries occurred between Derrick and me but I always felt inferior to him. I love my brother very much and if anything was to ever happen to him I would be devastated. As a child, though, I always felt worthless because I couldn't compete with him in terms of grades or anything else expected by society. My mother appeared to gain much frustration because she held high expectations for her children and I would often fall short of them. I remember that during my high school days she would often tell me that she was going to put me in a "Boys Home." I remember seeing the "Monroe Boys Home" pamphlet that was left on our dining room table. My godmother would later tell me that she would often engage in disagreements by telling my mother that she couldn't treat me like she treated Derrick because I was different. I was described as a "Special Needs" child that needed extra attention in my development. Derrick was adopted straight out of the hospital and I was 6-years-old when my adoption was completed. During the first five years of my life I had been passed through several foster families. During these early years my personality had already began to take form. Derrick, on the other hand, was privileged to have our parents shape him from his very beginning. Our father and I developed a very close relationship and I think it was formed somewhat due to his countering the negative relationship between my mother and me. Our father was a very special and caring man. I remember my last visitation when I drew very close to Mr. Burns and at that point I felt that I wanted to be a part of his family. He would often describe my struggles with my mother as her nervousness regarding me. I didn't realize exactly what that meant until after my mother's death. Derrick told me that he discovered my mother's tapes where she was speaking about the anxiety that I gave her due to the decisions that I made. Our Aunt Mae was like a grandmother and she raised her two sisters to become wonderful assets for their communities. I would often ask Aunt Mae if I could spend weekends with her due to being unhappy with my mother. Aunt Mae died during my freshman year of high school and I felt like I was once again abandoned. Other family members and close friends were instrumental in my upbringing.

The question that must be answered in the end is, "Did the adoptee end up better or worse as a result of being raised by the adopted family?" Although I have much respect for my biological mother and as I grow older I understand the events that forced my adoption, I strongly feel that I was better off being adopted into the Burns' family. Due to the values instilled by my parents I became an educated Christian person who is successful in my own way. I have been blessed to have been raised as part of my adopted family. There are many other people that ended up on the opposite end of the spectrum and did not achieve the same successes that I have.

Time Spent with My Biological Family

My childhood memories serve that my adopted mother would inform me several times that my biological family was trying to reconnect with me, but I was reminded that I was not mature enough to handle the reconnection. In 1989, I set out to find my biological family and as a result only received non-identifying information of my biological mother and father. I also received my medical information. My mother was described as a deeply depressed Caucasian woman that had a 3rd grade education level with a very low IQ. My father was described as an affluent African-American male that was well dressed. I was saddened to find out that both of my parents were institutionalized during my conception.

On March 24, 1972, I was blessed to be adopted by the family that I became a part of. My mother was a school teacher; my father successfully retired from the U.S. Government; and my brother received his bachelor's degree from Princeton University and went on to become vice president of three different companies. My surroundings were good, however I dealt with issues of depression, anger, abandonment, and trust. For fear of being ostracized and fear of getting beat up I kept my gender identity to myself. It appeared to me that my mother had expectations that placed her family above others. I felt as though I could never meet her lofty expectations. Therefore I felt as though I was a failure. As mentioned in the first section of this book, I often acted out in class in my quest to gain attention and be liked by others. Therefore I sacrificed some of the things that would have made me more successful because of me not giving 100% of my focus on my school lessons. I did not, however, understand what success was for me until I actually spoke with Gina, whom I deemed as a mother-figure. She told me that although I felt like a failure in comparison to Derrick, I was actually more successful in my specialty of sales whereas he may have been superior in other things like electrical engineering and computer science. I always felt that if I did not achieve a level of success such as being a company CEO I would have been a failure in my mother's eyes. This was my understanding of my mother's expectations. Therefore my goal was to become a regional vice president for Alltel Communications and that dream ended when Verizon purchased Alltel. In the end, though, I had it better than many children whom were raised by adopted families. I could have actually been worse off than I thought I was.

In July 2003, while my mother was expressing her disapproval of my gender transition she advised me to find my biological family and that I needed to end our relationship. While my mother was kicking me out of her life she was also giving me a gift which led to the reconnection of me and my biological family. She gave me the telephone number to a person at the adoption agency who had been trying to bring my biological family and I back together. On that July afternoon I nervously called the adoption agency and spoke to a lady that had information about the whereabouts of my mother Carla and my sister Patricia. After I received the phone number to my mother I felt a chill travel through my spine. I remember that I hesitated before calling the number that the woman from the adoption agency gave me. I did not have a clue of what to expect for the phone call that I was about to make.

Once I worked up enough nerve to call the number that I was given I anxiously began to tap the numbers on the phone's keypad. I remember trembling and recall how my fingers were shaking and the fact that I incorrectly dialed the number on two occasions. The first time I dialed I forgot to press the "1" key and the second time I actually transposed a digit. As soon I dialed the correct number I heard a woman's voice on the other end of the phone and I spoke very apprehensively to my mother for the very first time. Neither she nor I could speak clearly due to the emotions that we both had for this reunification. We both cried throughout the entire call and we only could tell each other how we loved and missed each other. I had always yearned for my mother's affection and always wanted to be part of her life. I didn't have a clue of what she was like; I only wanted to know my mother. I remembered the non-identifying information but I continued to say that it wasn't factual. After our attempted first conversation my mother told me that she was going to contact Patricia and have her contact me. Once my mother and I ended our phone conversation I took part in my daily routine of my walking exercise. I visibly remember walking with two of Blythe's friends and telling them about my experience and I kept crying while trying to inform them.

After my walk I showered and refreshed myself. As I was reapplying my makeup my phone rang and excitement once again ran through my veins. Once I answered the phone I discovered that the person on the other end of the phone had a very youthful and exciting voice. That person was my sister Patricia. She and I spoke for a while before she placed a conference call for our mother. We conversed on the phone for a while and then decided that Patty and I would talk later that night. During our second phone conversation I advised Patty that I was transitioning into the female that I had become and that I wasn't completely sure how our mother would accept the situation. Patricia told me that all they wanted was to reunite with me and that it probably would not be an issue.

After we became acquainted with each other we then planned to meet. The plans were for me to fly to Tampa, Florida within the next few days. My sister lived in Venice and my mother lived in St. Petersburg. We all agreed to stay at Patricia's house for our reunion. As soon as our conversation ended I called several airlines to get the cheapest air flight and I scheduled a flight for the following Sunday morning. During my flight I was a ball of nerves because I didn't know exactly what to expect once I was to arrive at the airport. I kept thinking, "What if this was some type of hoax and no one showed at the airport to pick me up." Well, once I got to the airport I found that no one was really at the airport to pick me up, so I became even more unsettled. I reached in my pocket and pulled out my cell phone so that I could try and get a hold of Patricia. She relieved my tensions by answering the phone and directing me to where she and our mother would pick me up. Then I thought that they wouldn't know what I looked like so I would make a sign on a piece of paper so I could easily be spotted. As I saw a long white 1989 Lincoln Town car pull curbside I saw two of the brightest smiles that I had ever seen. It was Mom and Patricia. Therefore July 13, 2003 was one of the happiest days of my life. I met my biological mother and sister. Before I knew it, all three of us were grouped together in one big hug. Patricia looked at the sign that I was carrying and laughed and stated that I didn't need the sign because they knew exactly how I looked. I was a very close resemblance of our maternal grandfather. Once our gathering ended we all climbed into Patricia's town car and headed to a restaurant for brunch. We participated in small talk while we ate. Then we headed to St. Petersburg to pick up Patty's dad so we could go to Venice. The drive was very scenic as we travelled along the ocean and over the huge Sky Way Bridge. The drive lasted for the better part of an hour.

Once we arrived at Patty's house I was introduced to her husband and kids. Up until this point, the only blood relative that I had was my son. Wow. This was very exciting. As we took part in activities for that evening we participated in discussion, viewed pictures, and played Spades. I discovered that I had a whole host of family members. I had a mother, two sisters, three brothers, and a whole host of nieces and nephews. Two important people missing from our family were our brothers Art and Randy. The evening was full of love as everyone was thrilled to be part of each other's lives. This exhilarating experience was one that I would cherish for a long time. I resembled many of the pictures that were in the photo albums that I explored. My visit lasted for the next couple of days and I returned to Fayetteville on Tuesday, July 15th.

My trip back home was very relaxing and my mind was filled with thoughts of how wonderful it would be for me to live my life as a piece of the magical puzzle that would bring our family all together as one. I had taken many pictures and videos. This was a true characteristic of the Burns' family. While I was being raised my adopted family would take many pictures. Once back in North Carolina I would show everyone my pictures. At this point many people informed me that I had a book to write because many people would be inspired about our story.

Upon my return to work I shared my story with nearly 800 of the employees at the Cingular Wireless Call Center in Fayetteville. I shared my recent experience with Blythe and her friends and everyone was excited for me.

Patty and I would talk during the night time hours on many days and decided that she would ask her husband if I could stay with them until I found an apartment. He agreed and then I decided to move to Florida so that I could be with my family. Cingular didn't have any Call Center positions available in Florida and my Call Center Director, the same one that appeared to block my advancement a few years prior, stated that we had a shortage of managers and wasn't supporting my request for a Personal Leave. Therefore I placed a two week notice and left Cingular on August 8, 2003.

I had arranged for one of Blythe's friends to move into my condominium as a precaution in case things didn't work out and I had to move back to North Carolina. The girl was supposed to pay rent and handle the ongoing utilities just like she would have done if the condominium was in her name. If I needed to move back to my place I would have been allowed the opportunity because it was still my home.

The next week I made that 13 hour drive back to Venice and decided to leave my belongings in North Carolina in case things didn't work out. I ended up staying at my sister's house for a week before I went back to Fayetteville to make sure that everything was being handled. It rained the entire week that I was in Venice; like folks say "It rained cats and dogs." Things appeared to be working okay in Florida so I began my job search. I had a few interviews in the Venice area before I went back to Fayetteville.

Upon my return to Fayetteville I found out that my rent hadn't been paid and that other business matters were not handled as they were supposed to have been. Therefore I was very hesitant in leaving my apartment and my return to Fayetteville lasted more than the week that I planned. I continued to apply for jobs both in Fayetteville and in Florida. In October I received a call from Alltel Communications and scheduled a telephone interview. The store manager was so impressed that she scheduled an in person interview for the next day. I drove back to Florida and prepared myself for the interview. After the interview I was informed that the regional store manager and the regional vice president wanted to interview me the next day. Everything went well with the interview and I was notified that Alltel was beginning their background investigation and that if everything checked out that I would begin my employment within the next 10 days. After passing the drug screen and background check I reported to work for Alltel on November 10, 2003. I spent a couple weeks completing the "in store training" and then I was sent to Tampa so that I could complete systems training.

The cost of living was very expensive in Florida and I found difficulty in getting an apartment for what I deemed a reasonable cost. Within the first month of my employment with Alltel, Patricia's father had suffered a heart attack and was hospitalized with a five-way bypass heart surgery. The entire family was in a panic due to our fear of whether he would make it through. After he spent time in the hospital things started changing for the better and he was able to go home. My mother and I started spending time with each other and I found that certain things were becoming too much for me. I struggled with her chewing tobacco and spitting into a jar and I thought that it was nasty and didn't like when she did it. My mother's depression was very apparent because it seemed as though every other word out of her mouth was a negative statement or a foul word. While living at Patty's house I had the opportunity to meet my brother, Reggie in person and my sister, Karen via telephone. Reggie took the bus down from Georgia and upon meeting him I thought that he was a very attractive man. Although this is somewhat conceded I thought that he was a spitting image of me and I thought, "Damn he is fine as hell." My brother-in-law was a very hard working man and spent a lot of his time off working in his garage or yard. I, on the other hand, didn't feel well and spent most of my time off laying in bed. I was still experiencing issues from my depression. In February 2004, I was informed that I had a week to find an apartment because it was time for me to move out of my sister's house. I didn't have anywhere to go, so I ended up staying in a hotel in Bradenton.

I gained a valuable education while living with Patricia. This experience was different from what I was accustomed to. My background included being indoctrinated into an African-American society; however I experienced the Caucasian way of life while living with my sister. For example, instead of us watching the BET Music Awards the family watched the Country Music Awards. We spent time together listening to each other's style of music. I found myself watching television shows different from what I had previously watched. Even though things seemed different we had a lot of common behaviors. Patricia and I had similar values in terms of education and Christianity.

While living in the hotel I decided that I wanted to hang out and still have fun. I went to a couple clubs but found that hanging at a club alone wasn't the same as clubbing with friends. Therefore I found that I didn't make the most out of my clubbing experience. I also decided to hang out at the Comedy Zone. So I dressed up in what I thought was a fine dress and knew that I had it going on. When I arrived at the Comedy Zone I was greeted by an usher and was asked if I wanted to sit up front at the corner of the bar. After being warned that the comedians normally picked on people sitting in those seats I agreed anyway. I thought that I was there to have fun and that comedians joke without trying to harm others. The show was great. It started out at a high peak of laughter and continued with the festive crowd in an uproar with laughter. Then suddenly, the star of the show, BET's very own Monique came on stage and lit right into me. As she greeted the audience, she unexpectedly stopped and looked directly at me and her jokes began mounting. In my early stages of my gender transition I wasn't very passable and Monique made it known. After pausing with her jokes with the audience, she looked at me and said, "What the fuck?" Everyone broke into laughter. I even laughed. She started talking about my dress and asked me if I thought that I was from the Flintstone Age. After telling more jokes she started telling the audience about performing oral sex and telling the crowd how to please a man. She paused and looked at me and said, "Bitch I'm talking to you too." Again everyone broke into laughter. I had been forewarned about the possibility of me getting picked on because of my seat location and Monique had her way. I took the jokes all in stride and had a night of fun.

After lodging in the hotel for a few weeks I had been informed that my store manager was going to try to help me relocate to North Carolina. The manager stated that she thought that I was good for the company and instead of losing me altogether she wanted to help me transfer back to North Carolina. Therefore I applied for a position in Lumberton and after successfully interviewing I moved back to Fayetteville. The girl that I allowed to move into my condominium decided not to pay the rent and therefore I was being evicted. After speaking with the owner he agreed to let me live in a small efficiency and told me that if I made good on my rent he would work something out so that my credit report would not be negatively impacted. After my return to North Carolina I continued to speak with Patricia, Karen, and Reggie by telephone. We spoke often for the next year or so and for some unknown reason we stopped communicating. I think that it was too much for me because I was really suffering from my depression. I also think that my illness may have been too much for them as well.

In May 2011, I was travelling to Douglasville to celebrate my cousins wedding engagement. As I was entering Georgia, I decided to call Patricia because although I had spoken with Karen on the phone I had never met her. Since I was heading into Georgia, I thought that it was a very opportune time to meet her. After speaking on the phone with her and then speaking with my cousin Playboy we decided to meet at Karen's house. Playboy loaded up his van with his daughter, her fiancé, her friend and me. When we arrived at her house five African-Americans got out of Playboy's van and decided to go meet her. My thought was "I wonder what her neighbors were thinking due to five black people crawling out of a van." Karen was a very short, pretty looking white woman in her forties. The guys went downstairs with Karen's fiancé and played pool, while us women stayed upstairs and chatted. Karen was due to get married in July and she invited me to attend her wedding in Gatlinburg, Tennessee. In July, I travelled four hours to Gatlinburg so that I could help her celebrate her wedding. We hung out and had a lot of fun. My cousin got married in August and I travelled with my son and while in Georgia I took him to meet his Aunt Karen. On May 6, 2012, while in Georgia recovering from knee surgery three of my siblings and I met at Karen's house in Woodstock, Georgia. This was monumental because it was the very first time that the four of us had ever been together. This was an awesome experience for we all gathered in the basement and socialized. We took pictures, looked at family pictures, and the guys played pool. Although this was exciting we were still not complete because we are still missing two of our brothers. Art and Randy, we truly want you back.

The following chapters will involve several interviews with my siblings. The intent of these interviews is to provide the readers with a full perspective of the experiences of the effects of adoption. I was thrilled to interview Derrick, Patricia, and Karen.

Adoption Questions
Derrick

Derrick is my beloved brother whom I had the pleasure to grow with over the past 40 years. He was adopted directly out of the hospital and immediately became a member of the Burns' family. Like me, it is believed that he was placed for adoption due to being biracial. Derrick has been blessed with a long pattern of success throughout his schooling and career. He has served as a vice president of several companies and currently has his own business. As readers have found he has been my mentor for many years.

Jala: Congratulations on the success that you have had during your lifetime. Tell me about your motivating factors. What drove you to your success level?

Derrick: For me it was the intellectual curiosity and the search for knowledge…it was the combination. Learning was always fun…it was a gift to find jobs that gave me more knowledge. The gift was to search for jobs that gave me knowledge. Jobs were an opportunity to learn. …it was important to learn to find jobs where you had to learn and you had to have the desire to learn.

Jala: How do you feel to know that Jala holds you in the highest regards and sees you as her mentor? Do you actually know how deep of a love that she has for her big brother?

Derrick: I think that I do and I really appreciate it and it makes me feel good.

Jala: How did you feel after you were old enough to know that you were adopted? What was your experience like?

Derrick: I always knew that I was adopted. I was teased by the kids in the neighborhood because they knew that I was adopted; but I never had a problem with it.

Jala: Do you remember the visitation that Dave (Jala) had prior to him (her) getting adopted? If so please elaborate on your feelings.

Derrick: I don't remember events; but I do remember feelings. I have a lousy memory. I was excited and I was lonely growing up. I was ostracized. I wanted a sibling, a brother to love and to love me back. I was excited.

Jala: What was your interaction like while you and your sibling were growing up? Were you two close at that time? Or do you think that your relationship developed over time?

Derrick: We played a lot and we wrestled a lot. We had a challenge with our mother being a tyrant and in her being demanding. She valued education. It came easier for me than for Dave. We tried to ignore it. It came up when selecting our high school. I went to a private school and Dave went to a public school where our friends were. For me it was like coming from the other side of the tracks when I was coming from across town. It all worked out. We definitely got closer when we had kids.

Jala: Jala writes in her book that she had a close relationship with your dad and that you had a close relationship with your mom. She also says that you were close to your dad as well. Please describe your thoughts towards your relationships within your family.

Derrick: Well, I didn't feel that adoption had any effect on the family until 1997. The issue came up between me and mom; but the relationship was good between Dad and you. I did feel a big change when I found my birth mother. Mom had an issue with color; we were her light skin kids. She felt that color was an issue. I didn't experience the problem because of color. It was not my issue. She had the problem.

Jala: Jala described her experiences growing up as a biracial child in a predominantly African-American Community. How do you think that your ethnicity (or skin tone) played a role in your community? Do you remember altercations? Please expound.

Derrick: I got in a lot of fights, almost daily. I had straight hair. I was a smart aleck. I was the teachers' pet. I found that being ostracized was very difficult and that was the reason that I wanted a sibling. I felt all alone and didn't want to be alone. That's why I wanted a sibling. I wanted to be loved and accepted.

Jala: At what age did you decide that you wanted to find your biological mother? Biological siblings? What impelled you to do so?

Derrick: I didn't seek to find them at all. Mom urged me to find my biological family in 1990 when Gina was pregnant with Maya. Mom initiated the process so Maya would know the genetics. This terrified Mom because she didn't know what I would discover.

Jala: What steps did you take in finding your biological family? How could you help other adoptees find their biological families?

Derrick: I can't say that I took any steps. There are many organizations that can help with this. The ALMA Society, Adoptees Liberating Movement Association, is a great organization for bringing families back together.

Jala: Please describe your emotions when you finally met your biological family.

Derrick: I don't know if I can describe emotions. It took me years and years for my emotions. In terms of meeting people for the first time it took me a while to process this.

Jala: How are your relationships with your biological family now? Has these relationships had any impact on Jala?

Derrick: No so great... not so great with my Birth Mother. She has many mood swings. She is up and down. I don't want to deal with this. I don't think that my biological family has any effect on Jala.

Jala: Does the fact that she has found part of her biological family impact you at all?

Derrick: No, I encouraged it. It's not easy. Never easy. People should be with people that embrace them. It's hard to be with people we don't know. I never wanted you to get hurt. It is a stage that we all have to go through as adoptees. I had a fear that you might get hurt. This is a part of the process.

Jala: Did you have any emotional effects such as depression, anger, or trust or any others due to you being placed up for adoption?

Derrick: Not anger. I know that I always had deep inside issues about abandonment. I always tested people because I thought that they would walk away from me. I don't trust people until they prove they want to be part of my life.

Jala: Do you know the reason for your being placed up for adoption? Please discuss.

Derrick: My mother was Jewish and my father was an African-American male and back then it wasn't accepted. It was taboo just like a woman getting married outside of wedlock was taboo; and so were many other things.

Jala: Was the reason that you were placed up for adoption due to voluntary or involuntary causes? Without getting too personal, I would like you to speak about your thoughts on this.

Derrick: I expect that my Birth Mother's parents urged her to give me up for adoption and they thought that this was the right thing to do. It didn't matter if she believed this or not.

Jala: While growing up did you see any feminine traits in Dave (Jala)? Please discuss.

Derrick: No. I didn't pay much attention to it.

Jala: Do you remember Jala ever dressing up?

Derrick: Yes vaguely. I didn't pay much attention to it. My memory is not as great as yours. You have a good memory and mine isn't as great.

Jala: At about what age did you know that she was struggling with gender identity? How did you feel about the issue?

Derrick: I didn't know that you were struggling until you told me that you were transgender. I just wanted you to be happy.

Jala: She mentions how she appreciates your overall support for her throughout her life. What is the underlying reason for your support for her?

Derrick: I didn't think that I needed a reason to support you. I would say why not; anything else wouldn't be love.

Jala: She appreciates you accepting her as your sister. Please describe the difficulty that you had dealing with her gender transition.

Derrick: The only difficulty I had wasn't with your gender; it was with your defensiveness when people refer to you as a male. You have to know that it is an adjustment for everyone. My whole issue is not your gender; but when other people make mistakes I hope that you wouldn't get upset. It shouldn't affect you. You shouldn't allow others to affect you. I want you to get comfortable and not allow others to affect you.

Jala: It must have been difficult for you to see Jala suffer from depression. She mentions how both you and Gina supported her through her turbulent times. At about what age did you see signs of her depression? What were your thoughts as she experienced these times? What lessons did you learn about dealing with family members that suffered from depression? In helping others what would you say to them so that they can also overcome depression?

Derrick: It's hard to see when you were depressed. I saw that you were depressed over a decade of time. I didn't see it, and that may have been my fault, during your childhood or early adulthood. What were my thoughts as you went through depression? Oh gee, I hated to see you suffer. When you are in depression it is the worse feeling. It doesn't go away without intervention. I wanted you to get some help. I was concerned about you and I didn't want you to do any physical harm to yourself. I know that it seemed like the end of the world. I had a lot of experience dealing with depression. The main lesson I learned was that you can't reason with a person in depression. You definitely can't reason with a depressed person over the telephone. Depression is anger turned inward. In helping others I would say that if you are depressed you should seek therapy and help. Understand when there are no options realize that you need help. It will pass. It's hard to see that when you are depressed; but it will pass. When in depression you can't see anything positive; everything is bleak.

Jala: Finally, what closing impressions would you leave for the readers of this book in their struggles with being adopted? How might you help those who experienced pain due to the adoption? What are your final thoughts?

Derrick: Adoption is not a disease; not an affliction. Adoption is a set of events that happened before you were born and ended after birth. It's a decision that your mom and/or dad made that was out of your control. You have to deal with it and move on. Being given up for adoption doesn't mean that you are not worthy of love. Being given up for adoption doesn't mean that you have to be afraid of trusting people. I go back to my personal mantra: the only thing that you can control in life is your attitude. You certainly cannot control events before or when you were born. You can't control circumstances as a child. One thing that you can control is your attitude and it's your responsibility to do so. If you believe that then you will look at adoption as another fact that is not in your control. Deal with it. All other things are out of your control. Focus on what you can control.

(Note: At this point of my book you already know that Derrick is my mentor. He catches onto things much quicker than I do but after I understand his approach and apply it I also reach a level of success. Due to his hectic schedule we divided Derrick's interview into three telephone conversations. He was very direct with his answers and this interview wasn't as emotional as the interviews with Patricia and Karen. Derrick, my message to you is that I am very proud of you and I am truly blessed to have you as my brother. You have taught me many things and I thank you.)

Adoption Questions
Patricia

My sister, Patricia has been a wonderful addition to my life. I met her is July 2003. I am very impressed with her dedication to bring our biological family back together. Due to her hard work and success I nicknamed her "Glue." She has made many strides in her education. Her goal is to become a teacher. Patricia was my only sibling that was raised by our biological family.

Jala: How would you evaluate your level of success throughout life? What is your definition of the word "success"?

Patricia: I wouldn't say that I'm too successful. I'm trying to become a school teacher. My definition is to be happy and have everything in your life fulfilled.

Jala: How do you feel to know that Jala is very impressed with your determination to work as hard as you do in bringing your biological family together? Do you know how much love she has for you as you being her younger sister?

Patricia: I am very glad you feel that way. I've been trying since a very young age. I always told mom that I would do everything to get us together. In terms of loving me as your younger sister I love you because you are my older sister. I'm ecstatic to have Karen, Reggie, and Jala as my siblings. In terms of the nickname "Glue" that you have given me, without all of us we wouldn't be a family. We all are like glue. We are like puzzle pieces.

Jala: How did you feel after you were old enough to realize that you had five brothers and sisters that were all given up for adoption? What was your experience like growing up with your biological mother and father? Without your brothers and sisters?

Patricia: I was excited that I finally realized that I wasn't the only child. When I found out that my siblings were adopted I was sad because I didn't have them. I placed them on a pedestal because they were my siblings and I put them first. It was a sad experience not having them. I was spoiled. My parents made extra sure that they made up for not having my siblings because I was the only one left and they didn't want to lose me. I cried at night and remember looking out the window wondering if my siblings were looking at the stars or if they were all together or separate. I was smothered and protected and loved because they didn't want to lose me.

Jala: What reasons were your siblings given up for adoption? What are your feelings towards these causes?

Patricia: There are two different stories why Jala wasn't with our family. Mom felt that her parents would not have accepted a biracial child; but later she found out that this wasn't true. The second story was that mom had you while she was in a mental institution and wasn't going back. She was going to be on the run and didn't think that she could be able to take care of you while she was running away from the institution. The reason that Art, Randy, Reggie, and Karen were taken was because mom and dad worked at the farm and they had to walk four to five miles to the store to get food for the family. When they returned to the house they took the kids. Either the family or the state took the kids. I had a lot of animosity. My parents were trying to feed the kids. The kids were safe. I still have a lot of animosity towards mom's side of the family and the State of Georgia.

Jala: How did you feel when Jala described the non-identifying information she received showing that your mother was in a mental institution when she gave birth to her first child?

Patricia: As far as mom giving birth while in the mental institution I feel that the state fabricated the non-identification information that they put on paper with Jala, Reggie, and Karen. In terms of childhood memories, I was always embarrassed to have mom around because she was a bad alcoholic. Up to the age around 10 years old my friends loved her. She would come to my recitals and baseball games. Mom and I fought and I got a lot of anger towards mom. She made efforts to be at my events in high school and things got better. As I had my own kids my animosity built. There were a lot of fights, lawsuits, and police reports. Mom was mom.

Jala: Jala described her experiences growing up as a biracial child in a predominantly African-American Community. How do you think your community would have treated her while she was growing up due to her being biracial? How do you feel about her being biracial? What causes you to feel the way that you do?

Patricia: That wouldn't have been a problem because my friends were a multi-diversity group. My best friend was an albino. Everyone outcast her until I joined the school. Then she was my friend then everyone became her friend. I have a friend that was a male friend who was white. Both his parents are white but one of his siblings was black. A paternity test was taken to show that the kid was theirs and it was. So somewhere in the family was African-American. Everybody accepted everybody so I know you would have been accepted. When I was young I never realized that you were biracial. It doesn't matter because you are blood. Everyone is human and deserves to have family. Skin color is nothing. It's an outer layer and people need to look at the inside.

Jala: The 1960s were a very turbulent time in terms of racial tensions. As far as you know was Dave (Jala) placed up for adoption because of race? How do you feel about the possibility that he (she) was given up because of race?

Patricia: I've heard two different stories. One was yes because she felt family wouldn't accept you but she didn't know at first. Mom was young and didn't understand. She should have gotten more information. It bugs me that she cared about what others said and not how she felt. I think that it was ridiculous that you were given up. I think that I resented mom because she didn't stand up for you. Now that I've gotten older I see how she was. She has mental problems that didn't allow her to stand up for you. The second story was that mom was on the run and she was running away from the mental institution and couldn't run with a child and it wasn't fair to the child. Even though you kids were taken she always talked about you kids and she wanted to find you. It wasn't 100% her fault. If she didn't move out of Georgia I would have been taken.

Jala: At what age did you decide that you wanted to find your biological siblings? What caused you to do so?

Patricia: I was about 9 or 10 when I first decided to do the search. I always wanted to find my brothers and sisters but I didn't know how until I got in school. I knew that I had a family out there and I knew that once they reconnected they would love me. They are a part of me and I wanted to fill my hole. I had an empty feeling in my hole. I found the piece to fill the hole and it was my brother and my sisters.

Jala: What steps did you take in finding your biological family? How could you help other adoptees find their biological families?

Patricia: The steps that were taken were: I went to family members to find out what they knew about the age and date of births of my siblings and I needed to find out the locations of where parents were at the point of when you were being taken. All of us were born in Michigan, but we all lived in different states. I then found out where mom and dad were when they lost the kids. They were in Chatworth, Georgia. Then I went to the agency. I called the state and found out that I didn't have any rights. It was up to the adopted kids to want to find the birth family. The State of Georgia told me to go online at georgiaadoptionregistry.com. I filled out the information and it was probably about two years later that mom got a phone call from Georgia. We lived in Tennessee. Frances, they named Karen that, had to come in and wanted to find her birth parents. Two years later, mom and dad took a trip to Georgia. It took four years to set up a date to meet with Karen. Reggie was too young; he was 16 and not old enough to find his family. I was 15. I noticed that a woman started to walk out the door as we were walking in to see her. Dad held the door for her because he didn't know it was her. He was just a gentleman and he always held the door for the ladies. As we went into the facility mom went to the information desk and told the lady the reason why we were there. The lady got on the walkie-talkie and told somebody to go get the girl that had just walked out of the door. We met Karen. We hugged and cried and bonded for a good two hours to get to know her. Karen made the suggestion to come to her house. Reggie was too young. Karen told Reggie that we were coming. He was just getting ready to turn 18 in August; he was three months from being 18. Then a couple days later we got together at Reggie's adopted house. We got a chance to see Nina, Reggie's daughter and Cody, Karen's son.

Jala: Please describe your emotions when you finally met your biological siblings.

Patricia: I didn't like it. No actually I am joking. I was happy because my life was partially complete but only because of the absence of Art and Randy. I wouldn't do anything different. If anybody lost your parents and tried to find your family I say that you should try to find them. I've seen both sides of the street. My husband was adopted and his family doesn't want anything to do with him; but you never know until you try. Sometimes I want to beat my brother if he doesn't straighten up. No matter what we all love our twisted sister. We are all a little twisted; we wouldn't be family if we weren't. We wouldn't be girls if we weren't twisted in some way.

Jala: How are your relationships with your biological family now?

Patricia: Great. It's like we have been together our entire life; other than talking about it. We are there for each other no matter what. I have a different relationship with each one of my siblings.

Jala: Does the fact that Jala is close to her adopted brother have any impact on you? What are your thoughts?

Patricia: I think that is a good thing because you need to have a good relationship with him. Your brother is part of our family because he took good care of you. We love him too. Like I said earlier you don't have to be blood to be family. Some parents can't give birth to kids so they adopt.

Jala: Did you have any emotional effects such as depression or trust or any others due to you losing your brothers and sisters?

Patricia: I had a lot of animosity towards the family. I was the black sheep of the family because I didn't accept them because of what they did to my family. I don't have anything to do with them today. I will forgive them like God says but I won't associate.

Jala: After meeting Jala for the first time how did you feel about her gender transition? How did you feel with your expectations were to reunite with your brother but instead you were reuniting with your older sister? Did this cause any sort of pain for you?

Patricia: It was hard to get use to at first. Every now and then we slip and say he. It was harder for Dad because he is older and set in his ways; but he is slowly coming around. Mom was happy to find one of her babies. We want to find Art and Randy before mom dies. I think that I took it better than most because what surprises life has. You are part of my family. We wanted you to be part of our family. Instead of finding a brother we found a sister and we love you anyway. So instead of having four boys and two girls we have three boys and three girls. We are like the modern day Brady Bunch.

Jala: She mentions how she appreciates your overall support with her transition. What is the underlying reason for your support for her?

Patricia: The reason that I accept your decision for transition is because I want my sister happy. If she wants to cut both legs off to be happy then I want her happy. We all make decisions. I will be there to support my family for what decisions they make. If you try and force an opinion you could push them away. Kids also learn from mistakes on paper but experience is learned in life.

You were born to be a girl and I was born to be educated. Family is support under a bridge helping a person to get across. I make decisions for my kids. Everybody has something that they aren't happy with. Some people aren't happy with who they were born. So they change. It doesn't have to be a sex change. I wasn't happy in life so I went back to school to be a school teacher. So if you need surgery to be happy then do it.

Jala: What were your feelings when you reunited with Karen and Reggie? Please describe your memories from the first time you three meet? Did you spend time as a child growing up with them? What was it like?

Patricia: When I was 15 I met them. I was giving mom and dad a problem so they sent me from Tennessee to Georgia. A friend came up with her to get me. We partied but we also worked. I didn't bond with Reggie because I heard that

Reggie's mom said that if he had anything to do with me she would take everything from him; like his job and everything else. I worked at Western Sizzler across from where Reggie lived. He would come see me often. I lived with Karen for two years. I almost went to Canada to get married but they stopped me.

Jala: How did you feel when Reggie, Karen, Jala and you met together for the first time?

Patricia: On May 6, 2012, three days before my son's birthday we all met for the first time. That was the highlight of my life. It was like the first time that I ever found you all; but I felt that something was missing. Mom, Art, and Randy were all missing. I would have liked for our mother and other two brothers to have been there as well.

Jala: How did you feel the very first time you spoke with Jala on the telephone?

Patricia: I was in tears. I was happy because it was like we found a piece of our lives. It was like finding Reggie and Karen. It was like finding a piece of our puzzle. We met in July 2003. You and mom spoke first and when mom tried to call me and tell me she couldn't speak because she was crying. I spoke to dad and drove an hour to their house. I drove from Venice to St. Pete. When I got there she was still crying so once I got her to calm down she told me.

Jala: How do you feel about not having Art or Randy in your life? What message do you want to send them? What would it mean to reunite them with all your siblings now?

Patricia: Like I was saying my life is not whole and I am missing pieces in my life. These are the pieces that were never put in place. Each piece has a point in life. There are still empty spaces in the puzzle. We search through millions and billions of pieces and never found them. I want to find them. The message that I want to send is that you have a family out here that loves you; your sisters and brothers; nieces and nephews; aunts and uncles; and cousins. We love you and there is more family. We all have room in our heart that we want you in our lives. (Jala started crying.) The message I want to say is that please give us a chance to be part of your lives.

Jala: It must have been difficult for you to see our mother suffer from depression. At about what age did you see signs of her depression? What were your thoughts as she experienced these times? How did you react when you found out that Jala was also suffering from depression? What lessons did you learn about dealing with family members that suffered from depression? In helping others what would you say to them so that they can also overcome depression?

Patricia: As far as how old I was, I was around 13 or 14. I was too young to acknowledge what it meant. I didn't know exactly what it was. The way mom acted and the way that I treated her. I didn't understand until I went through my divorce what it was. In October 1995 was when I acknowledged mom's illness. I didn't fully comprehend until I was 20. That's when it affected me. Then I realized I had been going through a divorce and my children. I felt bad how I treated her when I was young. When I realized it I felt like I got slapped in the face. I asked for forgiveness. I really didn't know how to handle your depression because we had a relationship but it wasn't a close bond at the time. I couldn't step in and I didn't know how to bring you out of it. I grew up with mom in depression. I didn't know how to handle it. It was like running away. I didn't feel like I built the relationship so I didn't know what to do.

Jala: Describe your maternal grandparents. What were they like? Did they force your mother to give Dave (Jala) up for adoption? Please explain what you were told. How did you feel about your grandparents?

Patricia: Grandma Lilly died when she was 50-years-old. Mom was barely 20 or 21 when Grandma passed. Mom and Dad were still together. They had been together though. The only memory I have of Grandpa was his face. I was 3-years-old. I remember him when I smelled a cigar or pipe. I remember sitting on his lap when I was three. He was smoking a cigar and drinking whiskey. He gave us kids a drink so I had a drink. Grandpa had a white hat and black band around the base of his head. He looked like a gangster. He wore color suites. He was always business. I was told that he was a drug dealer. He was an alcoholic. I don't remember him being mean to people. I've heard two stories. He was racist and he wasn't racist. I do not believe that our grandparents forced mom to give you up. I don't know which story to believe. I think the story of being on the run from the mental institution and not being able to care for you. I think that she wasn't forced to give you up. It was a decision that she had to make. In growing up everybody was different. There was no normal. I was brought up to accept everyone. If there was a racist thing in my family I would have had some type of racism in me. I dated a black guy and neither mom nor dad had a problem with it.

Jala: After finding out that Jala was writing a book which included a section on adoption what message did you want to send to the readers?

Patricia: Never give up. Follow every lead even if it leads to nowhere. Follow the lead. There is a purpose for every lead. I have talked to many adopted members that I thought were my family members but they weren't but we built a bond. Go on the chat lines because family members might be somewhere else.

Follow every lead that you possibly can. Family members can be anywhere. Like Karen and Reggie were in Georgia; Jala was in North Carolina; and Patricia was in Tennessee. We all were born in Michigan. I was told that you were in Michigan, but you were in North Carolina. I was told that you were a doctor. Art and Randy we don't know where you are. They could be in California. My message is to be patient. Don't get frustrated. It can be frustrating. Walk away if you get frustrated because you need to be able to enjoy them once you are back together.

Jala: Finally, what closing impressions would you leave for the readers of this book in their struggles with being adopted? How might you help those who experienced pain due to the adoption? What are your final thoughts?

Patricia: That all depends on the situation; if they are having bad thoughts or not. Each person is their own self. Be yourself and follow through with everything you do. You are a person and God loves you. You have a purpose in this life. Just follow your purpose and you just have to find that Golden Road to follow.

Jala: Please explain the rumor of mom being raped by my father while in the mental institution.

Patricia: What I think happened resulted when mom was at age of 10. She got hit by a truck by trying to save her sister. When mom got hit by the truck she started having medical issues which lead her to being in the mental institution. At that time she didn't have an education. She only has a third grade education. I was told for the longest that she was raped because she didn't know how to tell her family. Being raped was her excuse not to get in trouble. I don't think that she was raped. I think that your father was in the institution because of domestic dispute and for anger management. I think that there are a few pieces missing. Mom was 19 when she gave birth to Jala; her mentality was 12 or 13 years old. I'm slowly bringing the pieces together, but I don't think that she was raped by your father.

(Note: Patricia and I cried some. The emotional part of the interview for Patricia was trying to put it together and putting the truth in the right terms. "The whole thing is emotional in trying to see why mom is the way she is," says Patricia. I became emotional when Patricia was sending the message to Art and Randy about us wanting to find them.)

Adoption Questions
Karen

My biological sister, Karen, has been a wonderful big sister to our brother Reggie. She has worked in the restaurant business for many years. Although I had spoken with Karen via telephone we finally met in person in May 2011. I was very excited about attending her wedding in July 2011. She and I speak on the telephone quite a lot and I have seen her several times within the last year. I am very impressed with her personality and strength. She is a true blessing that is now in my life.

Jala: How would you evaluate your level of success throughout life? What is your definition of the word "success"?

Karen: I give myself an 8 on the level of success. I had to overcome obstacles from the very beginning and I did the best with what I had. That's what I did. I didn't have a very good start in life and I knew that no one was going to do it for me. I had a difficult road from the time I was adopted on down the road. I made it though.

Jala: How do you feel about being placed up for adoption? What information do you have for the reason that you were placed up for adoption? Was it a voluntary or involuntary adoption?

Karen: It was meant to happen. They wouldn't have placed me there if they thought that it was a bad idea. Bad people usually go to jail. The state took me from my mother. I'm not exactly sure why I was taken from my mother. It's unknown.

Jala: What information do you have for the reasons that your siblings were placed for adoption?

Karen: Art and Randy were taken by the state with Reggie and me. I had no idea that you existed. I think all four of us –Art, Randy, Reggie and I went to the same foster family. Then my adopted mother couldn't handle all four of us kids and we were separated.

Jala: What memories do you have being raised with your brother, Reggie?

Karen: I babied him like he was my own. I felt that my adopted mother didn't like me much. She was supposed to be the mother, but I was. I knew Reggie long before she did so I thought that I was suppose to take care of him. That was my job.

Jala: What were your emotions when you were reunited with Patricia? Were you and Reggie still together when you and Patricia were brought back together?

Karen: I wasn't allowed to tell Reggie that I talked to Patricia or my mom. I was shocked when I reunited with Patty because I thought that I was the only girl. I always had brothers and I was the only princess.

Jala: Were you ever placed in foster care prior to being adopted? If so please share your memories.

Karen: I was placed in foster care prior to my adoption. I have memories but they aren't worth talking about. It was just nothing.

Jala: Share your experience that you had while growing up in your adopted family?

Karen: I want to skip that conversation.

Jala: What memories do you have being with Art, Randy, and Reggie all being together?

Karen: It was like a slumber party every night because we didn't know how long it would last or if it would last. It didn't last. We were just four little kids that were together.

Jala: What would it mean to you to be reunited with Art and Randy?

Karen: I don't know what it would be like. They may be successful or they may be needy. I would be overjoyed to see them.

Jala: What steps do you plan on taking in your efforts to find Art and Randy?

Karen: If they want to find me they can. They were older than me and they know our phone number. Our phone number never changed over 35 years. They know where we are. At least I believe that they know where we are. It would be easier for them to find me than for me to find them.

Jala: Some people that were placed for adoption have had different impacts than others. Jala mentions her depression, trust, and abandonment issues. Do you think that you experienced any of these or other effects from being placed up for adoption?

Karen: No. (She started crying and laughing at the same time.) This was a hard event, but I knew that my mom was always coming back to get me. I was taken away, but I always knew that she was coming back. My adopted mother couldn't stand for that.

Jala: Do you want to share your emotions with me?

Karen: I'm crying because of my past and because I had missed my mother. I'm laughing because we still rejoined a few years later.

Jala: What would you say to someone that was adopted and was depressed because of the adoption?

Karen: I look at it in two different ways. It could be good or it could be bad but you must turn the bad into good.

Jala: If you would have stayed with your biological mother how might you think that you may have turned out different?

Karen: I don't know that answer. I could have been screwed or I could have been the same as I am today. One mother had money and the other didn't. If I wasn't the strong willed person that I am I wouldn't be the person that I am today.

Jala: I understand that different fathers were involved in the birth of you and your five siblings. Please explain your understanding of the different biological fathers.

Karen: Carla said that we all had the same father but I think that it was different. There were at least three different last names. We all had different shades of skin tones. One day Patty told me that mom wasn't perfect and we had a black boy in the family. I thought that Patty was mad at mom and was making up things. I thought that she was just being a spoiled brat. Patty said that mom was raped in the mental institution and that's how you came about.

Jala: Describe your relationship with Reggie.

Karen: He is always going to be my little brother and I will always love him. I will always be here for him; but I can't enable him or he will never grow up.

Jala: What were your emotions when you were united with Jala? How did you feel to find out that your brother was actually transitioning into your sister? What are your overall feelings about Jala?

Karen: I really wasn't surprised. At this point I knew you existed and when I saw you there you were. I talked to you on the phone as a brother then I found out that you were transitioning. Then I was okay with you. I now see you as a girl. My overall feelings about you? Wow. I'm roasting your ass now. I wish that your leg didn't hurt. You fall into place. I love you. We playfully call each other names like "Bitch" but we know that we are joking. I say "Another freaking girl." You are a friend. It was like we were never really apart. We talk about things like what we are doing today. I am so proud of you for writing this book. My friends have always told me that I need to write a book. We should write another book about our adoption later.

Jala: How did you feel about the first time that you spoke with Jala on the telephone? Why did it take so long for you two to meet in person? How did you feel when you finally met her?

Karen: At first you sounded like a guy and you did it on purpose. Then you told me that you were a girl. I didn't know what to expect. When you got out of the van you looked like a girl. So you are a girl. You scared my husband because he wasn't used to this.

Jala: After finding out that Jala was writing a book, what message did you want to make in the book regarding your adoption?

Karen: I am proud of you for doing something that I should have done. My life kept changing and I have a lot to tell people about. In talking about adoption I would tell adults to adopt children if you really want them. I would also say to be open minded if the kids want to reunite with their families. I have a friend that has a great adopted family that is so supportive.

Jala: What do you have to say to those that were adopted and are frustrated because they can't find their biological families?

Karen: If it's going to happen it's going to happen. I didn't make much effort to find my family. The only reason that I did anything was because I was threatened to be put back in foster care. They (the agency) took me in the back and told me to put my name on a list if I wanted to find my biological mother. If she also placed her name on a list and was trying to find me then we could be reunited.

Jala: What were your feelings after you found out that your biological mother had been in a mental institution?

Karen: I think that I knew this before I was adopted. A little piece of me always knew that. When I found out about you she was in an institution.

Jala: Do you think that you are better or worse overall because of you being placed in an adopted family?

Karen: Either way they have different backgrounds. I am still me. I was told to hang around the most normal people that I could so I hung around my aunts and uncles. What was in my adopted life wasn't normal, but I can control my part of life as I get older. I got a job the first day after my 16th Birthday. I was around mentors at Long John Silver's. They raised me as an adult. Once I started working I didn't need my adopted mother anymore.

Jala: Finally, what closing impressions would you leave for the readers of this book in their struggles with being adopted? How might you help those who experienced pain due to the adoption? What are your final thoughts?

Karen: I don't feel sorry for people who are adopted. People used to feel sorry for people who were adopted. Times have changed and things are much better. I tell those people to keep their heads up high and don't dwell on it. It's no big deal. God has all us kids in this world and everybody is related in some kind of fashion.

Jala: What were your emotions when you reunited with your mother? What childhood memories do you have of her?

Karen: This was in Atlanta. When I was reunited with her I had two friends take me there. I didn't see Patty or mom for a few minutes because my friends smothered me. So I went outside and sat on a bench with my friends. I finally saw her and she was wearing a green pants suite. Carla wanted the newspaper to take our pictures just like you wanted us on television. Like I told you I didn't want to. My childhood memories were that I was very special. I was her little princess. I was everybody's princess. Then I looked at Patty and said "How did you get here." I was supposed to be the only princess. Momma must have loved having sex. I always thought that my mother was pretty.

Bringing It All Together
Adoption and Finding My Biological Family

Children are adopted for many reasons. There are two different stories for why I was given up for adoption. One story involved my biological mother leaving me at the hospital due to her refusal to return to the mental institution where she became pregnant with me. The other story was very similar to Derrick where we both were placed for adoption due to racial reasons during the 1960s. Both Derrick and I were biracial children that were presumably placed in adoption due to pressure placed on our biological mothers by our maternal grandparents. Karen, Reggie, Art, and Randy were forcibly taken by the State of Georgia.

There were certain factors that contributed to the development of us all. For example, Derrick did not spend time in foster care; he was adopted directly out of the hospital. Therefore our adopted family was able to direct him through his formative years. I, on the other hand, spent the first five years of my life in various foster families. Thus my formative years were very unstable. My biological siblings also spent time in foster care prior to them being split apart. Although we do not know the outcome of Art and Randy we can tell from Karen's interview that she and Reggie had a difficult time. Karen stated that she could not answer whether she turned out better or worse due to being raised by her adopted family. Patricia, the only child out of all my siblings who was not adopted, also struggled during her childhood. Her education may not have been as traditional as others, but I am proud to say that she continues her focus on gaining her college degree. There are various levels of success for all of my brothers and sisters and I am honored to have them as a part of my life. I really value Derrick because he has been a very instrumental part of my life for 40 years and he has continued to support me with his unconditional love. During our interview he stated that he didn't think that he needed an underlying reason to support me because he supported me because of his unconditional love for me. (Wow. Man I love you more than anything.) As Patricia stated she doesn't even know Derrick but she also loves him because of the great care that he gave me.

All of my siblings had different thoughts when it came to the urge of being brought back together. Derrick mentioned that he was very excited when he found out that he was getting a sibling. Patricia stated that as a young child she was always wondering how her brothers and sister were and if they were gazing out the window at the stars like she was accustomed to. Her anger mounted due to not having us in her life. Karen always felt like she was the only princess and always knew that our mother would come back for her. I was blessed with a wonderful relationship with my adopted father and never cared to meet my biological father. My relationship with my adopted mother was different and I always yearned to have my biological mother in my life. One of the contributing factors in my depression was the absence of my biological mother.

Each of our families, both biological and adopted, were impacted differently because of the different adoptions. As Derrick mentioned he thought that things were normal for him while growing up as part of the Burns' family. He discovered an issue in 1997 when he was reunited with his biological family. Derrick realized that our adopted mother, although she raised two biracial children, actually had a problem with color. I, on the other hand, felt different. Although I was close to my adopted father, my relationship with my adopted mother was difficult. Patricia became very upset with the majority of her biological family because she felt that her siblings were separated from her unnecessarily. Karen felt as though she was responsible for taking care of Reggie because that's all she knew and therefore she felt that it was her duty to care for him. She states that she was also closer to her adopted father than she was to her adopted mother. I could only imagine the feelings that my biological mother had due to losing five of her six children.

Deep rooted issues resulted for us all due to being adopted. Derrick stated that he felt abandoned at first because his biological mother left him immediately after his birth. Derrick also stated that he had difficulty trusting others. He feels that others have to prove that they want to be part of his life. I also developed issues of abandonment and trust. I am so glad that Derrick has been so instrumental in my life. I have a deep appreciation and love for him. I don't always agree with him but I know that he gives his instruction because he genuinely cares for me and wants the best. People are not designed to agree with 100% of everything someone else believes, however I am very open to Derrick's direction and normally follow his advice. Our parents are deceased and there is only us remaining as adopted siblings. My fear is that one day I will lose Derrick and I will not be able to handle the lost. I suffered early in my depression due to not having my biological family. As an adult I have problems trusting people because of my trust being violated during my early age. Patricia says that she developed issues of both anger and depression due to the loss of Karen, Reggie, Art, Randy and I. Although Karen shared mixed emotions during the interview she stated that she didn't suffer from depression but she always knew that our mother was going to reunite with her.

There comes a time when adoptees want to find their biological families. My discovery in speaking with Derrick was that even though he urged me to find my biological family he was afraid that I would end up being hurt. He wanted to guard me against being harmed. Derrick also stated that our adopted mother initiated the process of him finding his biological mother due to genetics. She wanted Derrick's daughter, Maya, to know her biological family. In speaking to both Patricia and Karen, I find that once we knew that each of us existed that all three of us were very interested in coming back together. Patricia and I are very eager to locate Art and Randy but Karen doesn't seem as eager. Although Karen says that she would like to reunite with them she also says that they should know her phone number and address and if they wanted to reunite they should take the necessary action.

There are several measures that adoptees can take in their efforts to find their biological families. For example, Derrick and I were assisted by our adopted mother. My adopted mother actually gave me the telephone number to a contact at the adoption agency which put me in touch with my biological mother. Our adopted mother also urged Derrick to find his biological mother and she initiated the bulk of the work. Derrick mentions that agencies are very willing to help adoptees find their biological families. The agency that he used is called ALMA. I remember when Derrick went to various courthouses to review birth and marriage certificates and other records during his search in 1997. Patricia explains that she often goes on various websites in her attempt to locate Art and Randy. She also outlines her steps in searching for her biological family members. She says that she researches the place of birth; the age of the adoptee when placed for adoption; and location of where the adoptee's parents were when the adoptee was placed for adoption for either involuntary or voluntary reasons. She then contacts the adoption agencies that are located in the state in which the child was given for adoption. Patricia will then register on the various websites that she finds useful in her search. She also visits various chat rooms and communicates with others that are searching for their biological families. Due to difficulties that Karen had with her adoption she was taken back to the adoption agency. While at the agency Karen was taken in the back by an agent and signed some paperwork stating that she wanted to find her biological family.

In my final thoughts I urge adoptees to stay strong in their faith and know that God is in control. Derrick often tells me to not allow things or others to control me. So I pass the word to you and say that you are in control of your destiny. Patricia states that those searching for biological family members should check every avenue and never give up because you never know what the results of your search will be. Finally I say be prepared to deal with the unknown when you meet your biological family. For example my biological family could have turned me away due to my gender identity disorder. I had difficulty with my biological mother's depression.

At this time I extend many thanks to my audience and I hope that this entire book fulfilled its original purpose of helping others with gaining an education, becoming active politically in both the work place and the community in which you live, overcoming depression, understanding gender transition, and understanding and finding an adoptee's biological family. This writing was very therapeutic for me and helped me understand many patterns which formed my life. I look forward to writing other books in the near future. Once again many thanks.

Langston Hughes' poem "Midnight Raffle" is a wonderful description of life. I live my life by Faith and firmly believe that we have so many choices that life is like a raffle.

Dave Edward Morris

Howard L. Burns, Derrick R. Burns,
Dave B. Burns,
And Willa M. Burns
Mid-1970's
Detroit, MI

Dave B. Burns
1970's
Detroit, MI

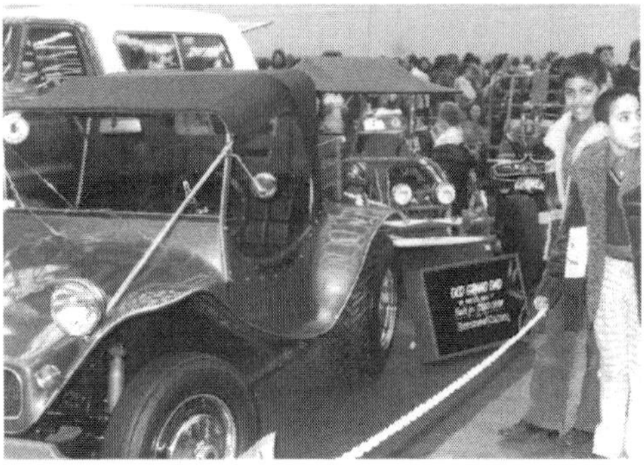

Derrick and David at
Car Show

Ausley Carla Morris
Jala's Biological Mother
2008 in Florida

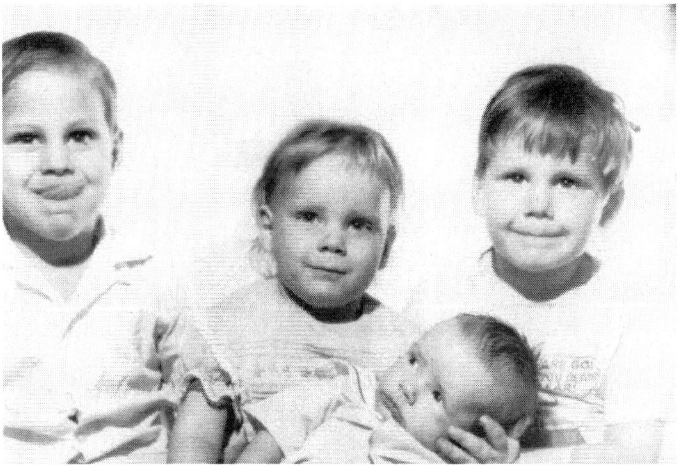

Art, Karen, Randy and Reggie

Rear from left: Patricia, Karen. Jala in front.
First time siblings came together at once
May 6, 2012 Woodstock, GA

Karen (Biological Sister's Wedding) and Jala
Gatlinburg, TN

Questions to Peak Your Interest

Preface

It is a great possibility that Jala and Derrick were both placed for adoption due to being biracial. Jala and Derrick had different biological families. In Derrick's interview he stated that in 1997 he discovered that his adopted mother may have had an issue with color. Does racism still exist in today's era? Is there such a thing as reverse racism? Is it less likely, more likely or about the same chance that a biracial child would be given up for adoption due to today's societal acceptance? Please explain the above.

Jala mentioned that during her writing she discovered that there were patterns which developed during her childhood. She stated that she saw patterns for her gender identity disorder, depression, and the lack of discipline of her mouth. What patterns do you recognize in your development?

Education

Which is more valuable: In class education, out of class education, or both? Please explain.

Jala has several family members who were born in the early 20th century who became educators. She viewed this as a very monumental accomplishment due to these relatives being African-American. Did she overstate this or do you agree?

Jala is moved by her predecessors due to their involvement in the Civil Rights Movement. She also believed that people of the younger generation do not value the struggle that those individuals fought. For example she mentions the right to an equal education; the right to drink from the same water fountain; and the right to sit at the front of a city bus. What are your thoughts on this matter?

Jala mentioned her interest in pledging for a fraternity and also wished that she could have been in a sorority. Should a person of gender transition be allowed to pledge an organization that matches the person's gender? Do you think that transgender females should be allowed to pledge a sorority? Should transgender males be allowed to pledge in fraternities? Do you think that this will ever be allowed?

Community Involvement

Jala described her experience with the labor movement and she said that there is a lot of apathy towards labor organizations in the United States. Do you agree or disagree? Please elaborate.

What are today's hot topics in your community? If you have an issue with anything that occurs in your community what role do you have in deciding the outcome? Are you a person that will only discuss the issue or are you one who would get involved in an attempt to resolve the issue? Are you politically active?

Overcoming Depression

Jala shared her experience with depression in Section 3. Are you close to anyone that suffers from depression? Do you provide any support for that person? Did you notice any signs of that person's depression? How does that person's depression impact your relationship?

Have you ever experienced any behavioral health issues such as depression, anxiety, anger or any other illness? If so what was your experience like? Did you overcome your battle? If so what steps did you take to overcome?

Jala discussed both healthy and unhealthy coping mechanisms that she took part of with her depression. What are some healthy coping mechanisms that you have experienced? What are the unhealthy coping mechanisms?

Gender Transition

Jala stated that she had an internal conflict with her gender from a very early age but she was scared to share her issue with others due to either placing herself in danger or becoming ostracized. She also stated that her experiences show that although she tried to keep her feelings to herself others may have already been aware of her struggle. Ms. McKenzie raised the question of whether she should have just announced her gender identity at an early age or if she should have fought her issue. How do you feel about how she handled the topic? Do you think that her situation would have been easier for her in today's society?

Is a person's gender an innate or learned experience? Is it both? Please explain.

In her book she and other transgender people pointed out that there is a difference between gay, lesbian, and transgender. Do you agree or disagree?

Her adopted mother told her that she was doomed to hell due to her gender transition. A pastor stated that he didn't agree because he wasn't sure if her condition is a sin or not, but he stated that if it is a sin she is saved by Grace. Without judging her on a personal level, what are your thoughts?

Adoption and Finding My Biological Family

Do you know anyone that has been adopted or that has adopted a child? What impact does the adopted person or adopted family have because of the adoption?

Do you know anyone who gave a child up for adoption? What impact does the biological family face?

Do you know an adoptee that has found his/her biological family? If so what steps were taken during the search? How can you help adoptees with their search?